WITHDRAWN

HISTORY

OF

PICKENS COUNTY

BY

LUKE E. TATE

THE REPRINT COMPANY, PUBLISHERS

SPARTANBURG, SOUTH CAROLINA

1978

This volume was reproduced from a 1935 edition in
The Reese Library, Augusta College,
Augusta, Georgia.

Reprinted: 1978
The Reprint Company, Publishers
Spartanburg, South Carolina 29304

ISBN 0–87152–287–X
Library of Congress Catalog Card Number: 78–13223
Manufactured in the United States of America on long-life paper.

Library of Congress Cataloging in Publication Data

Tate, Lucius Eugene, 1879–
  History of Pickens County.

  Reprint of the 1935 ed. published by W. W.
Brown, Atlanta, Ga.
  Includes index.
  1. Pickens Co., Ga.—History. 2. Pickens
Co., Ga.—Genealogy. I. Title.
F292.P57T3 1978   975.8′255   78–13223
ISBN 0–87152–287–X

HISTORY

OF

PICKENS COUNTY

BY

LUKE E. TATE

PRESS OF
WALTER W. BROWN PUBLISHING COMPANY
ATLANTA, GA.

• CONTENTS

LIST OF ILLUSTRATIONS

• PREFACE

In Georgia there are older counties than Pickens, and there are counties that are larger, or wealthier, or more populous. But I do not think there is any other county that is richer in the traditions of its common people or in the spiritual heritage of its pioneers.

It is a matter of gratification to all loyal Georgians that the year 1933, the bicentennial of the founding of the Georgia colony, should have witnessed an enthusiastic revival of popular interest in the historical affairs of our state. It was gratifying to me personally that my home county of Pickens was one of those counties which responded to the appeal of the legislature and made provision for the writing and preservation of its own historical traditions.

My choice as historian of the county was an unsought honor, and one that I not only debated whether to accept— but am still debating whether I should have accepted! The time and labor which it appeared would be necessary—and my early estimates fell far short of the actual requirements— had something to do with this attitude; but the chief reason was my feeling that I lacked qualifications for the work. In the course of a somewhat varied career, I seemed to have overlooked one business entirely: the gentle art of producing a book. So now I can only beg the reader to don the mantle of charity as he scans these pages, and try to balance their defects with whatever merits may result from the fact that they were written as a "labor of love."

In the preparation of this history I have received valuable aid from many persons—in fact, no book of this kind could be written without such aid. To all who have so kindly helped, I tender appreciative thanks. Especially to Miss Ruth Blair, official historian of Georgia, do I acknowledge my indebtedness for her kindness in searching for matters of interest and special application to Pickens County as contained in the records of the Department of Archives and History, and for her valuable advice in the general preparation of the book. I also wish to thank the three members of the county's historical committee, appointed by the grand jury, for their cooperation in this work.

The present volume has been written for Pickens Countians—those now living here and those who have gone out to other scenes of endeavor but still cherish memories of good days spent in Pickens. It has seemed more important to me that the county's traditions should be perpetuated among her people than that any effort should be made to impress others. My purpose in this book has been to pass on something of those traditions and to describe, as best I could, the notable heritage left by the pioneers of our county. The student of Georgia history may find added light on his subject from matters mentioned herein—I hope that will be the case; the general reader will no doubt find that the history of Pickens has been distinctive and interesting; but the citizens of the county have been my imaginary audience, because they best understand the things that I have written of. I sincerely hope they will find the book not entirely unworthy of its subject.

LUKE E. TATE

Tate, Ga.
March 1, 1935

REPORT OF PICKENS COUNTY
HISTORICAL COMMITTEE

The following committee was requested by the grand jury to review the County History written by Col. Luke E. Tate.

We have carefully reviewed this history and find it to be a very complete statement of facts relative to the County and he is to be commended for collecting the data and in giving to the present and future posterity a clear record of our county from the beginning to the present date and we gladly subscribe to the record he has made and commend him for his noble piece of work.

M. S. LONG
SAM TATE
DR. M. C. MCCLAIN

HISTORY OF
PICKENS COUNTY

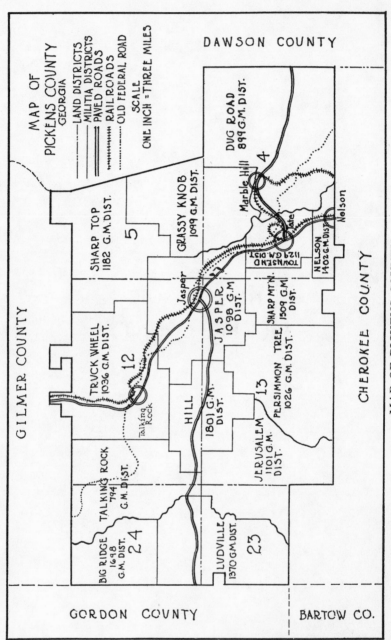

MAP OF
PICKENS COUNTY
GEORGIA

LAND DISTRICTS
MILITIA DISTRICTS
PAVED ROADS
RAILROADS
OLD FEDERAL ROAD

SCALE
ONE INCH = THREE MILES

DAWSON COUNTY

GILMER COUNTY

CHEROKEE COUNTY

GORDON COUNTY

BARTOW CO.

SHARP TOP
1182 G.M. DIST.
5

GRASSY KNOB
1099 G.M. DIST.

DUG ROAD
899 G.M. DIST.
4

Marble Hill

Tate

Nelson

TOWNSEND
1124 G.M. DIST.

NELSON
1402 G.M.DIST.

TRUCK WHEEL
1036 G.M. DIST.
12

Jasper

JASPER
1098 G.M.
DIST.

SHARP MTN.
1509 G.M.
DIST.

Talking Rock

HILL
1801 G.M.
DIST.

PERSIMMON TREE
1026 G.M. DIST.
13

JERUSALEM
1101 G.M.
DIST.

TALKING ROCK
794
G.M. DIST.

BIG RIDGE
1698
G.M. DIST.
24

LUDVILLE
1370 G.M.DIST.
23

MAP OF PICKENS COUNTY

Chapter I ★ ★ ★ ★ ★
EARLY HISTORY

●

THE OFFICIAL history of Pickens County, Georgia, began on December 5, 1853. That was the day on which Governor Herschel V. Johnson, of Georgia, signed an act passed by the legislature then in session, creating, out of the southern part of Gilmer County and the northern part of Cherokee, a new county "called and known by the name of Pickens, in honor of General Andrew Pickens."

It has now been eighty years since the meeting of that memorable session of the legislature—which created six other counties besides Pickens, one of them being Fulton. Eighty years is not a long time as the histories of Georgia counties go—some of them are twice that old. And yet Georgians will recognize a certain antiquity in the beginnings of their now most populous and prosperous county, and of their metropolitan Capital—which in the year 1853 was just getting used to its new name of Atlanta and was probably without an inkling of its future greatness. One realizes, also, that if 1853 was only fifteen years after the Indian Removal, and little more than a generation after our last war with England, then Pickens is hardly to be regarded as an "upstart" among counties, and her history not only can be said to be honorable but can claim as well a certain degree of length.

To confine the scope of this book to the eighty years of the county's *official* life, however, would be as inadequate— if hardly so dry—as it would be to list in it only official events from courthouse records. The true history of a coun-

13

try, or of a county, is the history of its people; and—to quote another aphorism—the value of history lies in its explanation of the present. So, to formulate a true and anywise valuable history of Pickens County, we must begin at the beginning and discover the backgrounds, racial, social and moral, of the county's earliest citizens; and we must also examine the natural environment which has formed the setting of her citizens both past and present, for its effect on their activities and characters.

First in the true history of Pickens County, therefore, comes the land—the setting; here when the first actors enter on the stage; continuing almost unchanged as successive acts, with ever new characters, unfold and draw to a close; playing a part throughout in the molding of lives, characters, and destinies. First, then, the natural characteristics—the "geography"—of Pickens County.

NATURAL CHARACTERISTICS

The "Land of the Cherokees" was a charming one. We do not have to be told how the Indians clung to it and refused to give it up, to know this, because the evidence is still here. It is still a charming land; though it must have been even more beautiful when its only inhabitants were the "untutored savages" who loved it for itself, and not for the timber they could cut from its hills, the gold they could dig from its valleys, or the waterpower they could harness from its sparkling streams.

Yet all these things were put here for the use of man; and the Indians were not the first unprofitable servants to be deprived of their talents. In one respect, indeed, they have continued to be served by them. For if it were not for these hills and valleys and streams, and the "pleasing prospects" they offer, the place in history of the Cherokee tribe

of Indians would have fallen considerably short of martyr-
dom, the historical status they are apparently destined to
occupy. Though there are other reasons for the romantic
attitude of their biographers, the fact that the Cherokees
lived in one of the most beautiful sections of the South is
one of the most potent; and while such an attitude is scarcely
to be wondered at, it has meant that the recriminations against
Georgia for her part in the Removal have been much more
bitter than those which less favored states have had to put up
with.

At any rate, the territory that now forms Pickens County
was a part of the "Land of Cherokee," and, none will deny,
one of its most scenic. Wooded hills in the east, some of
them rising to the stature of mountains in the northeast, over-
look green valleys and the fertile table-lands to the west;
while over all spreads a network of picturesque streams.

The geology of the county shows a very hard lime rock in
the west end, where it leaves Gordon County's limestone
and slate area. Coming east, one notes the transition to a
very broken country of shale, but soon arrives at a table-land
of fine agricultural country with a variety of fertile soils.
This table-land, or plateau, is broken by many small streams:
Talking Rock Creek and its tributaries on the north, and on
the south, Sharp Mountain Creek and the small streams
flowing into it, as well as tributaries of Salacoa Creek in
Cherokee County. Jasper, the county seat, is located on the
east brink of this plateau country.

In the northern part of the county, other creeks and
branches descend to the Cartecay Valley of Gilmer County;
in the southern part flow the tributaries of Long Swamp
Creek. In the beautiful valley of the Long Swamp are famous
marble deposits and the thriving villages of Marble Hill,
Tate, and Nelson.

The chain of mountains which rises in the northeastern part

LAKE SEQUOYAH

of Pickens County is a part of the Georgia Blue Ridge, which itself forms the southernmost range of the Appalachian system. Several magnificent peaks, visible many miles away, rise within the boundaries of Pickens. These include the two high points of the southern end of the Appalachians: Mount Oglethorpe (formerly called Grassy Knob) and Burrell Top of Burnt Mountain, each approximately 3,300 feet above sea-level. In the same vicinity is Sharp Top Mountain—aptly named in view of its steeple-like shape—with an elevation of 2,650 feet; and in the southwestern part of the county is a fourth peak, Sharp Mountain, which is 2,450 feet high. Geologists tell us that all these mountains consist principally of graywacke, the oldest known sandstone; while the marble deposits at their base are said to have been formed many thousand years later.

The mountain district of northeast Pickens is the setting for a summer colony known as Tate Mountain Estates. Two interesting features of this development are Lake Sequoyah —named after the inventor of the Cherokee alphabet—a large artificial lake 2,800 feet above sea-level, and an 18-hole golf course, at an average elevation of 2,900 feet, which has received high praise from many professional players. On Burrell Top is situated Connahaynee Lodge, the handsome center of the summer colony, constructed chiefly of logs gathered from the nearby woodland.

Atop Mount Oglethorpe stands one of the most interesting historical monuments in the state, dedicated to the memory of James Edward Oglethorpe, the founder of the Georgia colony. When the monument was proposed several years ago, the legislature by request changed the name of this mountain from "Grassy Knob" to its present name. The monument, a beautiful shaft of white Georgia marble thirty-eight feet high, was erected by Col. Sam Tate and dedicated before a distinguished gathering in 1930. It bears the fol-

lowing inscription: "In grateful recognition of the achieve-
ments of James Edward Oglethorpe, who by courage, industry, and endurance founded the commonwealth of Georgia
in 1732. Dedicated July 25, 1930."

Marble, of course, is the mineral for which Pickens County
is most noted, the Long Swamp Valley area containing a
great ridge of the pure stone five miles in length, of which
more will be said in a later chapter. There are a number of
other minerals of commercial value to be found in the
county, including gold, mica, flagstone, iron, copper, gra-
phite, kaolin, pyrites, silica, sericite, and others. For various
reasons, however, whether inaccessibility, impurity, or in-
sufficient quantity, no systematic attempts are now being
made toward their extraction or manufacture, although such
operations have been carried on to some small extent in the
past. Gold-mining has been limited chiefly to the panning
of gravel from small streams, the county being a little north of
the main gold belt of Georgia and containing no large deposits of the precious metal. Mica is found extensively in the
county and received some little attention in earlier days. A
flagstone deposit said to be one of the finest in the United
States is located near Jasper.

Two mineral springs of considerable local fame occur in
Pickens County, one about a mile and a half northwest of
Jasper, known as the Simmons Mineral Spring, the other
about five miles southeast of Jasper, called the Tate Mineral
Spring. The water from both these places is said to have been
valued for its healthful properties by the Indians, as well
as by later residents of the section. The Simmons spring
gives out about two gallons of water a minute, of an irony
taste. The other is a very bold chalybeate spring furnishing
six gallons a minute, and this water also tastes distinctly of

iron. An analysis of the water from the Tate Mineral Spring, made some years ago by the state geologist, is given here:

Constituents	Parts Per Million	Grains Per U. S. Gallon
Silica (SiO_2)	9.5	.554
Chlorine (C_1)	8.6	.502
Sulphur trioxide (SO_3)	11.5	.671
Carbon dioxide (CO_2)	48.4	2.822
Sodium oxide (Na_2O)	6.4	.373
Potassium oxide (K_2O)	1.7	.099
Lime (CaO)	22.6	1.318
Magnesia (MgO)	9.6	.560
Alumina (Al_2O_3)	2.4	.140
Ferric oxide (Fe_2O_3)	4.6	.268*

Included in a discussion of the geology and topography of Pickens County should be some mention of the three very interesting caves to be found here. One is on the west branch of Long Swamp Creek east of Jasper, and one on Sharp Mountain southwest of that town. The third of these caves is at Marble Hill near one of the Georgia Marble Company quarries. It abounds in stalagmite and stalactite, covered with crystal. This cave was closed on account of its nearness to a quarry and the danger incident thereto, and has not been fully explored.

The location of Pickens County in Georgia is the central northern part, Jasper, the county seat, being sixty-five miles directly north of Atlanta. The county lies between 34°23′ and 34°34′ north in latitude; and is bounded on the east by Dawson County, south by Cherokee, west by Gordon, and north by Gilmer. In its present shape, which it has retained substantially since its formation, Pickens County is twenty-three miles at its greatest distance from east to west, and thirteen and a half miles at its greatest distance from north to

*Table from Bulletin No. 20, Geological Survey of Georgia, p. 144.

south. It contains two hundred and forty-one square miles, being somewhat smaller than the average county in Georgia.

In spite of the comparatively small size of the county, its latitude, climate, and diversity of elevations—ranging from 1,000 to 3,300 feet—allow of a very extensive flora, so that a remarkable number and variety of plants thrive or may be grown within its borders. This is illustrated in a very striking manner by the long list of trees that are found in the county, which I will give here:

alder	hickory, several kinds
beech	holly, evergreen and deciduous
birch	honey-tree
box elder	laurel or ivy
buckeye	leatherwood
catalpa	linn
cedar	locust
chestnut	maple
chinquapin	oak, several kinds
cherry, wild	paw-paw
dogwood	pine, several kinds
elm	poplar or tulip
gum	rhododendron
hackberry or ironwood	sassafras
haw	sycamore
hemlock	witch-hazel

Even this list can not be called complete, but it gives an idea of the natural beauty and luxuriance of the section. One of the rare trees which grow here is the chinquapin oak, commonly accepted as belonging to the pin oak family. A fine specimen of this tree stands near the Tate homestead and has a spread of more than one hundred feet.

One of the most beautiful of the flowering shrubs in this section is the wild azalea, which grows in great abundance and variety of color, from the early-blooming light pink to the rich red and bronze of the dwarf type, which blooms as

CONNAHAYNEE LODGE

GOLF COURSE, TATE MOUNTAIN ESTATES

21

late as July. Other flowers and shrubs which flourish here
include the trailing arbutus, galaxia, wild hydrangea, daisy,
violet, phlox, lady-slipper, wild iris, passion flower, golden-
rod, wild aster, and many varieties of honeysuckle; while
there may also be found ginseng and other medicinal plants.

On account of diversity of soils, elevations, etc., Georgia
is said to have eleven distinct crop belts, of the thirteen which
exist in the United States; and she can grow the products of
the other two belts—citrus and semi-tropical fruits in the
extreme southern part of the state, and buckwheat and similar
crops in the northern part. Within the boundaries of Pickens
may be grown every type of crop found in the United States,
except semi-tropical fruits. Therefore the county may be
said to have twelve of the thirteen belts. Farm production
here consists chiefly, however, of cotton, corn, wheat, rye,
oats, hay, potatoes and cabbage. Some apples and peaches
are grown.

A very interesting fauna was also presented by the county
in the early days, when the forests abounded in game of many
kinds. Black bears, deer, beavers, red and gray foxes,
squirrels, opossums, raccoons, muskrats, groundhogs, wild
turkeys, pheasants, and quail were here in abundance, and
it is told that when the wild pigeons were migrating one year
they came in such great numbers that many limbs were
broken from the forest trees by their weight.

With the coming of civilization, of course, the greater part
of the wild life disappeared from this section, although many
parts of the county still offer good hunting and fishing.
Many different kinds of birds may be found today in Pickens
County, however, and I am giving a partial list of them here:

cardinal	mourning dove
bluebird	bob-white
flicker	starling
Carolina wren	red-winged blackbird

wood-thrush
indigo bunting
mocking-bird
brown thrasher
joree
goldfinch
blue-jay
English sparrow
red-headed woodpecker
downy woodpecker
robin
night-hawk

tufted titmouse
humming-bird
black-and-white warbler
prairie warbler
cat-bird
peewee
olive-backed thrush
meadow-lark
field-sparrow
white-throated sparrow
whippoorwill
chickadee

THE CHEROKEE INDIANS

The first inhabitants of the territory just described, and of all north Georgia, were the Cherokee Indians. At least, that is the more commonly accepted theory. The belief is held by some that long ago a strange tribe of white men, called the "mound-dwellers," lived in this section of the South, but the evidence in support of this belief is so small, as yet at least, that scientists have been able to form few if any definite conclusions about this half-mythical people.

There is no way of telling how long the Cherokees lived here. It is certain that during the time of which we have any knowledge, no other tribe of Indians ever inhabited the territory that is now North Georgia. The boundary between the Cherokees and the Creeks, who lived to the south of them, never extended very far north of the present Atlanta; and the northern boundary of the Cherokees, reaching at the time of the Revolutionary War to the Ohio and Tennessee Rivers, still included part of North Carolina and Tennessee when the Indians were removed to the west. References to the Cherokees are made in the first recorded history concerning this section, the accounts written by companions of DeSoto, who traversed North Georgia in 1540 on his march to the Mississippi. How many centuries the Cherokees had then lived here, none can say.

In spite of the interesting character of the topic, there is really no need to go into great detail here about the Cherokees. Their story has been well and completely told by a number of competent authorities* (whose works the reader may consult, if interested, with both pleasure and profit), so that one is constrained to believe they are one of the best-known and most publicized Indian tribes in the United States. It will, however, be proper to give here some idea of the life and customs of this very remarkable tribe.

It was the civilization of the Cherokees that has so intrigued their biographers. Even as early as the sixteenth century, they were said by chroniclers of DeSoto to have been surprisingly intelligent and friendly. When the first white men came to live among them, early in the last century, the Cherokees rapidly acquired many of the customs of the whites. One of these customs was slave-owning. A census taken of the Cherokee nation in 1825, showing 13,563 Indians, gave the number of negro slaves owned by them at 1,277. This example of "civilization," striking as it is, is less to the point, however, than their achievement of literacy. The invention by Sequoyah of the Cherokee alphabet, its quick adoption and use by the entire tribe, and the subsequent establishment of a national newspaper printed in this now literate language, form a chapter said to be unparalleled by any other so-called savage tribe in modern history.

In other fields, also, the Cherokees during their latter days in Georgia made notable progress. They developed proficiency in the use of looms, spinning wheels, and various farm implements; most of them adopted the Christian re-

---

*Including James Mooney, *Myths of the Cherokee*, in 19th Annual Report of the Bureau of American Ethnology; Wilson Lumpkin, *Removal of the Cherokee Indians from Georgia*; George R. Gilmer, *Sketches of Some of the First Settlers of Upper Georgia, of the Cherokees, and the Author.*

ligion and worshiped regularly at the churches which they built under the direction of white missionaries; they passed laws regulating the use of liquor, and made other moral advances; and they enjoyed an efficient method of self-government.

As we are reminded by most of the commentators on the Cherokees, they owed the greater part of their advance in civilization to the precept and example of white men, not only the missionaries who went among them to live and teach and, in some cases, dabble in their government, but also the whites who intermarried with the Cherokees. The census of 1825 before referred to showed that 73 women and 147 men of the white race were living in the Cherokee nation in that year after such intermarriage. It is accepted that practically all the chieftains and wealthy men of the tribe had white blood in their veins. Sequoyah—who had also the Caucasian name of George Guess—was at least three-fourths white, we are told, some of his biographers giving him as little Indian blood as one-sixteenth. John Ross and John and Major Ridge, head chieftains, and Elias Boudinot, the editor of the Cherokee newspaper, all were partly white, it is well established; and so were most of the wealthy, slave-owning class of Indians.

Of course, the fact that the Cherokees were able to take and assimilate the ideas of their leaders—red or white— proves that these Indians were of uncommonly good stock. It would be as idle to deny this as it would be to deny—on the other hand—the influence of the white blood among them. Everything considered, they must be regarded as superior to the average American Indian; and they are in fact so regarded by every student of the tribe.

That they were a "super-race," however, as their highly romanticized history might lead one to think, will stand a good deal of proving. Probably this was more evident to the white settlers who first lived among them than it is to us of today. Since the "civilization" of the Cherokees developed only after their contacts with the white race, we may rest fairly certain that these earliest pioneers underwent much the same inconveniences arising out of abode among Indians, as did our forefathers in other parts of the United States. If there were few Indian atrocities suffered in this section, as was the case, there was still no great amount of satisfaction, and a good deal of uncertainty, in having Indians for your neighbors. We are assured that the depredations of thieving Indians were nowise infrequent during the early days, and that their openly suspicious attitude was rather uncomfortable, to the pioneer women especially.

And there is nothing whatsoever to indicate that any actual white resident of the section, up to the time of the Removal in 1838, ever expressed the opinion that the rank and file of the Cherokees had partaken to any alarming degree of the civilized customs for which the upper class of the tribe became so celebrated. On the contrary, they were regarded by the whites with a mixture of distaste and pity, rather than as equals. We know this by official records, for one thing, since the court presentments of the early days took cognizance of the "state of degradation to which the Indians are fast approaching," (due to the use of liquor); and "the miserable existence" which they were being forced to lead among "an alien race, with strange customs and manners." These expressions, which are taken from the grand jury presentments of Cherokee County, Georgia, in 1835, would indicate not only that the Indians of this section were taking very slowly to "civilization" but that it did not agree with them.

Of course, it was to be expected that with the increase of white population the Indians would become more subdued and tractable, and that with the increasing scarcity of wild game in the forests, due to the encroachments of white civilization, a large part of the Cherokees would be forced to some extent to desert their nomadic ways of life and turn to agriculture, and some types of industry, for a living.

Going back into the "pre-settler" days, though, we find the Cherokees lived in much the same way as did the other Indian tribes of the continent. Hunting, fishing, a perfunctory kind of agriculture—the women worked patches of corn, beans, pumpkins, and the like—occasional fighting, and frequent game-playing, formed their main pursuits. Lacking some of the warlike temperament of most other tribes, the Cherokee men were inclined to take their energy out in sports, such as horse-racing and ball-playing. Legend says the site of the present Ball Ground, in Cherokee County a few miles south of the Pickens line, was once the scene of a great "ball-play" between Cherokees and Creeks to settle a point of land ownership, the former winning. Such procedure between Indian tribes—if this legend is true—was, to say the least, unusual.

While the habits of the earlier Cherokees were nomadic, the various clans often had villages for their headquarters, each village or "town" being under the nominal rule of a chief. Of the numbers of Indian towns which existed in North Georgia, only one of these seems to have been in what is now Pickens County. This was Sanderstown, the place at which the Indians of this locality were collected by General Scott's soldiers for removal to the west. The present town of Talking Rock is located at or near the old site of Sanderstown. It is not known what the Indians called this village before it became known to the white settlers as Sanderstown —which of course is not an Indian name. There appears to be no evidence that it was known by them as Talking Rock —or *Nunyu-gunwaniski*, in their tongue—this name apparently having been first used to designate a town by the white people. The name itself is undoubtedly of Indian origin, but does not seem to have been applied by them to anything except an actual rock, concerning which there are various stories. The account given by Professor Mooney, one of the best-known authorities on the Cherokees, is quoted here:

Talking Rock: A creek in upper Georgia flowing northward to join Coosawatee River. The Indian settlements upon it were considered as belonging to Sanderstown, on the lower part of the creek, the townhouse being located about a mile above the present Talking Rock station on the west side of the railroad. The name is a translation of the Cherokee *Nunyu-gunwaniski*, "Rock that talks," and refers, according to one informant, to an echo rock somewhere upon the stream below the present railroad station. An old-time trader among the Cherokees in Georgia says that the name was applied to a rock at which the Indians formerly held their councils, but the etymology of the word is against this derivation.*

Another account of the origin of this name is found in a story familiar to some of the older residents of Pickens County, dealing with a prank of the Indians. According to this version, there was once a rock, in the locality referred to, on which had been carved the words, "Turn me over!" The rock was so big and heavy that this was hard to do, but everyone who saw it would try. When, after a great deal of pushing and panting, someone would succeed in turning the stone over, he would read on the other side, "Turn me back over and let me fool somebody else!" This, according to the story, was the "talking rock."

It has been the impression of a few persons that there was once an Indian town called "Long Swamp" in what is now Pickens County, but the only historical reference to this town that I have been able to find is a map in Professor Mooney's book showing Long Swamp to have been in the northern part of the present Cherokee County, near Ball Ground. Another Indian town, Hickory Log, was in the same

---

*Myths of the Cherokee, p. 417.

MOUNTAIN SCENE, PICKENS COUNTY

vicinity, both villages being situated on Long Swamp Creek, which flows from Pickens into Cherokee. There is a strong local tradition to the effect that Long Swamp town was the place where an early Indian treaty was signed, and in view of this tradition I am quoting the following from Prof. E. Merton Coulter's recently-published book, "A Short History of Georgia" (p. 167):

Near the end of the Revolution a group of these dangerous characters [banished Tories, outlaws, and adventurers] led by Thomas Waters settled among the Cherokees on the Etowah River at the mouth of Long Swamp Creek and carried out a reign of terror on the frontiers of Wilkes County [the nearest settled region] until the combination of Clarke and Pickens went against them in the latter part of 1782, broke up the settlement, and forced, without right, upon the Cherokees a treaty ceding lands from the Tugaloo to the Chattahoochee.

Elijah Clarke and Andrew Pickens, both of them Revolutionary heroes and the latter the man after whom Pickens County was later named, were the "Clarke and Pickens" referred to in this excerpt. The actual place where the treaty was signed may have been either in the present Cherokee County or in the present Pickens, having undoubtedly been somewhere along Long Swamp Creek.

It is interesting to note here that this Treaty of Long Swamp was not between the United States and the Cherokees, but between Georgia and the Cherokees. Also it is apparently the first treaty among the very few ever signed between the two parties. The right of a state to enter into Indian treaties soon became a much disputed point, but a federal commission in 1789 investigated the matter and found that the state had been honest and open in its dealings with the Indians.

Enough has been said here to show what manner of people the Cherokee Indians were when the white men came to settle among them, and how the Indians were affected by the intrusion. Regardless of the nature of their relations with these new neighbors or of their reactions to civilization, the Cherokees were a doomed race from the time the white man first cast his covetous eyes on their land. Their ultimate departure was inevitable, as it would have been in any other state east of the Mississippi. That this departure had to be a Removal was due to several reasons, which will be mentioned a little further on.

THE OLD FEDERAL ROAD

When the newly-created county of Pickens was laid out in 1853, almost the entire distance of the Old Federal Road which had been in Gilmer and Cherokee Counties—a stretch of over thirty miles—was now found to be in Pickens. After traversing a small corner of Gilmer County, the road proceeded through Pickens from the northwest to the southeast corner, touching Cherokee only briefly on its way east.

The great importance of this early thoroughfare in the building up of the territory through which it passed gives it a prominent place in our history. At the time it was built —somewhere between 1812 and 1820, according to differing accounts—this road was the only direct route between the Cherokee country and the nearest trading point, Augusta. It connected Tennessee, to the north, with the thriving centers of East and South Georgia—and made Pickens County the gateway. You realize, of course, that there were few or no settlers here when the Old Federal Road was built—much less any Pickens County. So it is easy to see that the effect this road had on the settlement and early development of the county can scarcely be overestimated.

The credit for building this road, authorities agree, goes to General Andrew Jackson—"Old Hickory"—who passed

through this section with his army early in 1818 on his way
to punish the Seminoles of Florida for their recent uprisings.
There is some difference of opinion as to whether Jackson
cut the road on his way to Florida or on the return trip in
1819—or, as some accounts have it, as early as the time of
his southern operations in the War of 1812. According to
this latter version, the road was cut in the course of a forced
march which Jackson made to Savannah for the purpose of
defending a threatened attack by the British on that place.
The consensus of historical opinion, however, seems to be
that the road was not built until the time of the Seminole
expedition; and this opinion is further supported by an old
Indian treaty, dated March 22, 1816, by which the Cherokees
ceded to the United States the right to build roads through
any part of the Cherokee nation. In this same treaty, incidentally, the Indians agreed "to establish and keep up, on the
roads to be opened under the sanction of this article, such
ferries and public houses as may be necessary for the accommodation of the citizens of the United States"; which is
an interesting commentary on the character of these Indians.

As to whether the Old Federal Road was cut out in 1818 or
1819, one of the accounts handed down concerning the origin
of this road says that it was built by "the Pioneer Road Company," which preceded Jackson's soldiers on the trip southward. While it would of course have saved trouble thus to
cut the road on the first trip, it is possible on the other hand
that Jackson's haste to get to the Seminole country would
have prevented the construction of anything like an actual
road on this leg of the expedition. At any rate, we have
nothing to indicate that the words on a granite marker at
Tennga, Ga., erected by the Dalton chapter of D. A. R. in
1929 and stating that "Near this spot General Andrew Jackson first entered Georgia by the Old Federal Road—1818,"
are incorrect.

The point of the exact date when the road was built is interesting, but not of any especial importance for our purposes. What *is* important is the fact that along this early highway were built the very first houses and settlements in what is now Pickens County, as well as in practically all of northwestern Georgia. The taverns established by the Indians in compliance with the treaty referred to, were probably the first buildings along this road. As white settlers began to drift into the territory they also erected their homes near the road or, in some cases, bought out the Indian tavern-keepers and continued the business themselves. As the country opened up and industry and agriculture became active, towns and settlements grew up along the road and it became in reality an artery of commerce.

As I have stated, the Old Federal Road ran from Tennessee —Cleveland was one of the towns on it in that state—to Augusta, Ga., and southward. Spring Place, Ga., was an important point on this road in the early days, and to this place over the Old Federal Road travelled the Indians and the United States agents to attend the last council of the Cherokees in 1837. In Pickens County, the early settlements on the road were Carmel Station, Love's, Harnage's (later Tate's), and Daniel's. These places are shown on an old map published in 1839. The first two were not far distant from the present Jasper, Harnage's was at the present site of Tate, and Daniel's was a little further east.

I have been able to get together a list of a number of early Pickens County families who settled on this road, some earlier and some later. Entering Pickens from the north-west, the road passed the Silver's home, Preacher Chadwick's, the Atherton place (and later Atherton Mills), Jim Bryant's, the Coleman place, Jim Stephens', the Morrisons', Jack Glenn's, John E. Price's, the Mullinax home, the Morrison home, John Taylor's, and James Simmons', all in the order named; then came Tate's, Faulkner's, Herndon's, Howell's, Grogan's, and Arthur's, and so to the southeast corner of the county.

To bring the picture up to the present time, along the course of the Old Federal Road are three of Pickens County's towns—Talking Rock, Jasper, and Tate—as well as a number of smaller places and landmarks, including Blaine (Old Talking Rock), Covington Hang, Four-Mile Church, and the Faulkner and Grogan settlements.

Not only in the upbuilding of Pickens County but in the everyday life of its early settlers did the Old Federal Road naturally play an important part. It was by this route that the farmers of Northwest Georgia, and many from Tennessee, drove their livestock and hauled their produce to the southern markets. It was no unusual sight in the early days to see hogs in droves of hundreds, great droves of cattle, horses, sheep, and turkeys being driven to market along this road, the drovers selling or trading stragglers to the people along the way; and a great business grew up in the sale of feed for the animals and food and entertainment for the drovers. When the settler wished to do some "trading"—first at Augusta and later on at Athens—or even when he had business at the state capital (then Milledgeville), the Old Federal Road was his route.

On account of its accessibility by this road, as well as for its central location, the house of the early settler Ambrose Harnage—located at the present site of Tate in Pickens County—was selected as the place for holding in 1832 the first election and the first court in the newly organized Cherokee County, which then included all of the Cherokee territory. More will be said about this later in the book.

The property at this place was purchased in 1834 by Samuel Tate, who settled there and opened up an inn for travelers. Some interesting sidelights on the early days in this section were written by G. W. Featherstonhaugh, a well-known English geologist, writer and traveler of the last century, who stopped at this inn in 1837 on his way to Gainesville and back to the Indian council at Spring Place. The following is quoted from his book, *A Canoe Voyage Up the Minnay Sotor*:

At 4 p. m. we reached a poor settlement near a place called Carmel, where I got a drink of water, and our animals having rested awhile, we pursued our dreary and fatiguing journey, occasionally enlivened by bands of Cherokees on horseback and on foot going with their women and children to Red Clay. After a very hot and exhausting [day's] journey of forty-five miles, thirty of which I had to walk, we arrived at 8 p. m. in a valley where there was a tolerable tavern kept by one Tate; and having refreshed myself with some good food and got a bath for my feet, I was most glad to lie down . . . . Having slept comfortably, we resumed our journey at 4 a. m. I was informed that gold-dust was found near this place, and gold-veins worked a few miles off, so that, as I suspected from the prevalence of the talcose slate, I was now in the Gold Region. We passed a tolerable good-looking house belonging to a half-breed named Robert Daniel, whose drunken son, the driver told me, it was whom I saw at Spring Place with his eye almost stamped out by his horse. I got a miserable breakfast at one Field's, a Georgian. The people about were tall, thin, cadaverous-looking animals, looking as melancholy and lazy as boiled cod-fish. This, no doubt, is to be attributed to their wretched diet and manner of life, for the better class of Georgians, who lead more generous lives, contains many fine-looking individuals. . . . Their miserable attempts at farming, when compared with the energy, foresight, and neatness of the people of the Northern States, are as absurd as they are ridiculous.

I am quoting the latter part of this excerpt by the good Mr. Featherstonhaugh mostly for its entertainment value, as his derogatory remarks about the people he saw are not to be taken too seriously. There are people everywhere like the ones he describes, and moreover, I am afraid he was some-

thing of a snob. Being a good observer, however, he does
bring out the very true point that the lives of the settlers
in this part of the country were rather less than "generous,"
just as pioneer life has always been. There are many hardships in conquering even a land as friendly as North Georgia.

The business of our early commentator having been
finished at Gainesville, he returned by stage-coach—as he
had gone—and again stopped on the way at the "tolerable
tavern of Tate."

> We reached Tate's [he wrote] in time for me to visit a deposit
> of white marble I had been informed of. It was of a very fine
> quality, and the quantity immense, there being a ridge of at least
> six miles long, entirely consisting of this mineral, of which I
> brought several specimens away.

It is interesting to note here that Harnageville (later Tate)
was the first postoffice in Pickens County and for many
miles around. Mail was brought by stage-coach, and the
early citizens paid for the letters they received on a sliding
scale, the postage amounting sometimes to as much as twenty-
five cents for a single letter. The postoffice of Harnageville
was established, according to the records of the Post Office
Department, on February 28, 1832.

SETTLEMENT OF THE TERRITORY

Between the time when the first white persons began to
settle along the Old Federal Road in the region of what is
now Pickens County, and the formation of the county in
1853, there elapsed a period of—we may say—about twenty-
five years. It seems to be the opinion of everyone who has
any information on the subject, and to be borne out by such
records as are available, that there were very few, if any,
actual settlers here before the latter half of the 1820's. Even
that would be a decade before the removal of the Indians,

and from what evidence can be obtained it is safe to say that the settlers did not begin to come in appreciable numbers until the early 'thirties.

These twenty-five or so years covered what might be called the formative period of this section—the time when it was being settled and built up and its resources beginning to be developed. During this era occurred a number of events which were of great influence on the future history of the section, such as the Gold Rush of 1829-31, the ensuing immigration of settlers, the Land Lottery of 1832, the formation of the original Cherokee County in 1831 and the division of this territory into ten counties in 1832, the first courts and county elections of Northwest Georgia, the final removal of the Cherokee Indians in 1838, the Land Lottery of that year, and the subsequent development of the region up to the year 1853.

Truly this was an active period, and one of the most interesting with which we have to deal in this history. For the reason that it preceded the actual creation of Pickens County —and also because the events mentioned already have a prominent place in every history of our state, as well as having been brought together with some detail in Rev. L. G. Marlin's recent *History of Cherokee County*—I am making this part of my book brief; but I will try to give a general idea of this period, starting here with the early settlement of the territory and the reasons therefor.

In dwelling as I have done on the subject of the Old Federal Road, it has been my purpose to emphasize that this road was not only the earliest but one of the most potent factors in the settlement of Pickens County. We may reasonably assume that the land along the borders of this road, by reason of greater accessibility, was the first to attract settlers as being desirable for their new homes; and, consequently, that the period of earliest settlement in Pickens County was a trifle earlier, possibly by a few years, than that in some of the counties of Northwest Georgia through which the road did not pass.

Regardless of this point, however, we know that the attractions of a territory such as this part of the state then was —a virgin expanse of forest, plain, and mountain, unpenetrated for the most part by white men, and peopled by a half-savage tribe of Indians—were not sufficient to induce many people to settle here before the third decade of the last century. For more compelling causes of population, therefore, we will have to look to some of the events shortly before referred to. The first of these was the Georgia Gold Rush.

It is a disputed point as to whether the Indians actually mined gold in North Georgia before the days of the first settlers. That they were aware of its existence in their country is beyond doubt, but not knowing its value they probably did not make any systematic attempts to reclaim it from the earth. If they did, they hid their knowledge and their operations remarkably well, for it was not until the year 1829— according to most accounts, and certainly not before 1828 —that the white man learned of the existence of gold in the Cherokee country.

Two discoveries of the yellow metal were made in 1829, almost simultaneously. One was on Duke's Creek, in Habersham County, and the other on the banks of a stream near Dahlonega, in Lumpkin. The effect of this news, when it got out, was to start the first actual gold rush in the history of our country. Into the Land of the Cherokees poured adventurous men from every part of the nation—by the hundreds and even thousands.

Already, in 1827, the legislature of Georgia had recognized the need for law and order in the state's frontier territory by extending the jurisdiction of Carroll and DeKalb Counties over the Cherokee nation. This legislation, incidentally, was

designed also as a reply to the very embarrassing action of the
Cherokees, a few months before, in proclaiming themselves
a distinct, self-governing nation within the boundaries of
Georgia!—a proclamation which they backed up with a
written constitution of their own denying that the laws of
Georgia had any authority over them. In the following year,
1828, the state legislature took the further step of dividing
up the Cherokee territory and adding it to the counties of
Carroll, DeKalb, Gwinnett, Hall, and Habersham, again "extending the laws of this state over the same."

Such was the status of the territory when the "Twenty-
Niners" began pouring in on their eager quest for gold. The
situation immediately became very difficult for the state
to handle. The land belonged to the Indians, despite repeated
efforts by governors of Georgia to have the federal government remove them in accordance with a long-standing agreement. Many scenes of violence followed the entry of the
lawless element among the gold-seekers, all of whom were
violating three distinct sets of laws—those of the United
States, Georgia, and the Cherokee nation—in being there at
all without proper permits. It finally became necessary for the
state to pass a law prohibiting any gold-mining at all, by
either Indians or whites, without special permission, until
the land could be surveyed and distributed by lottery to
white settlers. This put an end to the Gold Rush—though
not of course to the pursuit of gold in North Georgia, a business that has continued, with varying degrees of enthusiasm
and success, ever since.

The number of actual settlers gained by this section during
the period of the Gold Rush was comparatively small. The
"Twenty-Niners" came looking for sudden wealth, not for
new homes. And by this time there were legal difficulties
in the way of acquiring the latter, though laws favoring
settlement were shortly to come into effect.

BOATING ON LAKE SEQUOYAH

That the state had some years before this time decided on a policy of encouraging the settlement of the Indian territory within its boundaries, as a step toward displacing the Indians, is evident from the legislation of 1827 and 1828 extending Georgia's authority over the territory. This policy had been interrupted by the Gold Rush, but the latter event also had something to do with speeding up the plan since it enhanced the desirability of the Cherokees' land. Accordingly, in 1830, legislation was passed ordering a survey to be made of the Cherokee territory and authorizing the governor to distribute this land by means of a lottery—the system of land distribution then in favor in Georgia.

The survey was completed in 1832, and drawing of lots began in the latter part of that year at Milledgeville, the state capital. The "gold region," which included thirty-three land districts out of the seventy-nine contained in the survey, was divided up into 40-acre lots, and the rest of the territory, including all of what is now Pickens County, into lots of 160 acres each. It is said that some 218,000 persons had applied for chances in the lottery, while we find that only about 58,000 lots were to be distributed; so three out of every four applicants necessarily drew blanks.

As to the method of procedure, one account states that slips of paper bearing the numbers of the lots were placed in a huge hopper, turned by a crank, and the numbers withdrawn by the officials; while another version relates that the slips were placed on two large wheels, one for the gold lots and the other for the larger lots. At any rate, the applicants who were fortunate enough to draw numbers instead of blanks were entitled to receive, upon payment of a small fee, a deed of original grant bearing the Great Seal of Georgia waxed to a blue ribbon. (These original deeds are of course very scarce now, but I understand that a number of families in this section still retain specimens.)

In trying to give a clear description of how the Cherokee lands were lotteried off—and of how the first settlers in this region obtained their lands—one is tempted to wish that some historian would go to the original state records and spend enough time to get complete details on this very interesting subject. My own excursion into "secondary" history has been rather unsatisfactory on this point for the reason that no available account of the land lotteries seems to cover all the facts that are shown by even a moderate research in original records. From the latter it is certain that there were three distinct lotteries of the territory in question; no account I have seen mentions more than two, and some of them only one.

Without exhaustive research, the following facts, however, come to light from old, records. In 1830 the act of the legislature* ordering the original survey (and division thereof into 160-acre lots) provided also that upon its completion the governor should order a lottery of the entire Cherokee territory. In 1831 an amendment† to this act required that all districts in the gold region be divided instead into 40-acre lots, or "gold lots," and specified the "gold districts." Thus the terms used in the legislation: Gold Lottery and Land Lottery. Both these lotteries were held in 1832-33 (the drawing requiring seven months). But in 1838, just prior to the removal of the Indians, another drawing, entirely of 160-acre lots and called the Cherokee Land Lottery, was held.

An old book published in 1838‡ and giving the names of the fortunate drawers in the lottery of that year, shows that only 287 out of the 969 land lots in what is now Pickens County were drawn prior to the 1838 lottery. The fact that less than one-third of the lots in this county (and the proportion holds true for the entire 160-acre-lot region) were ac-

*Acts, Georgia, 1830, p. 127; approved December 21, 1830.
†Ibid., 1831, p. 164; approved December 24, 1831.
‡The Cherokee Land Lottery, by James F. Smith.

tually owned by individuals prior to 1838 has led some persons to believe that there was no general lottery of the 160-acre parcels until that year. "Individual state grants" answers the question nicely—allowing as it does for the circumstance that most of these 287 lots were well located, as for instance near the Federal Road, and so would have been logical "homestead" lots—but does not take into consideration the fact that such a method of disposal would have been contrary to the legislation already mentioned. From the act of December 21, 1830, we know that *all* the 969 lots in our county were ordered to be lotteried off in 1832; and we can only assume that the 287 persons whose ownership of lots was already of record by January 1, 1838, were the only ones drawing lots in this county who had perfected their title claims by paying the necessary fee to the state and keeping up the taxes. On this theory, the balance of the lots drawn in 1832 had been forfeited, and were drawn all over again in 1838; which was probably the case.

Of course, title to many of the 40-acre or gold lots also must have gone unperfected, particularly since there were three times as many of them; and yet there appears to have been no second lottery of the gold lots. While this does not directly concern Pickens County, it shows that the whole subject needs a general clarification.

Like every other part of Cherokee Georgia, the Pickens County region derived unprecedented increases in population from the lotteries of 1832 and 1838. It is of course impossible to estimate the figures with any degree of accuracy, because it is not known how many of the fortunate drawers became actual settlers. But even if one had not drawn a free tract in one of the lotteries, lands were easily and cheaply available from many who had. Moreover, titles, being derived from state grants, were now legally perfect, as they could not have been with any other origin. There was no drawback as far as obtaining lands was concerned. And the very fact that new settlers were coming into the section and building their homes here meant that the recognized advantages and resources of the region were no longer outweighed by its lack of white population, and were therefore more attractive to developers. Settlement of the territory that was to become Pickens County was now beginning in earnest.

In the meantime, though, there had occurred another event that was also significant in the development of this section, through its influence on law and order. While the surveying of Cherokee Georgia had been going on prior to the drawing at Milledgeville, the state legislature, in further preparation of the territory for settlement, had taken the land of the Cherokees out from under the jurisdiction of the five counties it had been added to in 1828, and made from it one huge new county—called Cherokee. The Indian territory thus became, for the first time, a single unit of government under the direct jurisdiction of the state of Georgia.

What is particularly interesting, here, about the creation of the original Cherokee County is that its "county site" was located in what is now Pickens. The house of Ambrose Harnage, before referred to, was named in the creating act as the place at which the first election and first court of Cherokee County should be held. This house was located at the present site of Tate, Ga., on approximately the same spot of ground now occupied by the Tate homestead.

The date of the act creating the original Cherokee County was December 26, 1831. On February 6 of the following year an election of county officers was held at the Harnage place, and on March 26 began the first court session of the new county, then a part of the Western Judicial District.

The first words in the earliest court-minutes book of Cherokee County are: "On the 26th day, it being the fourth Monday

in March, in the year 1832, at a court begun and holden at
the house of Ambrose Harnage, now Harnageville, in and
for the county of Cherokee, in the state of Georgia, etc." The
"now Harnageville" doubtless refers to the fact that on the
28th of the preceding month the house of Ambrose Harnage
had been made a postoffice, and was now officially "Harnageville."

A few of the members of the grand jury at this term of
court are recognizable as having been residents of the vicinity,
and the names of the entire panel may be of interest here:
They were: James Hemphill, John Dawson, James Cantril,
Franklin Daniel, Green B. Durham, Robert Fowler, John
Jack, Reuben Sams, John P. Brooke, Charles Haynes, George
Baber, Noble Timmons, John S. Holcomb, Leroy Hammond,
Samuel Means, William H. Ray, Hubbard Baskin, William
Smith, and William Lay.

The first officers elected in the original Cherokee County
were: Oliver Strickland, clerk of the superior court; William
T. Williamson, clerk of the inferior court; John Jolly, sheriff;
Jesse Watkins, surveyor; Asa Keith, coroner; John McCon-
nell, John Witcher, Robert Obarr, Genubath Winn, and Henry
Holcombe, justices of the inferior court.

But the original Cherokee County lasted only one year.
In December of 1832, the territory which it had comprised
was divided up by act of legislature into ten different counties: Cass (now Bartow), Cherokee, Cobb, Floyd, Forsyth,
Gilmer, Lumpkin, Murray, Paulding, and Union. It was
from two of these, Cherokee and Gilmer, that Pickens County
was formed in 1853; and in a similar manner other new
counties have been formed from time to time, so that in all
there are now more than twenty counties in "Cherokee
Georgia."

Thus was the entire Indian territory then remaining in

AERIAL VIEW OF TATE, GA., IN THE LONG SWAMP VALLEY. MARBLE WORKS IN THE FOREGROUND

46

Georgia brought under the state's control and jurisdiction, divided into counties and duly organized, and partially populated with white settlers. There remained one other object to be accomplished before the proper development of the section could be brought about—an object which Georgia had long sought but without any appreciable results. This was the removal of the Cherokees.

Removal of the Cherokee Indians

A great deal has been said and written about this topic. Georgia's part in the Removal, particularly, has long been a favorite subject for discussion among the historians—with Georgia usually getting the little end of the argument. In view of the facts in the matter, this is a little hard to understand, as I shall try to point out.

It is not so difficult, however, to understand the universal interest which has attached itself to the subject of the Removal. The Cherokees were not only the last Indian tribe in Georgia, but the last in any state east of the Mississippi, with the exception of the Seminoles, who still live in Florida. Their departure thus marked a sort of era in our national history—a history in which the Indians of the East and South had been conspicuously present as the first owners of the land. In addition, the Cherokees have always been regarded as one of the superior Indian tribes of the continent, and the degree of civilization which they achieved was so astonishing as to win them permanent fame. Romance could not help but follow the footsteps of such a people as they plodded sadly along the journey from their beautiful home in the South to the unknown "Land of the Setting Sun."

The reader may have decided, from some of my previous remarks about the Cherokees, that I am trying to make out a case against them and show that their removal from Georgia was not only necessary but attended with the highest degree of justice, poetic and otherwise. If so, he will have mistaken my real purpose, which is simply to show that this chapter in the history of our state has been more than a little exaggerated— and twisted—by certain outside historians whose ability and reputations are high enough to lend a certain amount of credibility to their versions of the affair. Worse, some of Georgia's ablest historians either concur or else give the impression that no defense is possible against this slight to their state.

It were hypocrisy, of course, to contend that the Indians were removed for any other reason than that the white people *wanted the land*. The land belonged, by every test of equity and law, to the Indians. And so, be it now said, the removal of the Cherokees and the seizure of their land, as it was allowed to happen, was entirely wrong and unjust.

It is right here, though, that commentators add, "—and a permanent blot on the fair pages of Georgia's history," or words to that effect. This does not necessarily follow. In order to place the blame in this affair with any accuracy, it is necessary that one have more than a superficial knowledge of the circumstances surrounding it. When the facts *are* known, one is inclined to wonder just what course the state of Georgia could have followed to come out of the matter more creditably.

Here, briefly, was the situation:

A great many years ago, in 1785 to be exact, the United States entered into an agreement with the Cherokee Indians known as the Hopewell Treaty, by which the Cherokees lost a large tract of their northern territory as a result of having helped the British in the Revolutionary War, but in which, for the consideration of their promise of future peace and friendship, the federal government confirmed their title to the lands that remained. From that time on, the United States recognized and held as lawful the title of the Cherokees to the lands confirmed to them by the Hopewell Treaty. During subsequent years the Indians ceded various tracts of this territory to the federal government, by means of properly executed treaties and upon payment for the lands by the government, but no thought was entertained by the latter of obtaining such lands without proper conveyance of title by the Indians.

In 1802, however, the United States obtained the cession from Georgia of a great tract of territory then within the bounds of our state and reaching all the way to the Mississippi River. In return for this territory, the United States expressly agreed, then and there, to extinguish the Indian titles to all lands in Georgia "as early as the same can be peaceably obtained on reasonable terms."

On the interpretation of this modifying clause rests the only slightest excuse to condemn Georgia for the removal of the Cherokees. It may be said that the United States was not bound to extinguish these Indian titles if it could not be done peaceably and at a reasonable cost. If this technical reasoning is sound reasoning, then it must be admitted that the blame is Georgia's.

I am sure, however, that no court of equity would sustain such an argument. The fact is, when the agreement of 1802 was made the federal government had no reason, in view of its former cessions from the Cherokees, to believe that it could not also buy their Georgia lands. At least, this must certainly have been the case, for had there been any doubt on the point at the time of the agreement, then the acceptance by the United States of Georgia's valuable cession would have been a very questionable action, under the kindest interpretation. There can be no doubt that Georgia entered into the contract believing that the consideration involved was unequivocal extinguishment of the Indian titles; and that the federal government obtained her cession through this understanding. To contend that the latter willfully offered a doubtful consideration is to cast reflection on the integrity of the United States in its methods of obtaining the contract; to contend, after the United States had assumed the responsibility of extinguishing the Indian titles, that the responsibility —and blame—was Georgia's, is to imply that this consideration was in fact doubtful. Which I am sure the historians do not wish to do; they have merely overlooked some of the facts.

Of course, it might also be argued that Georgia was at fault in seeking the extinguishment of the titles in the first place. This reasoning fails to stand up inasmuch as Georgia had no more cause to believe the Indian lands could not be purchased "peaceably and reasonably" than did the federal government. Here a third "villain" introduces himself into the plot—the Indian himself, who would not listen to reason and enable the United States to fulfill its agreement. But Georgia's skirts yet seem to be clear, and so they remain— her only fault is to protest, albeit long and loudly, that the promise made to her be carried out.

These are the true circumstances underlying the Removal —that alleged "blot on Georgia's history." They fail dismally to uphold the criticism our state has received in this connection. Concerning the Removal itself, and the manner in which it was carried out, there has been further criticism, by persons apparently without realization of the great difficulties bound to be connected with such a procedure. Here again it seems the facts have been ignored by the critics.

But we are getting ahead of the story. In the meantime, we find a great reluctance on the part of the government at Washington to disturb its constitutional wards, the Cherokees, in the possession of their Georgia homes. Georgia, however, was determined that the promise of 1802 should be fulfilled. Various governors and legislatures urged the matter on Congress from time to time, with indifferent results. Finally, federal agents succeeded in obtaining a removal treaty from the Creeks of South Georgia, and in 1828 this tribe departed to the Indian Reservation west of the Mississippi.

The Cherokees, however, steadfastly refused to give up their lands, although they were offered equivalent territory in the West as well as a large cash payment and other inducements. The attitudes of the Cherokees, the United States, and Georgia all are shown at this point by a message from President Monroe to the House and Senate on March 30, 1824, as follows:

By the paper bearing date of 30th Jany. last which was communicated to the chiefs of the Cherokee Nation in this city, who came to protest against any further appropriations of money for holding treaties with them, the obligation imposed upon the United States by the compact with Georgia to extinguish the Indian titles to the right of soil within the state, and the incompatibility with our system of their existence as a distinct community within any state, we pressed with the utmost earnestness. It was proposed to them at the same time to procure and convey to them territory beyond the Mississippi in exchange for that which they hold within the limits of Georgia, or to pay them for it its value in money. To this proposal their answer, which bears date of 11th of Feby. following, gives an unqualified refusal.*

There are voluminous records of the events and negotiations that transpired in the course of Georgia's efforts to reclaim her Indian territory, and I can not take the space even to outline them here. To arrive at the climax, on December 29, 1835, there was signed at New Echota (the Cherokee capital, in the present Gordon County) a treaty under the provisions of which the Cherokees were to receive five million dollars and a large tract of land in the West in return for all their holdings east of the Mississippi. These were prin-

---

*Messages and Papers of the Presidents, Vol. VI, p. 2971.

cipally in Georgia, though parts of Alabama, Tennessee, and North Carolina were included. It was agreed also that the Indians were to be paid for the houses and improvements they left behind, and were to be transported to their new homes at the expense of the federal government and "subsisted" there for one year.

The treaty of 1835 was to go into effect two years after its ratification by Congress, but when that period had passed it became evident that the Cherokees did not intend to abide by their agreement. Their defense was that the treaty had not been approved by the majority of the tribe; and it is claimed, in fact, that the federal agent who obtained the treaty admitted himself that only three hundred Cherokees were present at the signing. However, things had gone too far to be halted at this late date, and neither the United States nor Georgia entertained any idea of relenting from the terms of the treaty.

So the military was called into action. General Winfield Scott, of the United States Army, brought a detachment of soldiers into Georgia and was joined here by General Charles Floyd with two Georgia regiments. The soldiers scattered out over the Indian territory and gathered the Cherokees into forts at convenient locations (Sanderstown was the place where the Indians of this county were gathered). The work of rounding up the Indians took a little over a week, being finished early in June, 1838. All the Cherokees—there were over 15,000—were then taken to Ross' Landing, in Tennessee, where they were to begin their long march to Indian Territory under military escort. Due to what can only be considered as inexcusably improvident arrangements, the Indians were held at Ross' Landing until fall, so that their march was completed in the dead of winter. Many of them perished on the way, from exposure, sickness, and other causes, the number of deaths being put by some authorities at as high as four thousand. Finally the remainder, footsore and weary, arrived at their strange new homes beyond the Mississippi.

There is real tragedy in the story of the Cherokee Removal, especially this last phase of it. Of course, Georgia can not be held responsible for the deaths that occurred on this journey, her connection with the matter ceasing after the Indians were turned over to federal authorities at Ross' Landing, in plenty of time to make the trip during the mild months. For the "inhuman" manner in which the Indians were collected and gathered into forts, however, Georgia has received a great deal of abuse.

The classic account is given by Prof. James Mooney, probably the most noted authority on the Cherokees. It be-begins: "The history of this Cherokee removal may well exceed in weight of grief and pathos any other passage in American annals." He then gives a very dramatic description of Cherokee families being interrupted at meals, at work, or at whatever they were doing, to be forced at the points of bayonets to leave their homes and accompany the soldiers to the various forts. In only one particular, however, does he indicate any action of the soldiers not absolutely necessary under the circumstances—he alleges "blows and oaths," and these are flatly denied by the statements of actual eyewitnesses, one of which he was not. As there is great dispute about the treatment accorded the Indians by the soldiers, we can not accept any one account as the whole truth; but the evidence seems to point to the fact that humane treatment was not only ordered—we know that—but used, for the most part, except in the extremest emergencies. I do not presume to decide this much-disputed question, however.

If I had the space, I would like to quote the rather lengthy address which General Scott made to his soldiers before they went out to round up the Indians, and also his address to the Cherokees after arriving in their territory with his army. In the former, he leaves no room for doubt as to the humane manner in which the soldiers were expected to carry out their work. "Every possible kindness," he ordered, "compatible with the necessity of removal, must be shown by the troops; and if a despicable individual should be found capable of inflicting a wanton injury or insult on any Cherokee man, woman, or child, it is hereby made the special duty of the nearest good officer or man instantly to interpose, and to seize and consign the guilty wretch to the severest penalty of the law." In his address to the Cherokees, General Scott reminded them that they had been constantly warned the treaty would be carried out, and that he had now come for that purpose, but assured them that if they submitted peaceably they would be treated with the utmost consideration. Thus the official attitude in the matter, at least, is established as completely humane.

This is a good deal more than can be said for some of the Eastern states in the treatment of their own Indian problems. Georgia had as little reason as they to want a large part of her territory made a permanent Indian reservation. No other state, furthermore, ever had an Indian tribe to attempt the setting up of an actual foreign nation within her borders. And yet, when the evidence is all in, few of the states in the Union can point to a record as favorable as Georgia's in the treatment of Indian affairs.

The Cherokees, in the final analysis, were so unfortunate as to stand in the way of white civilization; and it is in the nature of things that they should have had to yield, brave as their battle was. Wise men saw at the time that the injustice of the Removal would turn out to be justice in the end; that future generations, both red and white, would be better off for the step. We know today that this has been so; and we also have the interesting knowledge, today, that the "untold millions" in yellow gold which the Indians thought their

Georgia land contained has dwindled into insignificance be-
side the actually computed millions in "liquid gold" that
the Cherokees have derived from their Oklahoma oil lands.

EARLY SETTLERS

In subsequent portions of this book are given the names
of many of the citizens of Pickens County during the period
of its creation and organization, as taken from the early
county records; and a complete census of the residents of
the county in 1860 is also furnished (see Chapter III). It
is impossible, from lack of records on the point, to give
anything like a complete list of the early settlers who came
to this section before the formation of the county in 1853;
but from the information of older citizens I am able to furnish a good many of these names and the following list is
thought to be fairly accurate, if hardly complete. Federal
Road settlers have already been mentioned, and a list of
settlers on other roads and in other parts of the county is
now given.

The Jasper community, which as explained in the next
chapter did not become a town until the site was chosen as
the county seat, contained the early residences of the McHans,
A. Tribble, the Fanns, Mrs. Duck, Jerry Sosebee, Dr. Ben
Hanie, and Grafton Adair—all on the Federal Road. On the
street leading to Talking Rock, were the Wm. T. Day residence, the John Brock residence, the James Simmons
residence, the McHan store, the Gordon store and residence,
Nix's hotel, Adin Keeter's store and residence, and a Masonic
hall. On the road leading west from Jasper toward Fairmount in Gordon County were Dr. John Lyon's residence, a
Methodist church, and the residence of George Harmon. On
the road leading south to Canton in Cherokee County were
the Castleberry home, Bales Bruce's store and residence, the

Drawing by Jeanne Wythe

THE OLD SIMMONS HOME, TWO MILES NORTH OF JASPER. BUILT BY "UNCLE JIMMY" SIMMONS BEFORE 1834, THIS IS ONE OF THE OLDEST HOUSES IN NORTHWEST GEORGIA; AND IS TYPICAL OF THE PIONEER ARCHITECTURE OF THE SECTION

Knight Blackwell residence, the Glasco shop and residence, the homes of Mike Stoner and W. H. Simmons, and just off this road or street were located the residences of Griffin Heath, W. Hill, and Grafton Adair. The places mentioned were all in the Jasper vicinity, many of them before the county was created.

Between Jasper and Talking Rock were the homes of James Simmons, John Taylor, the Widows Morrison, the Mullinaxes, John E. Price, Jack Glenn, the Morrison sisters, Jim Stephens, the Colemans, Jim Bryant, and the Taylors, the latter living just south of Old Talking Rock.

Out of Talking Rock and up Ball Creek were the houses of Preacher Shadwick and the Silvers. Up Talona Creek from Talking Rock lived John Gartrell, Henry Gartrell, Joe Simmons, Hiram Reed, and Andrew Morrison. Also near Talking Rock were the residences of Zeke Akins, Moses Jones, and Josiah Reese.

From Jasper out the Fairmount Road were the homes of Jimmy Lovelace, Clark McClain, John Burgess, Ira Dunegan, John Lambert (who was a preacher), Andrew Jones, Zeke Forester, Bill Thompson, Lewis Thompson, Elisha Bennett, Joe Neal, Lewis Larmon, and Hiram Mills.

South of Ludville lived the Mosses, the Chastains, and the Evanses. Around Philadelphia were Crawford Cowart, John Lambert, Riley B. Strickland, and William Reeves.

Along the Old Federal Road from Jasper to the Dawson line were the Tates, John Nelson, the Faulkners, the Herndons, Jim Grogan, Bethel Disharoon, Elias Allred, and Jimmie Howell. Along the east fork of Long Swamp Creek, out from Tate's, lived the Stegalls, Erve Disharoon, Tom Monroe, and Jack Lovelady; and slightly west of this section were the homes of Rev. Isaac Padgett and Jasper Pettett. Close to Corinth Church was Mark Disharoon's.

Between Tate and Marble Hill was the residence of John

Darnell and Sion Darnell, and near this place were the homes of Tom and Harrison Pendley.

Near Long Swamp Church lived John Hendrix and Jasper White. Back toward Jasper from this section was the house of Jim Swafford and the Cale Griffith Settlement. North of the latter were the Lewis Quinton place and that of the Hurlick family. Up Bull Gap Road were the homes of Tom Norton and David and Jonathan McArthur.

Near what is now Tate Mountain Estates were the Landsdown place, Bill Fitzsimmons, and Isaac Burlison. At the foot of Mount Oglethorpe were the homes of Otis Dover and the Hammontrees.

Down the Ball Ground Road from Jasper lived Miles Berry, "Dad" Lyons, a preacher, "Aunt" Polly Tarbutton, Dred Patterson, Ben Davis, Gray Whitfield, Garland Green, Ned Townsend, Abe Crow, John Worley (who lived at what is now called Worley's Cross-roads), Alfred Spence, Samuel McCutcheon, Frank Manley, Hicks Patterson, and Buck Dowda. Down the creek from Abe Crow's place were the homes of the Cagles—Bill, John, Levi, and Frank—the Jordan place, Mike Stoner, Dick Cook, Mark Turner, and George Little.

On Bethany Road were the homes of Middleton Turner and his two sons, John and Hayden, Tom Cantrell, John C. Cornelison, John M. Allred, Pink Arwood, the Cook family, John Payne, and Wilkey McHan.

On the road leading southwest from Jasper were the residences of Absalom Lovelace, Thomas Johnson, the Alanson home and mill, Leonard Bearden, and William Davis.

LIFE AMONG THE PIONEERS

The word "pioneer" will always have a noble meaning for Americans. With it we associate strength of character as

well as strength of body; high ideals, as well as resourceful-
ness. The pioneers built our nation, and they built well;
and we honor their names.

The pioneers of North Georgia were such people. Hardy
of stock, adventurous of spirit, they took up their abode far
from the centers of civilization to wrest a living from the
wilderness and carve out a place for future generations in
a new section of America. Cherokee Georgia was one of the
last frontiers of the eastern states; most states near the sea-
coast had been entirely settled long before the Cherokee
Indian became accustomed to the sight of the white man.
Thus do the adventurous pioneers of North Georgia command our greater admiration; they chose the life of the frontier over that of the comfortable places, not through necessity,
but because they were that kind of people.

Pickens County exists and prospers because they were.

There is little need to dwell here on the oft-pictured details
of pioneer life—to tell how the early settlers arrived in horse-
or ox-drawn wagons bringing their families and what they
owned of worldly goods; how they set to work erecting cabins
from trees they felled in the forest; how they laboriously
broke the new soil and sowed their precious seed; how both
the women and the men toiled endlessly at the innumerable
tasks of setting up and maintaining homes in the wilderness.
This picture of frontier life has been much the same the
country over, and its details are familiar.

Somewhat less familiar, I think, and yet highly illuminat-
ing as to the character of the early settlers of this section,
are descriptions of their sports and diversions—the things
to which they turned for social recreation in the infrequent
spaces they allowed themselves for such indulgences. Not
entirely indulgences, either, and certainly not free from
honest work, as you will see, were some of these diversions;

but recreation they most certainly were, and their value as such was great.

Some of the sports and games I have gathered descriptions of to present here were not local by any means, being common to pioneers of nearly all sections; others seem to have been more or less peculiar to this region. There was one diversion in particular, which if not local, at least was not recognized by any other county besides Pickens to the extent of getting an act of the legislature passed against it. Incidentally, this sport does not belong to the period, exactly, that I am trying to describe; the law was passed in 1860; but mention of the matter will doubtless be interesting at this point.

The diversion which was translated by the law of the state into such a grievous crime—in Pickens County only—was the game of "Crack-a-loo." Now I am not an authority on Crack-a-loo, which was evidently a very corrupting game, but one gathers that it was played with cards and that sums of money often changed hands during the process. Here is the law passed against it by the 1860 legislature:

No. 165. An Act to Add Another Section to the Penal Code, so far as Relates to the County of Pickens.

SECTION I. BE IT ENACTED, [etc.] That from and after the passage of this act, that if any person in the county of Pickens shall throw and bet money on any game of "Crack-a-loo," or game of like character, such person shall be guilty of a misdemeanor, and, on indictment and conviction thereof, shall be punished by fine of not more than twenty-five dollars ($25), or imprisoned in the common jail of the County for not more than ten days.*

And here you have the "news behind the news" on the Crack-a-loo Act, as given in a presentment of the Pickens grand jury at the September 1860 term of court:

---

*Acts, Georgia, 1860, p. 160.

We recommend our members to the legislature to have an act passed making it a penal offense with a heavy penalty to play Crack-a-loo or any other game of chance, whether of cards or in any other way by which men bet or gambol. If they cannot get a general law, then a special act for this county. If the people of other counties are anxious that their sons should have some games lawful by which they can make vagabonds and gamblers of them, well and good; it is a matter of taste.

We applaud the independent spirit of these good men and are glad to see that it bore fruit. An era which likes to "pass the buck" of law enforcement might profit by their example.

But as I said, Crack-a-loo was not a pioneer diversion, or at least we hope not. Getting back to the subject, and to pursuits uncommemorated by special legislative attention, I am furnishing herewith descriptions of some of the most prominent sports and games in the early history of our county.

The Turkey-Shoot: Each contestant deposited a sum sufficient in total to pay for the turkey, and at a distance of 125 yards began to shoot. The person killing the turkey claimed it as his reward for marksmanship. At one meet many turkeys might be used, and often when the available turkeys were exhausted the participants would shoot at a spot or target and put up money, which went to the best marksman.

Horse-Racing: A good stretch of road was selected and the race was on for whoever cared to enter. It was a sort of sweepstakes affair, each contestant contributing to the purse and the winner carrying off the laurels and the purse as well.

Gander-Pulling: This unusual sport seems to have been indigenous to the region, and was observed here in 1837 by G. W. Featherstonaugh, from whom I have already quoted. The following is his account*:

*A Canoe Voyage Up the Minnay Sotor, p. 196.

"Gander-pulling" is a sort of tournament on horseback, and is, I believe, of European origin. A path is laid out on the exterior of a circle of about 150 feet diameter, and two saplings are sunk into the ground about twelve feet apart, on each side of the path. These being connected towards the top with a slack cord, a live gander with his legs tied, and his neck and head made as slippery as possible with *goose* grease, is suspended by the feet to that part of the cord immediately over the path. The knights of the gander having each deposited a small sum with the manager of the game to form a sweepstakes and to defray the expenses, follow each other, mounted on horseback, at intervals round the ring, two or three times before the signal is made to pull. When that is done, the cavaliers advance, each fixing his eye steadily upon the gander's shining neck, which he must seize and drag from the body of the wretched bird before the purse is won. This is not easily done, for as the rider advances he has to pass two men, five or six yards before he reaches the potence, one of them on each side of the path, and both armed with stout whips, who flog his horse unmercifully the instant he comes up with them to prevent any unfair delay at the cord. Many are thus unable to seize the neck at all, having enough to do to keep the saddle, and others who succeed in seizing it often find it impracticable to retain hold of such a slippery substance upon a horse at full speed. Meantime the gander is sure to get some severe "scrags," and for a while screams most lustily, which forms a prominent part of the entertainment. The tournament is generally continued long after the poor bird's neck is broken before it is dragged from its body; but some of the young fellows who have horses well trained to the sport, and grasp the neck with such strength and adroitness, that they bear off the head, windpipe, and all, screaming convulsively after they are separated from the body. This is considered the greatest feat that can be performed at a gander-pulling.

The Rough-and-Tumble Fight was sometimes a meeting for settlement of personal differences, but generally was a test of prowess and strength. Each contestant, usually, had his second and the affair would be carried on very much after the manner of a modern prize-fight. There was no purse, however, and the successful contestant had merely added another laurel to his crown.

The Log-Rolling: To a people somewhat shut off from the outside world, work itself could constitute a phase of social life, and great occasions indeed were the log-rollings, corn-shuckings, and house-raisings. Word was sent out and all the countryside came to help out a neighbor and have a big time. It might mean that some citizen was going to clear a piece of land. Then all the men would lend a hand to the cutting of trees, rolling of logs, and burning of debris. When the job was finished, there would follow a great feast, prepared by the women from food that would be furnished by him whose land was cleared.

The House-Raising: At a call the neighbors would gather to shape and put in place the logs that had been cut for a house, and in a very short time the newly arrived pioneer would have a roof over his head and walls around him, to house him and his.

The Corn-Shucking carried far into the night and was a time of great merriment for old and young. Like the log-rolling, it was an occasion of much feasting and conviviality, there being a supply of the refined variety of corn for those who wished it. Of course there was great rivalry among the huskers, each trying to outdo the other, but among the youngsters the glory went not to the one who accomplished the most work, but to him or her who found the most red ears. Some perhaps were more interested in red lips—and I dare say that many a romance dates back to a corn-shucking, and that many golden-wedding days have been brightened by the memory of the glow of an autumn moon around a pile of newly-husked corn. The fiddler might be there, too, and before the shades of night are driven away by the glimmer of dawn the happy couples have danced to the tunes of the Highland.

The Barn-Dance: One of the great occasions of settler life was the barn-dance, which was generally given at the completion of a barn of sufficient proportions to accommodate the gentry. Here the tuneful scrapings of the country fiddlers resounded merrily into the small hours of the morning while young folks and old expressed their exuberance in such steps as the Highland fling and the old-fashioned square-dance.

The Box-Supper: Other forms of recreation and amusement included candy-pullings, candy-knockings, and box-suppers. The gustatory appeal found in all three probably reached its height in the justly-famous box-supper. In the event money was needed for some worthy cause, the young ladies of the settlement prepared and brought to the party boxes of food carefully calculated to delight the palates of their sweethearts, and these boxes were auctioned off to the highest bidder. Sometimes a box would be purchased by one who was a stranger to the young lady who had prepared it, but more often her special admirer had been told what color of ribbon the box was tied with and he would spend his last dime to secure it, if necessary. In the case of rivals, the bids would mount to such sums as to raise considerable money for the worthy cause. After the sales were made, the feast was on. Each purchaser found his partner, and together they proceeded to enjoy the food and the companionship.

An account of pioneer life in our county would hardly be complete without mention of the hardy and adventurous spirit illustrated by the numbers of early citizens who went to the Mexican War in 1846 and to California in the Gold Rush of 1849. As Pickens County had not been formed in 1846 we have no way of obtaining an accurate list of the Mexican War soldiers who went from here, but the Cherokee County roster of nearly one hundred includes the names of many men recognizable as residents of what later became a part of Pickens.

An interesting incident is related to me by a descendant of one of the men concerned, about several Pickens Countians who went to the Mexican War. These soldiers were William T. Fitzsimmons, a son of Henry Fitzsimmons who was an early marble-dealer of the county; a Mr. Pool, and Lieut. Allen Keith. According to the story, these three men and several of their companions once surprised General Santa Anna, of the Mexican forces, while the latter was asleep. The surprise was so near a capture that Santa Anna barely escaped on his horse, leaving behind his cork leg, military cap, and wardrobe. Lieutenant Keith brought home as a souvenir a silver star taken from Santa Anna's cap; Pool, one of the general's razors; and Fitzsimmons, a piece of the cork leg.

As to the "Forty-Niners," I believe that from North Georgia a greater percentage of young men went to California during the Gold Rush than from any other part of the country. This was a natural result of the adventurous pioneer blood in their veins as well as of the gold-mining atmosphere that was a part of their environment.

From Pickens went Sam Bozeman, William and Stephen Tate, Clark McClain, Bethel Q. Disharoon, Ed Lenning, John and Hensley Stegall, and others. The trip was made by Cuba and across the isthmus by the Nicaragua route, boats being poled up the river by natives; then, on the west side, the "argonauts" took vessel to San Francisco. With the exception of Ed Lenning, all the men named soon returned, some of them in a very prosperous condition. Before leaving home Ed Lenning had made the statement that he was going out there and make ten thousand dollars in gold, then come back to the "red hills of North Georgia," marry, and not work any more. He kept his word all the way through, reared a family in Jasper, and made a most worthy citizen, dying at a ripe old age.

Chapter II ★ ★ ★ ★ ★ ★ ★ ★
COURTS AND OFFICERS

●

THE ACT of the Georgia legislature creating Pickens County was approved on December 5, 1853.* It follows, in full:

ACT CREATING THE COUNTY

An Act to lay out and organize a new county from the Counties of Cherokee and Gilmer, and for other purposes therein specified.

SECTION I. BE IT ENACTED, by the Senate and House of Representatives of the State of Georgia, in general Assembly met, and it is hereby enacted by the authority of the same, That from and immediately after the passage of this act a new county shall be, and the same is hereby laid out from the Counties of Cherokee and Gilmer to be included within the following limits, to-wit: Beginning at the north west corner of lot number one hundred and fifty-four in the twenty-third district of the second section, on the line of Cherokee and Gordon Counties, and running due east to a line of the thirteenth district of Cherokee County, thence along the line of said district south, four ranges of lots to the north west corner of lot number two hundred and seventeen in the thirteenth district: thence due east to the line of Lumpkin County, at the north east corner of lot number two hundred and forty-seven in the fourth district of the second section; thence along the line which divides the Counties of Cherokee and Lumpkin to the corner of Gilmer County; thence west along the line of the fifth district

Pickens County

Boundaries defined

---

*Acts, Georgia, 1853-4, p. 306 ff.

of the second section, to the southeast corner of lot
number three hundred and fourteen of said district;
thence in a direct line nearly north, to the south west
corner of lot number one hundred in said district; thence
west, to the line of Gordon County; thence south, along
the line of Gordon and Cherokee Counties, to the starting point.

SECTION II. AND BE IT FURTHER ENACTED by the authority aforesaid, That the new county described in the
First Section of this act be called and known by the
name of Pickens, in honor of General Andrew Pickens,*
and shall be attached to the fifth congressional district,
and to the Blue Ridge Judiciary District, and to the
First Brigade of Georgia Militia.

Name, District, etc.

SECTION III. AND BE IT FURTHER ENACTED by the authority aforesaid, That the persons included within said
new county entitled to vote for the same shall, on the
first Monday in January next, elect five Justices of the
Inferior Court, an Ordinary, a Clerk of the Superior
Court, a Clerk of the Inferior Court, a Sheriff, a Coroner,
Tax Collector and Receiver of Tax Returns, a County
Surveyor and a County Treasurer for said County, and
that said election for officers shall be held at the several
places where Justices Courts are now held within the
limits of the said new county; and the Governor on the

County Officers elected and com- missioned

---

*"PICKENS, ANDREW, American soldier: born at Paxton, Pa., September 19,
1739; died at Tomassee, S. C., August 17, 1817. He removed with his parents
to the Waxhaw Settlement, S. C., in 1752, was engaged in the Cherokee War
of 1761, and at the outbreak of the American Revolution was appointed a
captain of militia, from which he rose to be a brigadier-general. He defeated
General Boyd at Kettle Creek in 1779, was engaged in the Battle of Stone's
Ferry in the same year, routed the Cherokees at Tomassee, and in 1781 so
distinguished himself at the Battle of Cowpens that Congress voted him a
sword. He compelled the surrender of the British forts at Augusta, Ga., fought
under General Greene in the Campaign of Ninety-Six, and by a successful
expedition against the Cherokees in 1782 gained from them a large strip of
territory which later became a part of Georgia. In 1783-94 he was a member
of the South Carolina legislature and in 1793-95 served in Congress. He was
a member of the State Constitutional Convention, a commissioner in many
important treaties with the Indians, and again was a member of the legislature
in 1801 and 1812."—*The Encyclopedia Americana.*
There are two other counties in the United States named for General Pickens:
one in Alabama and one in South Carolina.

same being certified to him, shall commission the persons returned as elected at said election, who shall hold their posts respectively, for the terms prescribed by law, and until their successors shall be elected and qualified; and said Justices of the Inferior Court, after they shall have been commissioned shall proceed as soon as **Militia Districts** possible to lay off said county into militia districts, and to advertise for the election of two Justices of the Peace in each district, in which no Justice now in commission may reside, and in case one Justice in commission shall reside in any one of said districts, then one other shall be elected for said district; and the Governor on being duly certified of the election of such Justices shall commission them according to law; and all officers now in commis- **Officers to hold over** sion within the limits of said new county shall hold their commissions and exercise the duties of their several offices within said county for the terms respectively for which they were elected, and until their successors shall be commissioned and qualified.

SECTION IV. AND BE IT FURTHER ENACTED by the authority aforesaid, That the Justices of the Inferior Court of said county, after they shall have been commissioned **County site, how selected** and qualified, shall have full power and authority to select and locate a site for the public buildings of said county; and the said Justices or a majority of them are hereby authorized and invested with full power to purchase a tract of land for the location of the county site; to divide the same into lots, and sell each lot at public sale to the highest bidder, for the benefit of said county, or to make such other arrangements or contracts concerning the county site, or the location of the public buildings as they may think proper.

SECTION V. AND BE IT FURTHER ENACTED by the authority aforesaid, That so soon as the Justices of the **Election precincts** Inferior Court for said county shall have laid off said militia districts, the places of holding Justices' Courts in said district respectively be and each of them is hereby established an election precinct.

SECTION VI. AND BE IT FURTHER ENACTED by the authority aforesaid, That all mesne process, execution and other final process, in the hands of the Sheriffs, Coroners and Constables of the counties of which the new county may be formed,' and which properly belong to said new county, and which may have been levied or in part executed, and said proceedings therein not finally disposed of, at the time when the officers of the said new county shall receive their commissions, shall be delivered over to the corresponding officers of the said new county, and such officers are hereby authorized and required to proceed with the same, in the same manner as if such mesne process, execution, or other final process had been originally in their hands: Provided, That in all cases publication of the times and places of sale, or other like proceeding in the new county shall be made for the time now prescribed by law; and all papers appertaining to all or any suits or prosecutions pending in either of the counties out of which said new county is formed, when the defendant resides in said new county shall be transferred to the proper officers of the said new county and there tried and disposed of.

SECTION VII. AND BE IT FURTHER ENACTED by the authority aforesaid, That the Superior Court of said new county shall be held on the second Mondays in May and November in each year, and the Inferior Courts on the third Mondays in January and July.

SECTION VIII. AND BE IT FURTHER ENACTED by the authority, That the county site of Cherokee County shall not be removed, or the public buildings transferred from the town of Canton, the present county site of said county, to any other place, on account of the laying out of said new county, or for any other cause; but the county site of said county with the public buildings, be and the same are hereby declared to be permanently and perpetually located at said Town of Canton, the present county site.

SECTION IX. AND BE IT FURTHER ENACTED by the authority aforesaid, That all laws and parts of laws mili-

Marginal notes:

Processes etc., how executed

Papers transferred

Courts

tating against this act, be and the same are hereby repealed.

JOHN E. WARD
*Speaker of the House
of Representatives*

JOHN D. STELL
President of the Senate

HERSCHEL V. JOHNSON
Governor

Approved December 5, 1853.

ORGANIZATION OF THE COUNTY

On January 2, 1854, the organization of Pickens County began with the election of its first officers. There were already a number of polling-places here—the justices' courts previously in Gilmer and Cherokee—and at these places, on the date named, the voters resident in the new county met in accordance with the law to select a set of officers.

The following men were elected as the first officers of Pickens County: William Tate, clerk of the superior court; John P. Wofford, clerk of the inferior court; William Sosebee, sheriff; Charles Marshall McClure, ordinary; Derrick S. McClardy, tax receiver; Elias W. Allred, tax collector; John A. Lyons, coroner; Benjamin M. Stephens, surveyor; and John H. Ammons, Jesse Padgett, Stephen Griffith, Willis West, and James Tally, justices of the inferior court.*

The officers being duly chosen, the next thing necessary was the selection of a place for the county seat. It was over this point that one of the hardest-fought political contests

---

*These were the first officers of Pickens County. I have seen a list which omitted the last three inferior court justices named here, giving in their stead the names of John Lambert, John Holcomb, and Elsberry Tarbutton. Reference to the list of inferior court judges on page 87, which is a compilation recently made by the state historian, shows that Lambert, Holcomb, and Tarbutton replaced Griffith, West, and Tally later on in the year.

ever to take place in Pickens occurred, one faction wanting
the county seat for the western end of the county, where
there was a considerable population in the Hinton and Ludville sections, while a second group contended that the seat
should be located in the eastern part of the county, the Long
Swamp Valley section also being well populated by that
time. The justices of the inferior court, in whose hands the
matter lay, decided to hold an election on it, and by a close
margin the second faction won. A group of men composed
of Sylvanus Hamrick, Stephen C. Tate, James Simmons,
William Tate, and possibly one or two others were chosen to
settle up the location of the county seat, in accordance with
the provisions of the legislature, and thus the site of Jasper,
Ga., was determined. The town was named after Sergeant
William Jasper, the Revolutionary War hero.*

With the laying out of the county into militia districts and
the election of justices of the peace for these smaller divisions
and determination of voting-places therein, all as provided
for by the act of legislature, the machinery of the new county
soon became duly established and its organization complete.

A full list of Pickens County officers up to the present date
is given at the end of this chapter.

---

*"JASPER, WILLIAM, American soldier: born in South Carolina about 1750;
died at Savannah, Ga., October 9, 1779. At the commencement of the Revolutionary War, he enlisted in the 2d S. C. Regiment, in which he became a
sergeant. Subsequently, in the attack upon Fort Moultrie by a British fleet,
he distinguished himself by leaping through an embrasure to the ground,
under a shower of cannon balls, and recovering the flag of S. C. which had
been shot off. Gov. Rutledge presented him with his own sword, and offered
him a lieutenant's commission; Jasper declined this, saying: 'I am not fit
to keep officers company; I am but a sergeant.' His commander gave him a
roving commission to scour the country with a few men and surprise and
capture the enemy's outposts. His achievement in this capacity seems to belong
to romance rather than history, and in boldness equal to any recorded in the
Revolutionary annals of the Southern states. . . . At the assault upon Savannah he received his death wound while fastening to the parapet the standard
which had been presented to his regiment. His hold, however, never relaxed,
and he bore the colors to a place of safety before he died."—*The Encyclopedia
Americana.*

EARLY COURTS

The first term of the Pickens County Superior Court began on May 15, 1854, at Jasper, the county seat. There was no courthouse yet—in fact there was no town, the site having just been laid out—and we are left to infer that when the minutes of this court state the business was conducted "under our spacious oak," they mean just what they say. Evidently it was an outdoor affair, but—in May—why not?

Judge David Irwin, of the Blue Ridge Circuit, was the presiding officer at this court, and Edward D. Chisholm the solicitor-general. An idea of who were some of the leading citizens of Pickens County at that time may be obtained from the list of grand and petit jurors at this session, who were as follows:

Grand jury: George R. Edwards, foreman; William Godfrey, Brown B. Bradley, Stephen Jordan, Ransom Collins, William J. Nelson, Jeremiah Lambert, James Ferguson, Bailey A. Chandler, Lewis Sams, Davis Collins, William Darnell, Erwin C. Disharoon, Hiram Reid, Bethel Bradley, Benjamin M. Stephens, William G. Brown, James Morrison, William Mullinax, John Morrison, Ezekiel Townsend, John Guyton, and Ira Dunnagan.

Petit Jury No. 1: Hiram Partin, Andrew Cowart, Jeremiah Holcombe, Andrew J. Pinson, John Hays, Levi Yancey, Leander J. McCarter, John Martin, H. B. Bozeman, Joseph Tankersley, William Parker, and Thomas Wilson.

Petit Jury No. 2: Stephen Brown, Spencer Darnell, William B. Pendley, Joseph H. Bradley, Reuben Hopkins, Martin Stanfield, John Akins, Asa Holcombe, Aaron Collins, Henry Fendley, Julian Parker, and Orval Davis.

The constables were Warren R. Pool for the grand jury, James M. Ferguson for Petit Jury No. 1, and Samuel Norton for Petit Jury No. 2.

COURTHOUSE OF PICKENS COUNTY, JASPER, GA.

A recommendation that suitable arrangements for the early construction of a courthouse and other public buildings be made by the inferior court judges, who presumably were working on the matter at that time in compliance with the creating act, formed the burden of the grand jury's presentments at this session. The presentments follow in part:

We would also in view of the numerous expenditures that must be made for the several improvements now necessary for the comfort and convenience of our citizens recommend to the honorable inferior court the necessity of making prudent as well as liberal appropriations for publick improvements, and to grant all their contracts guaranteed by good and sufficient security.

In conclusion we beg leave to tender to His Honor, Judge Irwin, our thanks for the patience with which he has indulged us in the completion of the business of the present term under our spacious oak.

Only a few cases came before the grand jury at this first court session, and they were all of a minor nature, with one exception. In this case, a true bill for murder was found against one Franklin Saterfield, who according to the evidence had "on the 3rd day of October, 1853, with force and arms in and upon William R. Young in the peace of God and said state, then and there being feloniously, wrongfully, willfully and of his malice aforethought," assaulted the said William R. Young with a stone which he "did cast and throw" to the mortal detriment of the said William R. Young, who had thereupon "languished" for five days and then died. This was the first murder case in Pickens County.

The second term of court was held in November of the same year, with Judge Irwin presiding and George N. Lester serving as solicitor-general pro tem. By the presentments of the grand jury we see that a courthouse has been started, but it is apparently not far enough along to hold court in yet. Quoting from the presentments at this term:

Our courthouse is going up slowly and we find some of the bricks of an inferior quality and recommend the Inferior Court see to it that the work progresses as steadily as possible and that it be done in good style and according to contract. We would also respectfully urge the inferior court to hurry the county jail so that our county may soon see all its public buildings finished in good order.

Slow progress on the courthouse is reported by the grand jurors at the third term of court, held in May 1855, and the inferior court is urged to speed the construction up a little. A recommendation is also made to put up signboards and mileposts on the various roads in the county, for the benefit of both citizens and travelers.

The fourth term, in November 1855, was presided over by Judge Joseph E. Brown, a Canton lawyer who had recently been commissioned to fill out the unexpired term of Judge Irwin when the latter had resigned. The choice of Judge Brown received popular confirmation in the fall election of 1855, and he continued to serve as Judge of the Blue Ridge Circuit until his election to the governorship of Georgia in 1857. The "War Governor" of Georgia was one of the most distinguished of a long line of distinguished products of the Blue Ridge bench.*

Returning to the business of the court, and the grand jury in particular, we see by the presentments of this term that a jail for the county has been "finished according to contract, except a small part of the work that is yet to do"; but that there is some difficulty in getting the courthouse completed.

---

*"BROWN, JOSEPH EMERSON, American statesman: born in Pickens County, S. C., April 15, 1821; died in Atlanta, Ga., November 30, 1894. He was educated at Calhoun Academy and was graduated at Yale in 1846. He settled in Canton, Ga., served in the State legislature and was elected governor in 1857, serving three terms. As war governor he opposed Jefferson Davis in the matter of the conscription laws and raised 10,000 recruits to oppose Sherman's march to the sea, but would not allow them to leave the State. After the war he gave hearty support to the reconstruction measures and supported General Grant for the presidency. He was chief justice of Georgia in 1868 and United States senator in 1880-91. He made large gifts for religious and educational purposes."—The Encyclopedia Americana.

The inferior court is severely taken to task in the presentments for allowing such a delay on the part of the contractors.

Not to drag the story out as the court minutes do, I will
say now that the courthouse was not finished until about
1860, the minutes showing that approval by the grand jury
of the contractors' work was finally secured in March of
that year. However, it seems to have been ready for occu-
pancy a little earlier than that, the first mention of its use
being in September 1859. No reason is given in the county
records why the final completion of the courthouse should
have taken so long.

The worries of the grand juries of this period included
not only the delay on the courthouse and the difficulty of
keeping the jail in repair—"There is no necessity for a jail
unless it is made safe," and "A stitch in time saves nine,"
were some of their comments on the jail situation—but extended also to the condition of the county's roads. In 1855
we learn that the roads were "in tolerable condition with some
exceptions," but this condition did not seem to improve very
fast despite repeated protests to the inferior court judges,
who were supposed to have charge of the matter. In 1857
a bridge was ordered by the inferior court across Talking
Rock Creek, "where it is crossed by the Federal Road," and
the contractor collected part of his pay and left the work
unfinished, the grand jury was told.

In 1858 the inferior court was again reminded about necessary road work, but the next year the grand jury again reported many roads in bad order. This jury was particularly
disgusted with the situation, their remarks indicate. "We
find many roads in bad order. We would recommend to the
Inferior Court to have the roads worked according to law,
but this has been done by so many grand juries we know
they won't do it."

The foregoing matters, which of course are not today of

notable importance except as they illustrate the first official
business of Pickens County, are supplemented in the early
court records by other transactions of county affairs as well
as by court cases of various kinds. There are, however, during this period and the period immediately following—that
of the Civil War—certain official records which hold more
than a passing significance for present citizens of the county.
This is true especially of certain presentments dealing with
early provisions for the education of the county's children,
and others illustrating the true spirit of Pickens County in
the Civil War—a spirit often misunderstood today. Mention of these, however, is reserved for later chapters to which
they more properly belong.

COUNTY LINE CHANGES

At no time since Pickens County was formed have its
legal boundaries been materially altered, the greatest changes
in this respect involving only six land lots (or 960 acres) in
1858 and the same number in 1863. The county therefore
retains practically the same size and shape given it by the
legal description in the creating act of 1853.*

The following changes, as enacted from time to time by
the legislature, bring the original description up to date:

Mar. 6, 1856: Lots No. 477, 478, and 479, in Land District No. 4, Section No. 1, transferred from Lumpkin County
into Pickens County. These lots were then owned by Daniel
P. Monroe.†

Dec. 22, 1857: Same three lots transferred from Pickens
to Dawson.‡ (Dawson County had just been created from
Lumpkin and Gilmer Counties at this same session of the

---

*Cf. p. 66 ff. and map of county.
†Acts, Georgia, 1855-56, p. 129.
‡*Ibid.*, 1857, p. 231.

legislature. Lumpkin had previously adjoined Pickens on the east.)

Dec. 13, 1858: Lots No. 114, 139, 140, 185, 211, and 212, 12th District, 2nd Section, from Gilmer to Pickens.*

Dec. 19, 1860: Lot No. 27, 23d District, 2d Section, owned by Sarah Bunch, from Pickens to Gordon.†

Apr. 18, 1863: Lots No. 101, 102, 103, 78, 79, and 80, 5th District, 2d Section, "containing the residences of James Cowart, Jasper White, Franklin Mealer, and Robert Cowart," from Gilmer to Pickens.‡

Mar. 19, 1869: Lot No. 231, 4th District, 2d Section, owned by Alfred Spence, from Cherokee to Pickens.**

1870 (became law by lapse of time): Lots No. 200 and 201, 13th District, 2d Section, owned by William B. Dowday, from Pickens to Cherokee.††

Pickens County Officers, 1854-1935

The names of all the men who have served as (commissioned) officers of Pickens County since the formation of the county in 1853, together with the dates on which they were commissioned by the governor, are given in the list that follows. This list has been compiled from the records of the governor's office, in order to get these dates of commission, and the spelling of the names is not guaranteed in all cases. Also there are one or two "gaps," and several discontinuations or changes of offices, which however I have tried to explain in footnotes wherever the explanatory legislation could be found.

---

*Ibid., 1858, p. 44.
†Acts, Georgia, 1860, p. 141.
‡Ibid., 1863, p. 208.
**Ibid., 1869, p. 179.
††Ibid., 1870, p. 24.

Clerks of the Superior Court

DATE COMMISSIONED

William Tate	Feb. 15, 1854
William Tate	Jan. 11, 1856
William Tate	Jan. 9, 1858
William Tate	Jan. 10, 1861
R. B. McCutchen	Jan. 24, 1862
R. B. McCutchen	July 16, 1864
William Pool	Jan. 22, 1866
A. P. Mullinax	Sept. 14, 1868
Glenn Cowart	Feb. 7, 1871
Glenn Cowart	Jan. 18, 1873
Eber Wofford	Jan. 15, 1875
William R. Allen	Jan. 26, 1877
William R. Allen	Jan. 16, 1879
Ezekiel Hood	Jan. 12, 1881
Marion C. McClain	Jan. 9, 1883
Samuel K. McCutchen	Jan. 15, 1885
Samuel K. McCutchen	Jan. 8, 1887
John F. Simmons	Jan. 11, 1889
John F. Simmons	Jan. 9, 1891
A. V. Jones	Jan. 7, 1893
A. V. Jones	Jan. 8, 1895
G. W. Owen	Oct. 19, 1896
G. W. Owen	Oct. 20, 1898
J. T. Atherton	Oct. 18, 1900
J. T. Atherton	Oct. 14, 1902
Elias Whitfield	Oct. 17, 1904
Elias Whitfield	Nov. 1, 1906
Elias Whitfield	Nov. 3, 1908
W. C. Allred	Nov. 5, 1910
W. C. Allred	Oct. 15, 1912
W. C. Allred	Nov. 30, 1914
W. C. Allred	Dec. 4, 1916

(Resigned Jan. 1, 1920)

W. T. Day	Feb. 18, 1920

(Resigned Aug. 30, 1921)

W. T. Day	Dec. 9, 1920
M. E. McWhorter	Oct. 12, 1921
M. E. McWhorter	Dec. 20, 1924

DATE COMMISSIONED

M. E. McWhorter_____Dec. 20, 1928
M. E. McWhorter_____Dec. 15, 1932

Sheriffs

William Sosbee	Feb. 15, 1854
George H. Turner	Jan. 11, 1856
William Sosbee	Jan. 9, 1858
B. F. Hanie	July 6, 1859
James Bruce	Jan. 10, 1861
B. F. Hanie	Jan. 24, 1862
D. S. McCrary	July 16, 1864
N. C. McClain	Jan. 22, 1866
J. E. McClain	Sept. 14, 1868
John G. Caffney	Sept. 14, 1868
A. W. Davis	Feb. 7, 1871
A. W. Davis	Jan. 18, 1873
John F. Lindsay	Jan. 15, 1875
John F. Lindsay	Jan. 26, 1877
John F. Lindsay	Jan. 16, 1879
Rufus S. Henderson	Jan. 12, 1881
Rufus S. Henderson	Jan. 9, 1883
Rufus S. Henderson	Jan. 15, 1885
John E. Johnson	Jan. 8, 1887
John E. Johnson	Jan. 11, 1889
James H. Pinyan	Jan. 9, 1891
J. D. Cowart	Jan. 7, 1893
J. D. Cowart	Jan. 8, 1895
C. T. Wheeler	Oct. 19, 1896
C. T. Wheeler	Oct. 20, 1898
C. T. Wheeler	Oct. 18, 1900
D. F. Taylor	Oct. 14, 1902
D. F. Taylor	Oct. 17, 1904
D. F. Taylor	Nov. 1, 1906
D. F. Taylor	Nov. 3, 1908
D. F. Taylor	Nov. 5, 1910

(Resigned Oct. 30, 1911)

W. C. Moss	Jan. 16, 1912
W. C. Moss	Oct. 15, 1912
T. E. Johnson	Nov. 30, 1914

DATE COMMISSIONED

T. E. Johnson	Dec. 4, 1916
D. P. Poole	Dec. 9, 1920
T. E. Johnson	Dec. 20, 1924
T. E. Johnson	Dec. 20, 1928
Jim Pool	Dec. 15, 1932

Ordinaries

C. Marshall McClure	Feb. 15, 1854
C. Marshall McClure	Jan. 11, 1856
Pascal T. Ferguson	Jan. 10, 1861
William H. Simmons	Jan. 25, 1862
William H. Simmons	July 16, 1864
William H. Simmons	Sept. 14, 1868
William H. Simmons	Jan. 18, 1873
Thaddeus Pickett	Feb. 2, 1877

(Contested and withdrawn)

William R. Allen	Jan. 12, 1881
Ezekiel Hood	Mar. 6, 1884
Ezekiel Hood	Jan. 15, 1885
C. J. Cornelison	Jan. 11, 1889
C. J. Cornelison	Jan. 7, 1893
C. J. Cornelison	Oct. 19, 1896
C. J. Cornelison	Oct. 18, 1900
J. C. Payne	Oct. 17, 1904
A. W. McHan	Nov. 10, 1908
T. A. Chastain	Oct. 15, 1912
M. S. Long	Dec. 4, 1916
C. Whitfield	Dec. 9, 1920
W. O. Westbrook	Dec. 20, 1924
W. O. Westbrook	Dec. 20, 1928
Olen Cagle	Dec. 15, 1932

Tax Receivers

Derrick S. McClardy	Feb. 15, 1854
Lawrence Bradley	Jan. 9, 1855
Carey S. Padgett	Jan. 11, 1856
Derrick S. McClardy	Jan. 12, 1857

DATE COMMISSIONED

Merrick H. West_____Jan. 9, 1858
           (Also tax collector)*
Merrick H. West_____Jan. 10, 1859
           (Also tax collector)
Thomas P. Forester_____Jan. 10, 1861
           (Also tax collector)
T. J. Bryan_____Mar. 1, 1862
           (Also tax collector)
William Pool_____July 16, 1864
Joseph H. Taylor_____Mar. 8, 1866
M. V. Coffee_____Sept. 14, 1868
Benjamin M. Cowart_____Feb. 7, 1871
           (Contested and withdrawn)
H. G. B. Turner_____Jan. 18, 1873
Caleb Jones_____Jan. 15, 1875
Benjamin M. Cowart_____Feb. 2, 1877
G. H. Little_____Jan. 16, 1879
William A. Simpson_____Jan. 12, 1881
Henry B. Stokes_____Jan. 9, 1883
L. F. Padgett_____Mar. 16, 1885
E. J. Allred_____Jan. 8, 1887
R. R. Bryan_____Jan. 11, 1889
James W. Eaton_____Jan. 9, 1891
J. M. Eaton_____Mar. 5, 1892
G. W. Owen_____Jan. 7, 1893
L. A. Moss_____Jan. 8, 1895
L. A. Moss_____Oct. 19, 1896
Geary W. Fitts_____Dec. 22, 1897
Marion Wilson_____Oct. 20, 1898
R. P. Fields_____Oct. 18, 1900
R. P. Fields_____Oct. 14, 1902
S. S. Fields_____Feb. 5, 1904
G. T. Hall_____Oct. 17, 1904
C. C. Goodson_____Nov. 1, 1906
C. V. Bruce_____Nov. 3, 1908
William Clark_____Nov. 5, 1910
Ed. McWhorter_____Oct. 15, 1912

*For a time the offices of tax receiver and tax collector of Pickens County were consolidated. (Acts, Georgia, 1857, p. 242; act approved December 15, 1857.)

DATE COMMISSIONED

Hardy Champion	Nov. 16, 1914
Will Wood	Dec. 4, 1916
S. Gaddis	Dec. 9, 1920
Frank Burton	Dec. 20, 1924
Sol. A. Tatum	Dec. 20, 1928
Sol. A. Tatum	Dec. 15, 1932

Tax Collectors

Elias W. Allred	Feb. 15, 1854
Elias W. Allred	Jan. 9, 1855
James M. Lenning	Jan. 11, 1856
James M. Lenning	Jan. 12, 1857
Merrick H. West	Jan. 9, 1858
(Also tax receiver) *	
Merrick H. West	Jan. 10, 1859
(Also tax receiver)	
Thomas P. Forester	Jan. 10, 1861
(Also tax receiver)	
T. J. Bryan	Mar. 1, 1862
(Also tax receiver)	
T. J. Bryan	July 16, 1864
S. A. Darnell	Mar. 8, 1866
John Penly	Sept. 14, 1868
Alfred M. Davis	Feb. 7, 1871
Stephen Richards	Jan. 18, 1873
R. R. Howell	Jan. 15, 1875
A. McHan	Jan. 26, 1877
Charles B. Price	Jan. 16, 1879
Charles B. Price	Jan. 12, 1881
James J. Harris	Jan. 9, 1883
George W. Little	Jan. 15, 1885
G. W. Fields	Jan. 8, 1887
Jeremiah Soseby	Jan. 11, 1889
George W. Hamrick	Jan. 9, 1891
C. C. Pettett	Jan. 7, 1893
C. C. Pettett	Jan. 8, 1895
H. Taylor	Oct. 19, 1896
J. H. Disharoon	Oct. 20, 1898

*See footnote on p. 82.

DATE COMMISSIONED

A. B. Bradley	Oct. 18, 1900
J. F. Pressley	Oct. 14, 1902
J. F. Pressley	Oct. 17, 1904
Robert G. Henderson	Nov. 1, 1906
R. L. Pettett	Nov. 3, 1908
J. L. Bagwell	Nov. 5, 1910
J. L. Bagwell	Oct. 15, 1912
J. W. Walker	Nov. 16, 1914
J. W. Walker	Dec. 4, 1916
Fred K. Stancil	Dec. 9, 1920
Fred K. Stancil	Dec. 20, 1924
Fred K. Stancil	Dec. 20, 1928
Fred K. Stancil	Dec. 15, 1932

Treasurers

Levi W. Hall	Jan. 10, 1861
Levi W. Hall	Jan. 24, 1862
J. M. Allred	Feb. 16, 1864
J. A. McCutchen	Sept. 14, 1868
J. A. McCutchen	Feb. 7, 1871
J. A. McCutchen	Jan. 18, 1873
James W. Grogan	Jan. 15, 1875
T. M. Johnson	Jan. 26, 1877
W. B. McCreary	Jan. 16, 1879
Henry K. Wood	Jan. 12, 1881
William B. Allred	Jan. 9, 1883
(1885-1895: see "Clerks of the Superior Court") *	
A. V. Jones	Jan. 8, 1895
G. W. Owen	Oct. 19, 1896
G. W. Owen	Oct. 20, 1898
G. W. Owen	Oct. 18, 1900
J. T. Atherton	Oct. 14, 1902
J. H. Hopkins	Nov. 1, 1906
D. S. Cook	Nov. 3, 1908
D. S. Cook	Nov. 5, 1910

*The office of treasurer in Pickens County was consolidated with that of clerk of the superior court—the latter becoming ex-officio treasurer—by an act of the legislature approved September 14, 1883, which became effective at the end of the then current officials' terms. (Acts, Georgia, 1882-83, p. 500.) The offices were later re-separated.

DATE COMMISSIONED

E. L. Lenning_____Oct. 15, 1912
J. L. Wiginton_____Nov. 30, 1914
                (Office abolished 1916)*

Coroners

John A. Lyons_____Feb. 15, 1854
Martin Collins_____Jan. 11, 1856
John A. Lyons_____Jan. 9, 1858
John A. Lyons_____Jan. 10, 1861
J. M. Lenning_____Jan. 24, 1862
G. Moss, Jr._____July 16, 1864
Absalom Wheeler_____Jan. 22, 1866
A. Wheeler_____Sept. 14, 1868
William Thompson, Sr._____Feb. 7, 1871
Jehoida Barnett_____Jan. 18, 1873
Jehoida Barnett_____Jan. 15, 1875
T. J. West_____Jan. 26, 1877
F. M. Cowart_____Jan. 16, 1879
F. M. Cowart_____Jan. 12, 1881
A. W. Richards_____Jan. 9, 1883
J. H. Dorsey_____Jan. 15, 1885
J. H. Dorsey_____Jan. 8, 1887
T. B. Barnett_____Jan. 11, 1889
James A. Newberry_____Jan. 9, 1891
J. H. Dorsey_____Jan. 7, 1893
W. W. Wright_____Jan. 8, 1895
L. D. Blackburn_____Oct. 19, 1896
L. D. Blackburn_____Oct. 20, 1898
W. W. Wright_____Oct. 18, 1900
J. A. Reese_____Oct. 14, 1902
W. W. Wright_____Oct. 17, 1904
W. W. Wright_____Nov. 1, 1906
W. W. Wright_____Nov. 3, 1908
W. W. Wright_____Nov. 5, 1910
W. W. Wright_____Oct. 15, 1912

*The act abolishing the office of treasurer in Pickens County (Acts, Georgia, 1916, p. 480; approved August 18, 1916) provided that the ordinary should designate some bank to act as county depository and disbursing agent and keep the treasurer's books.

DATE COMMISSIONED

W. W. Wright_____Nov. 30, 1914
W. H. Reece_____Dec. 4, 1916
T. A. Cox_____Dec. 9, 1920
T. A. Cox_____Dec. 20, 1924
T. A. Cox_____Dec. 20, 1928
T. A. Cox_____Dec. 15, 1932

Surveyors

Benjamin M. Stephens_____Feb. 15, 1854
Amos Allison_____Jan. 11, 1856
Andrew Steel_____Jan. 9, 1858
Andrew Steel_____Jan. 10, 1861
Andrew Steel_____Jan. 24, 1862
J. Williams_____Feb. 16, 1864
L. M. Hall_____Sept. 14, 1868
Levi W. Hall_____Feb. 7, 1871
William Cagle_____Jan. 18, 1873
James H. Roper_____Jan. 15, 1875
James H. Roper_____Jan. 26, 1877
Ezekiel Hood_____Jan. 16, 1879
Columbus C. Pettit_____Jan. 12, 1881
Columbus C. Pettit_____Jan. 9, 1883
Thomas Honea_____Jan. 15, 1885
Thomas Honea_____Jan. 8, 1887
J. H. Clark_____Jan. 11, 1889
William H. Reece_____Jan. 9, 1891
William H. Reece_____Jan. 7, 1893
F. A. Mullinax_____Jan. 8, 1895
Benjamin L. Mullins _____Oct. 19, 1896
Benjamin L. Mullins_____Oct. 20, 1898
Dick Grabley_____Oct. 18, 1900
(Failed to qualify)
M. F. Granely_____Oct. 14, 1902
(Failed to qualify)
Benjamin L. Mullins_____Feb. 14, 1903
(Appointed by Ordinary)
Benjamin L. Mullins_____Oct. 17, 1904
Benjamin L. Mullins_____Nov. 1, 1906
Benjamin L. Mullins_____Nov. 3, 1908

DATE COMMISSIONED

W. M. Dodson_____Nov. 5, 1910
(Resigned Nov. 7, 1911)
W. L. Brooks_____Oct. 15, 1912
(Resigned Mar. 11, 1914)
Charlie Peabody_____Nov. 30, 1914
T. A. Pitts_____Dec. 4, 1916
W. L. Wigginton_____Dec. 9, 1920
E. C. Perrow_____Dec. 20, 1924
E. C. Perrow_____Dec. 20, 1928
E. C. Perrow_____Dec. 15, 1932

Justices of the Inferior Court
(1854 to 1868) *

TERM

John H. Ammons	Jan. 24, 1854-
	Feb. 15, 1854-Feb. 12, 1857
Jessee Padgett	Jan. 24, 1854-
	Feb. 15, 1854-Feb. 6, 1855
Stephen Griffith	Jan. 24, 1854-
	Feb. 15, 1854-July 5, 1854
Willis West	Jan. 24, 1854-
	Feb. 15, 1854-July 5, 1854
James Tally	Jan. 24, 1854 (declined)
John Holcombe	Feb. 15, 1854-Feb. 12, 1857
Elsberry Tarbutton	July 5, 1854-Feb. 6, 1855
John Lambert	July 5, 1854-Aug. 2, 1856
Allison McHan	Feb. 6, 1855-Feb. 12, 1857
Samuel Tate	Feb. 6, 1855-Feb. 12, 1857
William H. Gordon	Aug. 2, 1856-Feb. 12, 1857
Samuel Tate	Feb. 12, 1857-Jan. 10, 1861
William H. Gordon	Feb. 12, 1857-Feb. 3, 1859
Baylis Bruce	Feb. 12, 1857-Jan. 10, 1861
James Ferguson	Feb. 12, 1857-Feb. 3, 1859

*The inferior court was the governing body of Pickens County, as well as of most other Georgia counties, until 1868, when it was abolished by the state constitution of that year. It was composed of five judges, or justices, whose powers were more of an executive than of a judicial nature. It was their business to authorize county expenditures, look after public buildings and roads, and generally manage the affairs of the county.—The foregoing list of justices is the compilation of Miss Ruth Blair, State Historian, and is here published for the first time.

TERM

Andrew Jones _____Feb. 12, 1857-Jan. 10, 1861
Allison McHan _____Feb. 3, 1859-Jan. 10, 1861
Philip R. Simmons_____Feb. 3, 1859-Jan. 10, 1861

Baylis Bruce _____Jan. 10, 1861—resigned 1862
Andrew Jones _____Jan. 10, 1861-Jan. 21, 1865
Allison McHan_____Jan. 10, 1861-Jan. 21, 1865
Philip R. Simmons_____Jan. 10, 1861-1862
Samuel Tate _____Jan. 10, 1861-Mar. 11, 1863
Ambrose K. Blackwell_____Jan. 25, 1862-Jan. 21, 1865
Joseph A. McCutchen_____Sep. 19, 1862-Jan. 21, 1865
A. Keeter_____Mar. 11, 1863-Jan. 21, 1865

Andrew Morrison _____Jan. 21, 1865—resigned May 14, 1866
William Forrester_____Jan. 21, 1865-1868
David Kayler _____Jan. 21, 1865-1868
William Tate _____Jan. 21, 1865-1868
G. L. Summey_____Jan. 21, 1865-1868
Samuel Hood _____May 14, 1866-1868

Clerks of the Inferior Court

DATE COMMISSIONED

John P. Wofford_____Feb. 15, 1854
William Partin_____Jan. 11, 1856
Abraham W. Tribble_____Jan. 9, 1858
Jeremiah Lambert_____Jan. 10, 1861
Jeremiah Lambert_____Jan. 24, 1862
B. F. Steel_____July 16, 1864
Jeremiah Lambert_____Jan. 22, 1866

(Office discontinued 1868)

Representatives
From Pickens County

1855/56—B. M. Stephens
1857-58—John E. Price
1859-60—John E. Price
1861-62-63 Ex.—Elias W. Allred
1863-64 Ex.-64—Elias W. Allred (resigned)
1865 Ex.—B. F. Hanie
1865/66-66—R. B. McCutchen

1868 Ex.-69-70 Ex.—Sion A. Darnell
1871-72-72 Adj.—J. M. Allred
1873-74—A. P. Loveless
1875-76—L. J. Allred
1877—L. J. Allred
1878-79 Adj.—Robert R. Howell
1880-81 Adj.—William Thomas Day
1882-83 Ex.-83 Ann. Adj.—Farish Carter Tate
1884-85 Adj.—Farish Carter Tate
1886-87 Adj.—Farish Carter Tate
1888-89 Adj.—E. W. Allred
1890-91 Adj.—William Cagle
1892-93—William M. Jones
1894-95—J. R. Allen
1896-97 Adj.-97—A. P. Mullinax
1898-99—L. J. Darnell
1900-01—Hardy Rhyne
1902-03-04—W. M. Jones
1905-06—E. Roper
1907-08-08 Ex.—J. W. Goode
1909-10—J. T. Atherton
1911-12 Ex.-12—Roscoe Pickett
1913-14—J. R. Allen
1915-15 Ex.-16-17 Ex.—A. B. Bradley
1917-18—Chesley Vincent
1919-20—Will Richards
1921-22—T. E. Johnson
1923-23 Ex.-24—G. W. Hamrick
1925-26 Ex.-26 2d Ex.—Edgar Wheeler
1927—Robert Lee McClain
1929-31 Ex.—Robert Lee McClain
1931—Luke E. Tate
1933—Luke E. Tate

Senators
From Pickens County
(1855-1860)
1855/56—Lemuel J. Allred
1857-58—Samuel Tate
1859-60—Elias W. Allred

From Forty-First District
(1861-date)

1861-62-63 Ex.—James Simmons

1863-64 Ex.-64-65 Ex.—James Simmons

1865/66-66—B. B. Quillian

1868 Ex.-69-70 Ex.—John B. Dickey

1871-72-72 Adj.—John A. Jervis

1873-74—John A. Jervis

1875-76—J. P. Chastain

1877—J. P. Chastain

1878-79 Adj.—William H. Simmons

1880-81 Adj.—Benjamin C. Duggar

1882-83 Ex.-83 Ann. Adj.—Thomas F. Greer

1884-85 Adj.—W. T. Day

1886-87 Adj.—Samuel Higdon

1888-89 Adj.—David Garen

1890-91 Adj.—C. B. Vincent

1892-93—W. D. Smith

1894-95—Thomas W. Craigo

1896-97 Adj.-97—J. R. Allen

1898-99—Thomas R. Johnson

1900-01—John M. Greer

1902-03-04—J. R. Allen

1905-06—G. W. Phillips

1907-08-08 Ex.—James L. Weaver

1909-10—W. T. Day

1911-12 Ex.-12—J. R. Kincaid

1913-14—A. H. Burtz

1915-15 Ex.-16-17-Ex.—Roscoe Pickett

1917-18—Thomas Avery Brown

1919-20—William Kimsey Reece

1921-22—Will Richards

1923-23 Ex.-24—J. B. Chastain

1925-26 Ex.-26 2d Ex.—Clifford Freeman Owen

1927—Will Richards

1929-31 Ex.—Wade Allen

1931—Nathaniel A. Pratt

1933—Steve C. Tate

Superior Court Judges
(Blue Ridge Circuit)

TERM

David Irwin _____Dec. 5, 1853-Oct. 8, 1855 resigned

Joseph Emerson Brown_____Oct. 8, 1855-Nov. 28, 1855

Nov. 28, 1855-Aug. 1, 1857 resigned

George D. Rice_____Aug. 1, 1857-Feb. 8, 1858

Feb. 8, 1858-Feb. 8, 1862

Feb. 8, 1862-Feb. 8, 1866

David Irwin_____Feb. 8, 1866-1868

William T. Crane _____July 21, 1868 appointment withdrawn

Aug. 19, 1868

Noel B. Knight _____Aug. 28, 1868-1870 resigned

Oct. 25, 1870-Jan. 1, 1877

George N. Lester_____Jan. 1, 1877-Jan. 1, 1881

James Rice Brown _____Jan. 1, 1881-Jan. 1, 1885

Jan. 1, 1885-Jan. 1, 1889

Will J. Winn_____Jan. 1, 1889-Oct. 21, 1889 died

George F. Gober_____Oct. 24, 1889-Jan. 1, 1893

Jan. 1, 1893-Jan. 1, 1897

Jan. 1, 1897-Jan. 1, 1901

Jan. 1, 1901-Jan. 1, 1905

Jan. 1, 1905-Jan. 1, 1909

Newton A. Morris _____Jan. 1, 1909-Jan. 1, 1913

Henry L. Patterson_____Jan. 1, 1913-Jan. 1, 1917

Newton A. Morris _____Jan. 1, 1917-Dec. 12, 1919 resigned

Daniel Webster Blair_____Feb. 1, 1920-Jan. 1, 1921

Jan. 1, 1921-Jan. 1, 1925

Jan. 1, 1925-June 16, 1926 died

John Stephens Wood_____June 24, 1926-Jan. 1, 1927

Jan. 1, 1927-Jan. 1, 1931

Jan. 1, 1931 resigned

John Harold Hawkins _____Mar. 1, 1931-Jan. 1, 1933

Jan. 1, 1933-date

Solicitors-General
(Blue Ridge Circuit)

TERM

Edward D. Chisholm_____Dec. 5, 1853-Nov. 27, 1855

TERM

William Phillips_____Nov. 27, 1855-Nov. 27, 1859

Nov. 27, 1859-Dec. 14, 1863

Dec. 14, 1863-Dec. 14, 1867

S. Calvin Johnson_____July 21, 1868-1870 died

James M. Bishop_____Oct. 22, 1870-Jan. 1, 1873

Carl Juan Wellborn_____Jan. 1, 1873-Jan. 14, 1874 resigned

Charles D. Phillips_____Jan. 19, 1874-Jan. 1, 1877

Thomas F. Greer_____Jan. 1, 1877-Jan. 1, 1881

George F. Gober_____Jan. 1, 1881-Jan. 1, 1885

Jan. 1, 1885-Jan. 1, 1889

George R. Brown_____Jan. 1, 1889-Jan. 1, 1893

Jan. 1, 1893-Oct. 28, 1896 died

Thomas Hutcheson _____Nov. 1896-Jan. 1, 1897

Jan. 1, 1897-Jan. 1, 1901

Jan. 1, 1901-1901 died

Berry F. Simpson_____Aug. 24, 1901-Jan. 1, 1903

Jan. 1, 1903-Jan. 1, 1905

Jan. 1, 1905-Jan. 1, 1909

J. P. Brooke_____Jan. 1, 1909-Jan. 1, 1913

Eugene Herbert Clay_____Jan. 1, 1913-Jan. 1, 1917

Jan. 1, 1917-Nov. 22, 1918 resigned

John Tucker Dorsey_____Nov. 26, 1918-Jan. 1, 1921

John Stephens Wood_____Jan. 1, 1921-Jan. 1, 1925

Jan. 1, 1925-June 24, 1926 resigned

George David Anderson_____Jan. 24, 1926-Jan. 1, 1929

Jan. 1, 1929-Jan. 1, 1933

Henry Grady Vandiviere_____Jan. 1, 1933-date

Congressional Districts

Following are the various congressional districts in which Pickens County has been from time to time:

1. Fifth District, from December 5, 1853, to March 23, 1861. (Acts, Georgia, 1853-4, p. 306.)

2. Ninth District, from March 23, 1861, to October 26, 1865. (Confederate Records, I, p. 732; Code of 1860, p. 12.)

3. Sixth District, from October 26, 1865, to July 30, 1872. (Confederate Records, IV, p. 146.)

4. Ninth District, from July 30, 1872, to date. (Acts, Georgia, p. 12.)

Chapter III ★ ★ ★
CENSUS OF 1860

●

IN THIS CHAPTER are given the names, ages and native States of every person who resided in Pickens County when the Census of 1860 was taken. The census of that year was the first taken after the formation of Pickens in 1853, and nearly all the pioneer families of the county are included.

The population of Pickens County in 1860 was: males, 2,353; females, 2,352; total, 5,705. (These figures were made up entirely of white persons, slaves not being listed in the census and there being no free negroes in the county in 1860.) The number of children of school age (then eight to seventeen, inclusive) was 1,219, of which number 919 had attended school within the year. The total value of real and personal property was given as $859,289.

In 1930, the population of Pickens County was: males, 4,959; females, 4,728; total 9,687. Of this number 795 were negroes (males, 426; females, 369). The number of children between the ages of six and eighteen, inclusive, was 2,491, and 2,101 of these had attended school within the year. The total valuation of real and personal property was set at $1,835,434.

The 1930 census also showed the following distribution of population for Pickens County: Talking Rock District, 568; Dug Road District, 1,055; Persimmon Tree District, 346; Truck Wheel District, 857; Town District, 1,298; Grassy Knob District, 725; Jerusalem District, 518; Townsend District, 1,628; Sharp Top District, 171; Ludville District,

93

585; Nelson District, 850; Sharp Mountain District, 343; Big Ridge District, 293; Hill District, 450.

CENSUS OF 1860 FOR PICKENS COUNTY

	NAME	AGE	OCCUPATION	BORN IN
1.	Harrison Pendley	34	Farmer	Ga.
	Kizera Pendley	40		Ga.
	Barnabas Pendley	10		Ga.
	Carter Pendley	6		Ga.
	William Pool	23	Farm hand	Ga.
	Sophia Pool	21		Ga.
2.	William Arthur	23	Farmer	Ga.
	Lucinda Arthur	18		Ga.
	Martha L. Arthur	6/12		Ga.
3.	Barnabas Arthur	60		Ga.
	Sophia Arthur	50		S. C.
	Rebecca Arthur	35		Ga.
	Felix Arthur	25	Farm hand	Ga.
	Malissa Arthur	18		Ga.
	Malinda Arthur	18		Ga.
	Sophia Arthur	21		Ga.
4.	Thomas Partin	61	Carpenter	Va.
	Catherine Partin	61		Ga.
	Jane Partin	21		Ga.
	Jesse Partin	22	Farm hand	Ga.
	Sarah J. Partin	24		S. C.
	John H. Partin	8		Ga.
5.	James Buchannan	50	Farmer	S. C.
	Lucinda Buchannan	51		S. C.
	Jane Buchannan	23		Ga.
	Jackson Buchannan	21	Farm hand	Ga.
	Mary Wilder	11		Ga.
	Amanda Wilder	4		Ga.
6.	Hiram Partin	31	Farmer	S. C.
	Eliza Partin	28		S. C.
	Mary Monroe	8		Ga.
	James Monroe	6		Ga.
	Perry Monroe	2		Ga.
7.	Verlinna Hutcheson	48	Tailor	S. C.
	John Hutcheson	20	Farm hand	Ga.
	Martha A. Hutcheson	17		Ga.
8.	Lucinda A. Smith	40	Domestic	Ga.
	James Smith	16	Farm hand	Ga.
	Lafayette Smith	14		Ga.

NAME	AGE	OCCUPATION	BORN IN
Reuben Smith	12		Ga.
Alfred Smith	9		Ga.
Rhoda Smith	8		Ga.
Caroline Smith	5		Ga.
Lucinda H. Smith	3		Ga.
9. Jackson Sherley	22	Farmer	Ga.
Sarah E. Sherley	20		Ga.
James H. Sherley	1		Ga.
10. Jacob Kirkingdall	21	Farmer	Ga.
Mary E. Kirkingdall	19		Ga.
Elias T. Kirkingdall	6/12		Ga:
11. Terissa Potts	40	Domestic	S. C.
James E. Potts	14		Ga.
John C. Potts	11		Ga.
Elizabeth A. Potts	9		Ga.
Young M. Potts	7		Ga.
William W. Potts	9/12		Ga.
Termima Hyde	74		S. C.
12. Samuel Buckhannun	34	Farmer	S. C.
Tempy M. Buckhannun	32		Ga.
Mary Buckhannun	14		Ga.
Narcissa J. Buckhannun	12		Ga.
Miles M. Buckhannun	9		Ga.
Sarah E. Buckhannun	8		Ga.
Susan D. Buckhannun	6		Ga.
Ruthey H. Buckhannun	2		Ga.
Martha L. Buckhannun	1/12		Ga.
13. James T. Green	33	Farmer	S. C.
Lucinda Green	22		Ga.
Malina C. Green	10		Ga.
Mary R. Green	7		Ga.
Alfred M. Green	8		Ga.
Thomas Green	5		Ga.
Elisha M. Green	4		Ga.
Doctor E. Green	3		Ga.
Josiah M. Green	2		Ga.
Jesse Z. Green	2/12		Ga.
14. Kimsey Padgett	26	Farmer	Ga.
Sarah Padgett	24		Ga.
Jacob A. Padgett	4		Ga.
Sanford Padgett	3		Ga.
Columbus A. Padgett	1		Ga.
15. John Martin	25	Farmer	Ga.
Minerva Martin	25		Ga.
William J. Martin	8		Ga.

NAME	AGE	OCCUPATION	BORN IN
Newton Martin	6		Ga.
Lavoanda Martin	5		Ga.
Rose Anna E. Martin	3		Ga.
Nancy A. Martin	1		Ga.
Sarah Jenkins	26	Domestic	Ga.
16. John Stegall	40	Farmer	S. C.
Elizabeth Stegall	36		Ga.
Martha R. Stegall	12		Ga.
Charlotte A. Stegall	11		Ga.
John H. Stegall	8		Ga.
Andrew H. Stegall	4		Ga.
Mary A. Stegall	3		Ga.
Sarah E. Stegall	1/12		Ga.
Reuben Loving	16	Farm hand	Ga.
Charles Chitwood	15	Farm hand	Ga.
17. Pickens Herndon	23	Farmer	S. C.
Sarah E. Herndon	22		N. C.
William T. Herndon	6		Ga.
Nancy E. Herndon	4		Ga.
Delphia J. Herndon	1		Ga.
18. Thomas Hudlow	32	Miller	N. C.
Susanna Hudlow	28		N. C.
Andrew J. Hudlow	9		Ga.
Miranda C. Hudlow	3		Ga.
William J. Hudlow	2		Ga.
19. Leander P. Allen	28	School teacher	Ga.
Winney A. Allen	24		Ga.
Thomas F. Allen	2		Ga.
20. Jesse Monroe	65		S. C.
Martha Monroe	72		S. C.
Delila Kerby	22	Domestic	Ga.
Margaret Colbert	6		Ga.
21. Thomas Monroe	40	Farmer	Ga.
Elizabeth Monroe	39		N. C.
Jesse Monroe	18	Farm hand	Ga.
Robert S. Monroe	15	Farm hand	Ga.
Perry D. Monroe	14		Ga.
Thomas L. Monroe, Jr.	13		Ga.
Martha D. Monroe	9		Ga.
Hiram K. Monroe	8		Ga.
Sarah J. Monroe	3		Ga.
Benjamin F. Monroe	1		Ga.
22. Jacob Hudgin	59	Farmer	S. C.
Elizabeth Hudgin	50		S. C.

NAME	AGE	OCCUPATION	BORN IN
William W. Hudgin	15	Farm hand	Ga.
James H. Hudgin	13		Ga.
23. Noah Biddy	21	Farmer	Ga.
Martha Biddy	21		S. C.
24. Richard Covington	55	Farmer	N. C.
Mary Covington	51		N. C.
Mahalia Covington	33		N. C.
Matsey H. Covington	23		N. C.
Bessey Covington	20		N. C.
Rebecca Covington	19		N. C.
Anna N. Covington	17		N. C.
Thomas Covington	16	Farm hand	Ga.
Mary J. Covington	14		Ga.
Richard M. Covington	13		Ga.
Doctor R. Covington	12		Ga.
25. Stephen Floyd	48	Farmer	S. C.
Martha Floyd	35		S. C.
Mary A. Floyd	16		Ga.
Jane E. Floyd	15		Ga.
Christopher C. Floyd	10		Ga.
Martha A. Floyd	6		Ga.
Joel T. Floyd	4		Ga.
Stephen D. Floyd	2		Ga.
26. Simon Huff	34	Farmer	S. C.
Mary A. Huff	34		S. C.
William Huff	10		Ga.
27. Francis Jones	35	Farmer	S. C.
Mary Jones	36		S. C.
James H. Jones	18	Farm hand	S. C.
Susan C. Jones	13		S. C.
Mary H. Jones	11		Ga.
Thomas P. Jones	6		Ga.
Sara J. Jones	1		Ga.
28. Susan Richards	39	Tailor	S. C.
Laura P. Richards	18		S. C.
Elizabeth J. Richards	6		S. C.
Martha E. Richards	3		S. C.
29. Silas Wilder	34	Farmer	S. C.
Dorkas Wilder	32		Ga.
Miranda E. Wilder	13		Ga.
John N. Wilder	9		Ga.
William L. Wilder	7		Ga.
Sarah N. Wilder	6		Ga.

Name	Age	Occupation	Born In
30. Verlina Monroe	26	Domestic	N. C.
Martha Monroe	26		Ga.
Mary H. Monroe	5		Ga.
Mary M. Monroe	3		Ga.
Terissa R. Monroe	1		Ga.
31. John Hagin	21	Farmer	Ga.
Sarah Hagin	24		Ga.
Elizabeth Hagin	1		Ga.
Joseph E. Hagin	6/12		Ga.
32. Washington Dobson	36	Farmer	Ga.
Margaret Dobson	30		Ga.
James A. Dobson	10		Ga.
David M. Dobson	9		Ga.
Caroline Dobson	7		Ga.
Albert T. Dobson	4		Ga.
Martha E. Dobson	1		Ga.
33. Elias Biddy	35	Farmer	N. C.
Mary Biddy	33		N. C.
Elias Biddy, Jr.	8		Ga.
John Biddy	6		Ga.
Sarah Biddy	4		Ga.
34. Nancy Biddy	65		N. C.
Jackson Biddy	25	Farm hand	Ga.
John R. Biddy	19	Farm hand	Ga.
George W. Biddy	15	Farm hand	Ga.
Jane Taylor	20	Domestic	Ala.
35. Andrew Eaton	28	Farmer	Ga.
Ruthey Eaton	31		N. C.
Jesse W. Eaton	6		Ga.
Nancy E. Eaton	4		Ga.
Mary L. Eaton	2		Ga.
Lewis Biddy	17	Farm hand	S. C.
36. William Blackwell	39	Blacksmith	N. C.
Martha Blackwell	30		N. C.
Martha L. Blackwell	13		Ga.
James A. Blackwell	10		Ga.
William D. Blackwell	8		Ga.
Malissa E. Blackwell	10		Ga.
Jasper Blackwell	1		Ga.
Newton Blackwell	1		Ga.
37. Joseph Blackwell	61	Blacksmith	N. C.
Mary Blackwell	62		N. C.
Rebecca Blackwell	36		N. C.
Joseph Blackwell	28	Farm hand	N. C.

NAME	AGE	OCCUPATION	BORN IN
Patsy Blackwell	26		N. C.
George Blackwell	23	Farm hand	N. C.
Martha A. Blackwell	18		Ga.
Thomas L. Blackwell	13		Ga.
38. Alfred Padgett	25	Farmer	Ga.
Sarah Padgett	21		Ga.
James W. Padgett	3		Ga.
39. James Howell	54	Farmer	S. C.
Jane Howell	52		S. C.
Liceney Howell	28		S. C.
Robert Howell	26	Farm hand	S. C.
Mary Howell	21		S. C.
Russell Howell	23	Farm hand	S. C.
40. John Taylor	39	Farmer	S. C.
Ary A. Taylor	31		S. C.
Lewis C. Taylor	13		Ga.
William Taylor	12		Ga.
William Colbert	16	Farm hand	N. C.
41. William Hogin	45	Farmer	Ga.
Malinda Hogin	43		S. C.
Frances C. Hogin	5		S. C.
42. John Buckhannon	19	Farmer	Ga.
Sarah Buckhannon	16		Ga.
43. James Darby	26	Farmer	Ga.
Caroline Darby	25		S. C.
Elizabeth Darby	11		Ga.
Mary C. Darby	10		Ga.
Emily Darby	5		Ga.
Madison B. Darby	2		Ga.
44. Charles Darby	65	Farmer	S. C.
Nancy Darby	50		S. C.
Newton Darby	17	Farm hand	Ga.
45. Reuben Darby	22	Farmer	Ga.
Frances Darby	24		Ga.
John H. Darby	2		Ga.
Charles L. Darby	4/12		Ga.
46. William Heath	40	Farmer	N. C.
Icey Heath (F)	34		Ga.
Mary C. Heath	14		Ga.
Nancy A. Heath	12		Ga.
Benjamin J. Heath	9		Ga.
Margaret J. Heath	7/12		Ga.

Name	Age	Occupation	Born In
47. Salom Abbot	27	Farmer	S. C.
Anna Abbot	30		S. C.
George Abbot	1		Ga.
48. Madison Strickling	29	Farmer	N. C.
Caroline Strickling	22		Tenn.
Thomas R. Strickling	2		Ga.
Joseph H. Strickling	10/12		Ga.
49. George Howell	44	Farmer	S. C.
Fanny Howell	33		Ga.
Josephine F. Howell	12		Ga.
Elihu Howell	11		Ga.
James F. Howell	9		Ga.
Jesse L. Howell	8		Ga.
John R. Howell	7		Ga.
Elizabeth E. Howell	5		Ga.
Eli C. Howell	3		Ga.
Cathrine A. Howell	2		Ga.
Julia R. Howell	1		Ga.
50. Rachel Worley	61		N. C.
Rebecca Worley	35		N. C.
Martha C. Worley	31		N. C.
Jiffen Worley	21	Farm hand	Ga.
51. William Byers	25	Farmer	Ga.
Jane A. Byers	27		N. C.
David E. Byers	4		Ga.
Jobenny Byers	1		Ga.
52. Pleasant Worley	35	Farmer	N. C.
Margaret Worley	34		N. C.
Thomas C. Worley	12		Ga.
Joel W. Worley	10		Ga.
Martha J. Worley	8		Ga.
James T. Worley	6		Ga.
John H. Worley	3		Ga.
Ambro J. Worley	1		Ga.
53. David Worley	28	Miller	N. C.
Caroline Worley	21		Ga.
Benton Worley	4/12		Ga.
54. Thomas Blackwell	29	Blacksmith	N. C.
Nicey Blackwell	28		Ga.
Benton Blackwell	8		Ga.
Marcus Blackwell	7		Ga.
Sarah E. Blackwell	4		Ga.
Emily Jarrott	28	Domestic	Ga.

Name	Age	Occupation	Born In
Samuel Jarrott	5		Ga.
55. Lewis Sams	52	Farmer	N. C.
Margaret Sams	52		S. C.
Martha J. Sams	13		Ga.
56. William Sams	28	Farmer	Ga.
Mahalia Sams	27		Ga.
Louisa Sams	7		Ga.
Frances Sams	5		Ga.
Columbus L. Sams	3		Ga.
Doctor B. Sams	2		Ga.
Nancy Sams	1/12		Ga.
57 John Sams	25	Farmer	Ga.
Jane Sams	27		Ga.
Sarah C. Sams	5		Ga.
John R. Sams	1/12		Ga.
58. James Worley	41	Farmer	N. C.
Frances Worley	40		N. C.
Thomas Worley	15	Farm hand	Ga.
Jason Worley	13		Ga.
Jasper Worley	11		Ga.
Mary Worley	8		Ga.
Jesse Worley	6		Ga.
Martha Worley	4		Ga.
Jane Worley	2/12		Ga.
59. Martha Biddy	20	Domestic	Ga.
Jesse Biddy	2/12		Ga.
Caroline Sams	34	Domestic	S. C.
Perliman Sams (M)	8		Ga.
Samuel F. Sams	3		Ga.
James C. Sams	5/12		Ga.
60. Elmira Monday	60		Ireland
Terry Fitzsimmons	20		Ga.
Patrick W. Fitzsimmons	19		Ga.
Lucinday Monday	12		Ga.
William Fitzsimmons	45	Stonecutter	Ga.
61. Franklin Baggett	24	Farmer	Ga.
Sarah Baggett	20		Ga.
Mary Baggett	1/12		Ga.
62. Leander McArthur	31	Blacksmith	N. C.
Mary McArthur	28		S. C.
Louisa A. McArthur	8		Ga.
Edy J. McArthur	4		Ga.
Sarah E. McArthur	2		Ga.

Name	Age	Occupation	Born In
63. Jacent Evans	29	Farmer	Ga.
Eliza Evans	30		S. C.
Mary J. Evans	11		Ga.
Frances M. Evans	9		Ga.
Sarah T. Evans	5		Ga.
64. Lucius Bradley	27	Farmer	N. C.
Adeline Bradley	27		S. C.
William J. Bradley	6		Ga.
John H. Bradley	1		Ga.
Rufus C. Bradley	26	Farm hand	N. C.
65. Robert Allen	63	Farmer	S. C.
Miranda Allen	48		S. C.
Aaronda H. Allen	19		Ga.
Jesse L. Allen	15	Farm hand	Ga.
66. Robert Allen, Jr.	37	Farmer	S. C.
Sarah Allen	33		Ga.
Marvel O. Allen (F)	15		Ga.
William R. Allen	10		Ga.
Harvey W. Allen	6		Ga.
Lucy A. Allen	3		Ga.
John W. Allen	1		Ga.
67. Robert Anderson	28	Farmer	Ga.
Salina Anderson	26		N. C.
Mary A. Anderson	5		Ga.
68. Dred Ledford	27	Farmer	Ga.
Mary Ledford	24		Ga.
George S. Ledford	4		Ga.
William B. Ledford	2		Ga.
69. David McArthur	66	Blacksmith	S. C.
Gences McArthur (F)	63		Va.
Elvira C. McArthur	13		Ga.
Leonard McArthur	20	Farm hand	Ga.
Elisa McArthur	24		Ga.
70. David McArthur	33	Farmer	S. C.
Amanda McArthur	18		Ga.
Elijah McArthur	67		N. C.
Elijah McArthur, Jr.	25	Farm hand	Ga.
71. Moses Jones	49	Farmer	S. C.
Malinda Jones	50		S. C.
William L. Jones	20	Farm hand	Ga.
Hugh A. Jones	20	Farm hand	Ga.
James C. Jones	17	Farm hand	Ga.
Levi Jones	14		Ga.

NAME	AGE	OCCUPATION	BORN IN
72. John Woodall	49	Farmer	S. C.
Catherine Woodall	49		S. C.
Elitha J. Woodall	23		Ga.
Malissa C. Woodall	18		Ga.
Anna A. Woodall	15		Ga.
John L. Woodall	13		Ga.
John P. Woodall	10		Ga.
Hampsey A. Woodall (F)	7		Ga.
73. Benjamin Akin	23	Farmer	N. C.
Louisa Akin	35		Va.
Isabella Akin	1		Ga.
74. Jackson Hearn	44	Farmer	S. C.
Loucinda Hearn	43		S. C.
Andrew J. Hearn	19	Farm hand	Ga.
Jemima M. Hearn	13		Ga.
Elizabeth M. Hearn	10		Ga.
John W. Hearn	8		Ga.
Mary E. Hearn	6		Ga.
Andrew Levi	38	Farmer	N. C.
Peter Ran	23	Farm hand	Ga.
Gilbert Lanxton	19	Farm hand	Ga.
75. Mathew Griffith	45	Farm hand	S. C.
Elizabeth Griffith	33		S. C.
William Griffith	15	Farm hand	S. C.
Mary Griffith	12		Ga.
Benjamin Griffith	10		Ga.
Martha F. Griffith	8		Ga.
Elizabeth J. Griffith	5		Ga.
Stephen Griffith	2		Ga.
76. William Ray	46	Farmer	Ga.
Nancy Ray	33		N. C.
Loucinday Ray	19		Ga.
Julia A. Ray	18		Ga.
Mary A. Ray	16		Ga.
Cynthia A. Ray	12		Ga.
Marion Ray	13		Ga.
Caroline Ray	10		Ga.
Catherine Ray	1		Ga.
77. Ephraim P. Dotson	47	Farmer	Ga.
Catherine Dotson	39		N. C.
Mary E. Dotson	22		N. C.
Sarah M. Dotson	20		N. C.

Name	Age	Occupation	Born In
Isabella J. Dotson	19		N. C.
Sarah E. Dotson	1		Ga.
78. Benjamin F. Stell	27	Blacksmith	N. C.
Malinda Stell	24		Ga.
Sarah E. Stell	6		Ga.
James M. Stell	4		Ga.
Elizabeth Stell	2		Ga.
Martha J. Stell	7/12		Ga.
79. Thomas Nicholson	43	Farm hand	La.
Louisiana Nicholson	38		S. C.
Elizabeth Nicholson	20		Ga.
William Nicholson	18	Farm hand	Ga.
Martha J. Nicholson	16		Ga.
Rebecca Nicholson	14		Ga.
Catherine Nicholson	12		Ga.
Mary Nicholson	10		Ga.
Andrew J. Nicholson	8		Ga.
John H. Nicholson	4		Ga.
80. Newton Ray	21	Farmer	Ga.
Sarah C. Ray	36		Ga.
William Carroll Ray	8		Ga.
81. Lakin Stephens	63	Farmer	S. C.
Anna Stephens	41		S. C.
Mary Hickman	21		Ga.
82. Wilbern Shepard	26	Farmer	N. C.
Mary Shepard	26		Ga.
Nancy C. Shepard	6		Ga.
Amos A. Shepard	2		Ga.
83. Leroy McCravey	34	Farmer	Ga.
Catherine McCravey	26		Ga.
Frances E. McCravey	2		Ga.
Thomas T. McCravey	5		Ga.
84. Harny Shires (F)	56	Domestic	S. C.
Thomas E. Shires	20	Farm hand	Ga.
Samuel C. Shires	17	Farm hand	Ga.
Thaddeus Shires	13		Ga.
85. Albert Langley	30	Farmer	Ga.
Elizabeth Langley	28		Ga.
Anna E. Langley	12		Ga.
William A. Langley	7		Ga.
Hawatha Langley	3		Ga.
86. Elbert Humphrey	40	Farmer	Ga.
Charlotte Humphrey	32		Ga.

Name	Age	Occupation	Born In
Elizabeth C. Humphrey	13		Ga.
Nancy J. Humphrey	12		Ga.
William Humphrey	10		Ga.
Elijah Humphrey	8		Ga.
Jesse L. Humphrey	3		Ga.
Mary A. Humphrey	9/12		Ga.
87. Allen Humphrey	60	Farmer	N. C.
Jane Humphrey	61		N. C.
88. Steward McCravey	29	Farmer	Ga.
Martha F. McCravey	24		Ga.
James L. McCravey	4		Ga.
Matilda J. McCravey	1		Ga.
William Harris	15	Farm hand	Ga.
89. William Godfrey	43	Farmer	S. C.
Mary Godfrey	30		N. C.
Mary E. Godfrey	9		Ga.
William H. Godfrey	3		Ga.
Thomas C. Godfrey	1		Ga.
90. Thomas Dean	37	Farmer	S. C.
Nancy Dean	37		S. C.
Sarah J. Dean	12		S. C.
John M. Dean	11		S. C.
William H. Dean	8		Ga.
Martha A. Dean	5		Ga.
Francis M. Dean	2		Ga.
91. Thomas Godfrey	33	Farmer	S. C.
Gilly Ann Godfrey	26		S. C.
Eleanor Godfrey	8		Ga.
Loucinda Godfrey	6		Ga.
Chasteen Godfrey	4		Ga.
Decater Godfrey	3		Ga.
McArthur Godfrey	2		Ga.
92. Green Payne	63	Farmer	Ga.
Rhoda Payne	16		Ga.
Alfred F. Payne	20	Farm hand	Ga.
Lewis Payne	15	Farm hand	Ga.
Calvin H. Payne	13		Ga.
Fanny J. Payne	11		Ga.
Samuel Payne	7		Ga.
John T. Payne	6		Ga.
93. Moses Herrin	50	Farm hand	N. C.
Zilla Herrin	38		N. C.
Augustus Herrin	11		Ga.

	Name	Age	Occupation	Born In
	William T. Herrin	9		Ga.
	Salina A. Herrin	7		Ga.
	Rebecca Herrin	7		Ga.
94.	Andrew Morrison	47	Farmer	N. C.
	Elizabeth Morrison	42		N. C.
	Adolphus Morrison	16	Farm hand	Ga.
	Columbus Morrison	7		Ga.
	Calvin Morrison	2		Ga.
	Mary A. Morrison	14		Ga.
95.	James A. Stephens	28	Farmer	Ga.
	Mary Stephens	21		N. C.
	Malissa E. Stephens	5		Ga.
	Francis E. Stephens	2		Ga.
96.	William Hammons	28	Farmer	N. C.
	Sarah Hammons	25		N. C.
	Angeline Hammons	2		Ga.
	Elizabeth Hammons	11/12		Ga.
97.	Francis Moon	31	Farmer	N. C.
	Martha Moon	18		Ga.
	James H. Moon	2		Ga.
98.	Hiram Roach	48	Farmer	S. C.
	Joanna Roach	46		S. C.
	Nancy W. Roach	25		Ga.
	Esther E. Roach	23		Ga.
	Mary J. Roach	21		Ga.
	Joanna Roach, Jr.	18		Ga.
	James K. Roach	15	Farm hand	Ga.
	Martha A. Roach	12		Ga.
	William L. Roach	10		Ga.
99.	Thomas Price	47	Farmer	N. C.
	William Price	42	Farm hand	N. C.
	Samuel Price	38	Farm hand	N. C.
	Nancy Price	45		N. C.
	Elizabeth Price	30		N. C.
100.	James Morrison	63	Farmer	N. C.
	Catherine Morrison	24		N. C.
	Elizabeth Morrison	23		N. C.
	Eliza J. Morrison	22		Ga.
	Margaret Long	5		Ga.
	John Ran	21	Farm hand	N. C.
101.	James Kell	36	Farmer	Ga.
	Jane Kell	38		S. C.
	Nancy A. Kell	13		Ga.

Name	Age	Occupation	Born In
Mary J. Kell	11		Ga.
Hannah C. Kell	10		Ga.
Susan E. Kell	8		Ga.
John E. Kell	6		Ga.
James B. Kell	3		Ga.
Ary Kell	2		Ga.
102. Frederick Price	32	Farmer	N. C.
Elizabeth Price	38		N. C.
Mary P. Price	13		N. C.
Martha B. Price	11		Ga.
Charles B. Price	10		Ga.
Nancy J. Price	8		Ga.
Caroline J. Price	6		Ga.
103. Susan Morrison	32	Domestic	N. C.
James D. Morrison	10		Ga.
Alonzo Morrison	8		Ga.
Charles E. Morrison	4		Ga.
Arabella Morrison	7/12		Ga.
Malissa Kenneman	29		N. C.
104. William Long	26	Farmer	N. C.
Rebecca Long	25		N. C.
Mary O. Long	3		Ga.
Jane A. Long	9/12		Ga.
105. William Long	33	Farmer	N. C.
Demima Long	31		N. C.
Camadon T. Long	9		N. C.
John L. Long	7		N. C.
Martin D. Long	6		N. C.
City D. Long	4		N. C.
Franklin Long	2		N. C.
Drewery S. Long	1		Ga.
106. James Shivers	33	Farmer	Ga.
Mary Shivers	33		N. C.
Arnerory Shivers (F)	10		Ga.
James F. Shivers	6		Ga.
Mahuldy C. Shivers	3		Ga.
107. Delilah Presley	40	Domestic	Ga.
Sophie Presley	14		Ga.
Robert M. Presley	13		Ga.
Mortester Presley	12		Ga.
Jackson Presley	9		Ga.
Lawson V. Presley	7		Ga.
John C. Presley	7		Ga.

Name	Age	Occupation	Born In
Joshua Presley	6		Ga.
Julius Presley	3		Ga.
108. John Tatem	37	Farmer	S. C.
Elizabeth Tatem	29		Ga.
Malinda Tatem	9		Ga.
Edward M. Tatem	7		Ga.
William R. Tatem	6		Ga.
John W. Tatem	3		Ga.
109. Eli Sumner	34	Farmer	N. C.
Josephine Sumner	29		N. C.
Isabella Kelley	10		Ga.
Susanna Kelley	13		Ga.
Nancy J. Kelley	12		Ga.
William T. Kelley	6		Ga.
110. Hugh Allen	60	Farmer	N. C.
Elizabeth Allen	52		N. C.
Mary A. Allen	25		N. C.
Nancy E. Allen	22		N. C.
Elizabeth Allen, Jr.	19		N. C.
Susan Allen	16		N. C.
William A. Allen	16	Farm hand	N. C.
111. Thomas Stokes	30	Farmer	S. C.
Elizabeth Stokes	30		S. C.
Mary A. Stokes	10		S. C.
Elizabeth Stokes, Jr.	7		S. C.
Harriett E. Stokes	5		S. C.
Andrew J. Stokes	4		S. C.
112. Harrison Gipson	45	Farmer	N. C.
Loucinda Gipson	37		N. C.
Asa Gipson	22	Farm hand	Ga.
Mary F. Gipson	20		Ga.
Rachel C. Gipson	17		Ga.
John D. Gipson	12		Ga.
Doctor R. Gipson	9		Ga.
Eda E. Gipson	5		Ga.
113. William Erwin	52	Farmer	S. C.
Nancy Erwin	42		N. C.
Malinda Erwin	20		Ga.
Susan Erwin	17		Ga.
Charles T. Erwin	14		Ga.
Juda H. Erwin (F)	12		Ga.
William H. Erwin	8		Ga.
Mary Summerour	18		Ga.
Nancy Summerour	6/12		Ga.

	Name	Age	Occupation	Born In
114.	Edward Tatem	68	Farmer	N. C.
	Rebecca Tatem	50		N. C.
	Parthenia Tatem	6		Ga.
115.	Robert Jordan	71	Farmer	Va.
	Susan Jordan	61		Va.
116.	David Oaks	34	Farmer	S. C.
	Mary Oaks	30		N. C.
	George W. Oaks	13		Ga.
	Elizabeth J. Oaks	11		Ga.
	Rachel C. Oaks	9		Ga.
	Sarah M. Oaks	7		Ga.
	Isaac L. Oaks	3		Ga.
	William E. Oaks	11/12		Ga.
117.	Jonas Gipson	34	Farm hand	N. C.
	Eliza Gipson	27		N. C.
	Adolphus Gipson	12		Ga.
	Leander A. Gipson	8		Ga.
	Sarah A. Gipson	10		Ga.
	Augustus Gipson	5		Ga.
	Eleanor Gipson	4		Ga.
	Richard Gipson	2		Ga.
	Eda Gipson	61		S. C.
118.	Caroline Duckett	43	Farmer	N. C.
	Amanda J. Duckett	18		Ga.
	Martha C. Duckett	16		Ga.
	James M. Duckett	14		Ga.
119.	Jackson Desley	35	Farmer	S. C.
	Elizabeth Desley	27		Ga.
	Marion T. Desley	4		Ga.
	Andrew J. Desley	4/12		Ga.
120.	Diar Burch	45	Farmer	N. C.
	Rebecca Burch	44		N. C.
	Jarase E. Burch	21	Farm hand	Ga.
	John T. Burch	17	Farm hand	Ga.
	Rebecca Burch, Jr.	14		Ga.
	Mary E. Burch	11		Ga.
	William M. Burch	8		Ga.
	Rutha H. Burch	4		Ga.
121.	William Bowen	28	Farmer	Ga.
	Mary Bowen	30		Ga.
	Malinda Bowen	4		Ala.
	John S. Bowen	2		Ala.
122.	Edwin Swanson	44	Miller	N. C.
	Sarah A. Swanson	27		Ga.
	William Swanson	9		Ga.

Name	Age	Occupation	Born In
Malinda C. Swanson	5		Ga.
James L. Swanson	4		Ga.
Joseph A. Swanson	3		Ga.
123. John Steel	28	Distiller	Ga.
Susan Steel	19		Ga.
124. Joseph Williams	40	Farmer	S. C.
Cynthia Williams	39		S. C.
Amanda E. Williams	14		Ga.
125. Jasper Johnson	47	Farmer	Ga.
Harriett C. Johnson	37		Ga.
Lucy Johnson	12		Ga.
James A. Johnson	11		Ga.
Caroline J. Johnson	9		Ga.
Sarah E. Johnson	5		Ga.
Frances Johnson	3		Ga.
William Ellington	23	School teacher	Ga.
Malinda Johnson	62		Ga.
Newton Johnson	37	Farm hand	Ga.
126. William Long	57	Farmer	N. C.
Mary Long	58		N. C.
Francis E. Long	24	Farm hand	N. C.
James A. Long	21	Farm hand	N. C.
Catherine L. Long	16		N. C.
127. Joseph Morrison	43	Farmer	N. C.
Delitha Morrison	40		N. C.
Mary E. Morrison	17		Ga.
Nancy C. Morrison	14		Ga.
Laura S. Morrison	7		Ga.
Alfred L. Morrison	4		Ga.
Elizabeth Morrison	48		N. C.
128. Lidya Steel	61	Domestic	N. C.
129. Henry Lankford	50	Bootmaker	S. C.
Elizabeth Lankford	26		Ga.
John H. Lankford	5		Ga.
Colitha Lankford	3		Ga.
Henry C. Lankford	6/12		Ga.
130. Mason Standfield	76	Miller	N. C.
Elizabeth Standfield	75		Va.
131. Count P. West	26	Farmer	S. C.
Sarah West	28		N. C.
Emma Jane West	7/12		Ga.
Caroline Hoyes	12		Ga.
132. Gardner Stearns	60	Farmer	Mass.
Nancy Stearns	48		N. C.
Thomas Stearns	21	Farm hand	N. C.

	NAME	AGE	OCCUPATION	BORN IN
	Caroline M. Stearns	19		N. C.
	Harvey Stearns	16	Farm hand	N. C.
	William E. Stearns	14		N. C.
	James F. Stearns	12		N. C.
	Eleanor L. Stearns	10		N. C.
	Lawson G. Stearns	7		N. C.
	Jane M. Idler	26		N. C.
	Lucy Idler	6		N. C.
	Nancy Idler	4		Ga.
133.	George Stearns	24	Farmer	N. C.
	Lucinda Stearns	24		N. C.
	Robert G. Stearns	2		Ga.
	Sarah Stearns	8/12		Ga.
	James Jackson	15	Farm hand	Ga.
134.	Willis West	45	Farmer	S. C.
	Jane West	43		S. C.
	Monroe West	14		Ga.
	Javan West (M)	10		Ga.
	Octavus West	6		Ga.
	Harvey West	3		Ga.
	Joseph Wooten	19	Farm hand	Ga.
135.	Benjamin West	54	Farmer	S. C.
	Elizabeth West	52		S. C.
	Susan M. West	21		S. C.
	Adolphus West	19		S. C.
	Amanda West	18		S. C.
	Columbus West	16		S. C.
	Frances West	13		Ga.
	Trapun A. West (F)	10		Ga.
136.	Isaac Mullinax	68	Physician	S. C.
	Rachel Mullinax	67		S. C.
	Isaac Stephen	7		Ga.
	Sarah M. Stephen	15		Ga.
	William Harris	23	School teacher	Ga.
137.	Andrew Mullinax	25	Farmer	Ga.
	Martha Mullinax	18		Ga.
138.	Allison Long	60	Farmer	N. C.
	Sarah Long	53		N. C.
139.	William Reeves	27	Farmer	N. C.
	Elizabeth Reeves	18		Ga.
	Mary Reeves	7/12		Ga.
140.	George Mooney	36	Farmer	N. C.
	Jane Mooney	29		N. C.
	Susan Mooney	12		N. C.
	Jonathan Mooney	18	Farm hand	Ga.

Name	Age	Occupation	Born In
William L. Mooney	6		Ga.
Mary Mooney	4		Ga.
John J. Mooney	2		Ga.
141. Samuel Stephens	50	Carpenter	Ga.
Catherine Stephens	39		Ga.
John A. Stephens	12		Ga.
142. Elijah Carroll	53	Mechanic	S. C.
Elizabeth Carroll	53		N. C.
143. Abram Shadwick	30	Farmer	S. C.
Nancy Shadwick	30		S. C.
Lazerus Shadwick	12		Ga.
Louisa Shadwick	18		Ga.
Henry S. Shadwick	13		Tenn.
144. George Head	43	Farmer	N. C.
Angeline Head	40		N. C.
Mary A. Head	18		Ga.
145. Andrew Carroll	28	Farmer	N. C.
Angeline Carroll	24		S. C.
Sarah J. Carroll	8		Ga.
Mary A. Carroll	7		Ga.
Columbus Carroll	5		Ga.
Thomas Carroll	4		Ga.
Amanda Carroll	1		Ga.
146. Abram Guyton	36	Farmer	S. C.
Dicey Guyton	23		S. C.
Jackson F. Guyton	1/12		Ga.
Aaron Parker	12		Ga.
147. Isaac Guyton	26	Farmer	S. C.
Martha Guyton	18		Ga.
Hester Guyton	14		Ga.
Jacob Guyton	10		Ga.
Linda Guyton	8		Ga.
Joseph Guyton	5		Ga.
148. George Whelchel	21	Farmer	S. C.
Mary Whelchel	21		S. C.
149. Jason Smith	62	Blacksmith	N. C.
Jane Smith	49		S. C.
Edward N. Smith	14		Ga.
Mary A. Smith	11		Ga.
Levi D. Smith	9		Ga.
150. Golden Mason	24	Farmer	N. C.
Mary Mason	21		Tenn.
John M. Mason	1		Ga.
151. Henry Smith	26	Farmer	Ga.

	Name	Age	Occupation	Born In
	Sarah Smith	24		Ga.
	Licy Smith (F)	2		Ga.
	Martha J. Smith	6/12		Ga.
152.	Thomas Smith	20	Farmer	Ga.
	Lucinda Smith	20		Ga.
153.	William Rassy	70	Farm hand	S. C.
154.	Daniel Kelley	28	Farm hand	Ga.
	Nancy Kelley	30		Ga.
	Nancy J. Kelley	8		Ga.
155.	Madison Dover	30	Miller	N. C.
	Susan Dover	25		N. C.
	Emma Dover	12		Ga.
	Harmon Dover	9		Ga.
	Manuel Dover	7		Ga.
	Willy Dover	5		Ga.
156.	William Abin	28	Farmer	Ga.
	Mary A. Abin	27		Ga.
	Mary A. Abin, Jr.	3/12		Ga.
157.	Levi Silvers	25	Farmer	Ga.
	Elizabeth Silvers	18		Ga.
158.	William Wilson	40	Farmer	N. C.
	Mary Wilson	37		N. C.
	John Wilson	13		Ga.
	Mary A. Wilson	10		Ga.
	Andrew Wilson	8		Ga.
	Sarah A. Wilson	6		Ga.
	Elizabeth C. Wilson	4		Ga.
159.	Jefferson Smith	23	Farmer	Ga.
	Jackson Smith	20	Farm hand	Ga.
160.	Marduke Sworn	22	Mechanic	Tenn.
	Lydia Sworn	36		Ga.
	William B. Sworn	9		Ga.
	Mary E. Sworn	6		Ga.
	Sarah J. Sworn	10/12		Ga.
161.	Eli Hudgens	45	Farmer	N. C.
	Caroline Hudgens	25		N. C.
	Hester Hudgens	8		Ga.
	Hamilton Hudgens	6		Ga.
	Arminda Hudgens	4		Ga.
	Ramon H. Hudgens	2		Ga.
	Elizabeth Hudgens	6/12		Ga.
162.	James McDaniel	19	Farmer	N. C.
	Rebecca McDaniel	22		Ga.
	Thomas McDaniel	2		Ga.

	Name	Age	Occupation	Born In
163.	Thomas McDaniel	22	Farmer	N. C.
	Rhoda McDaniel	24		Tenn.
164.	Reuben Jackson	42	Farmer	S. C.
	Rhoda Jackson	31		Tenn.
	William F. Jackson	11		Ga.
	John C. Jackson	10		Ga.
	Mary J. Jackson	8		Ga.
	General A. Jackson	6		Ga.
	Cornelius A. Jackson	4		Ga.
	Abbott R. Jackson	5		Ga.
	Miles N. Jackson	1		Ga.
165.	Daniel Buckhannon	30	Farmer	Ga.
	Susan Buckhannon	18		N. C.
166.	Abram Moss	55	Farmer	S. C.
	Mary Moss	27		S. C.
	Sarah C. Moss	11		Ga.
	James M. Moss	8		Ga.
	George W. Moss	7		Ga.
	Harriett M. Moss	4		Ga.
	John M. Moss	21	Farm hand	S. C.
	Pinkney L. Moss	31	Farm hand	S. C.
	Green Moss	29	Farm hand	S. C.
	Granderson Moss	26	Farm hand	S. C.
167.	John Boren	35	Farm hand	S. C.
	Rose Boren	27		Ga.
	Mary J. Boren	14		Ga.
	Nancy A. Boren	12		Ga.
	Indiana Boren	9		Ga.
	John H. Boren	7		Ga.
	Sarah F. Boren	5		Ga.
	James M. Boren	1		Ga.
168.	Thomas Stephens	55	Farmer	N. C.
	Martha Stephens	45		Tenn.
	George W. Stephens	17	Farm hand	Ga.
	Edward B. Stephens	12		Ga.
	Martha C. Stephens	10		Ga.
	Jane Stephens	5		Ga.
	Nancy Stephens	3		Ga.
169.	Elisha Ivery	42	Farmer	Ga.
	Catherine Ivery	42		Ga.
	Elizabeth N. Ivery	20		Ga.
	Samuel Ivery	18	Farm hand	Ga.
	Sarah A. Ivery	16		Ga.
	William N. Ivery	14		Ga.
	Myra M. Ivery	12		Ga.

NAME	AGE	OCCUPATION	BORN IN
Benjamin F. Ivery	8		Ga.
Martha E. Ivery	7		Ga.
John A. Ivery	4		Ga.
Harriett Ivery	1		Ga.
170. Barton T. Graveley	42	Blacksmith	Va.
Eda Graveley	35		Va.
Harriett F. Graveley	16		Va.
Frances A. Graveley	14		Va.
Verliza Graveley	12		Va.
William B. Graveley	11		Va.
Henry A. Graveley	8		Ga.
Luke W. Graveley	7		Ga.
Columbus Graveley	4		Ga.
171. William Collins	62	Farmer	S. C.
Mary Collins	23		N. C.
William J. Collins	22	Farm hand	N. C.
172. Williamson Forester	55	Farmer	N. C.
Celia Forester	50		Ga.
Mary S. Forester	20		Ga.
Emily Forester	18		Ga.
173. John Bradley	24	Farmer	Ga.
Nancy Bradley	25		Ga.
Martha A. Bradley	2		Ga.
Henry H. Bradley	6/12		Ga.
174. Thomas Johnson	64	Farmer	S. C.
Martha Johnson	65		S. C.
Thomas L. Johnson	20	Farm hand	Ga.
175. Nancy Sosebee	34	Domestic	Ga.
William Sosebee	16	Farm hand	Ga.
Mary Sosebee	10		Ga.
George Sosebee	7		Ga.
Massila Sosebee	3		Ga.
176. Marion Forester	26	Farmer	Ga.
Anna Forester	20		Ga.
Sarah E. Forester	8/12		Ga.
177. Bithel Bradley	48	Farmer	N. C.
Ann Bradley	47		S. C.
Rufus C. Bradley	15	Farm hand	Ga.
Ravester Bradley (F)	12		Ga.
Robert M. Bradley	8		Ga.
Hester Ann Bradley	5		Ga.
178. Martin Collins	30	Carpenter	N. C.
Derinda Collins	24		N. C.
James Collins	4		Ga.
Henry H. Collins	2		Ga.

	Name	Age	Occupation	Born In
179.	John Pack	22	Farmer	Ga.
	Sarah Pack	20		Ga.
180.	George Pack	48	Farmer	Ga.
	Elizabeth Pack	40		N. C.
	Sarah Pack	22		N. C.
	Mary Pack	20		Ga.
	Reuben Pack	16	Farm hand	Ga.
	Liney Pack (F)	13		Ga.
	James Pack	14		Ga.
	Joseph Pack	10		Ga.
	Clementine Pack	7		Ga.
	Rosanna Pack	5		Ga.
	William J. Pack	3		Ga.
181.	James Bowen	35	Farmer	S. C.
	Emeline Bowen	30		S. C.
	Sophie Bowen	12		S. C.
	Randolph Bowen	8		Ga.
	William P. Bowen	6		Ga.
	Andrew Bowen	5		Ga.
182.	Charles Jones	29	Farmer	N. C.
	Sarah Jones	23		Ga.
183.	Elizabeth Anderson	44	Domestic	Ga.
	Louisa Anderson	23		Ga.
	Silone Anderson	17	Farm hand	Ga.
	David Anderson	15	Farm hand	Ga.
	Martha J. Anderson	15		Ga.
	Frances E. Anderson	10		Ga.
	George M. Anderson	8		Ga.
184.	Franklin Lewis	34	Farmer	S. C.
	Sarah Lewis	24		S. C.
185.	William Jones	71	Farmer	N. C.
	Jinette Jones	63		S. C.
	Cynthia Jones	50		N. C.
	Mary Jones	47		N. C.
	John Jones	45	Farm hand	N. C.
	Lydia Jones	36		N. C.
	Jinette Jones, Jr.	30		N. C.
	Mable S. Jones	4		Ga.
186.	George R. Edwards	52	Farmer	S. C.
	Elizabeth Edwards	31		N. C.
	Mary A. Edwards	20		Ga.
	Lucinda J. Edwards	15		Ga.
	Sarah E. Edwards	12		Ga.
	George B. Edwards	2		Ga.
	Robert D. Edwards	8		Ga.

	Name	Age	Occupation	Born In
	William Edwards	60		Va.
187.	James Adair	37	Farmer	Tenn.
	Malissa Adair	31		N. C.
	William M. Adair	12		Tenn.
	Elijah S. Adair	10		Ga.
	George M. Adair	8		Ga.
	Mary J. Adair	6		Ga.
	Elizabeth K. Adair	1		Ga.
188.	Joshua McFarlin	70	Farmer	S. C.
	Nancy McFarlin	73		S. C.
	Sarah McFarlin	17		Ga.
	Mason McFarlin	12		Ga.
189.	George Moss	30	Blacksmith	S. C.
	James Moss	25		S. C.
	Frances Moss	2		Ga.
	Amanda Moss	1		Ga.
190.	James West	49	Farmer	S. C.
	Mary West	49		S. C.
	James E. West	24	Farm hand	S. C.
	Edward J. West	22		S. C.
	Christopher West	21	Farm hand	S. C.
	Thomas J. West	21	Farm hand	S. C.
	Mordica West	19	Farm hand	S. C.
	Maurice West	17	Farm hand	S. C.
	Willis West	14		S. C.
	Mary J. West	22		Ga.
	Mariman L. West	2		Ga.
	Frances West	1/12		Ga.
191.	Gabriel Moss	50	Wagonmaker	S. C.
	Selitha Moss	54		S. C.
	Richard Moss	26	Farm hand	S. C.
	Jane L. Moss	22		S. C.
	Mary M. Moss	18		S. C.
	Margaret Moss	13		Ga.
	John N. Moss	12		Ga.
	Martha C. Moss	10		Ga.
	Cynthia Moss	1		Ga.
192.	Elizabeth Hopkins	57	Domestic	S. C.
	Sarah Hopkins	30		Ga.
	Nancy Hopkins	27		Ga.
	William Hopkins	26	Farm hand	Ga.
	James Hopkins	23	Farm hand	Ga.
	Simeon Hopkins	22	Farm hand	Ga.
	Rebecca Hopkins	15		Ga.
193.	Richard McFarlin	45	Mechanic	S. C.

	Name	Age	Occupation	Born In
	Margaret McFarlin	32		N. C.
	John H. McFarlin	14		Ga.
	Zachariah T. McFarlin	12		Ga.
	William H. McFarlin	10		Ga.
	Mathew C. McFarlin	8		Ga.
	Peter P. McFarlin	5		Ga.
	Martha M. McFarlin	3		Ga.
194.	Ransom Collins	54	Farmer	S. C.
	Rhoda Collins	48		S. C.
	Sarah R. Collins	21		S. C.
	Elizabeth Collins	18		S. C.
	Berry M. Collins	16	Farm hand	Ga.
	Julia A. Collins	14		Ga.
	Dalimy Collins (F)	12		Ga.
	James B. Collins	9		Ga.
	Cynthia J. Collins	6		Ga.
	Anna J. Collins	17		Ga.
	Martha Collins	12		Ga.
195.	Lewis Moss	31	Farmer	S. C.
	Hannah Moss	23		S. C.
	Lewis T. Moss	5		Ga.
	Benjamin M. Moss	3		Ga.
	Willy R. Moss	6/12		Ga.
196.	John Boley	43	Farmer	S. C.
	Marintha Boley	36		S. C.
	James F. Boley	18	Farm hand	Ga.
	Margaret Boley	15		Ga.
	Bevergel H. Boley (M)	12		Ga.
	Rachel E. Boley	10		Ga.
	Martha A. Boley	10		Ga.
	John M. Boley	7		Ga.
	Sarah J. Boley	6		Ga.
	Elizabeth Boley	5		Ga.
	Samantha Boley	2		Ga.
	Robert McCutchen	38	Farmer	Ga.
	Thomas Jinkins	22	Blacksmith	Ga.
	Sarah Holtsclaw	16		Ga.
	Martha Pool	18		Ga.
197.	Marimon Moss	44	Farmer	S. C.
	Mary Moss	10		N. C.
	Mary Moss	16		Ga.
	Hulda Moss	14		Ga.
	Cardeny Moss (F)	12		Ga.
	Marion Moss	9		Ga.
	Jerome Moss	7		Ga.

	NAME	AGE	OCCUPATION	BORN IN
	Hannah Moss	5		Ga.
	Hiram F. Moss	1		Ga.
198.	Aaron Moss	64	Farmer	S. C.
	Elizabeth Moss	64		S. C.
	Vincy Moss (F)	30		S. C.
199.	Caroline Bell	40	Domestic	N. C.
	Robert Bell	24	Farm hand	N. C.
	James Bell	22	Farm hand	N. C.
	Mary Bell	20		N. C.
	Samuel Bell	18	Farm hand	N. C.
	Houston Bell	16	Farm hand	N. C.
	John Bell	14		N. C.
	Thomas Bell	12		N. C.
200.	Henry Loveless	24	Farm hand	Ga.
	Josephine Loveless	20		Ga.
	James E. Loveless	4/12		Ga.
201.	Andrew Jones	48	Farmer	S. C.
	Permelia Jones	31		S. C.
	Columbus F. Jones	17	Farm hand	Ga.
	Nancy N. Jones	15		Ga.
	Upson N. Jones	13		Ga.
	Pretty E. Jones	12		Ga.
	Andrew V. Jones	10		Ga.
	Ancel C. Jones	6		Ga.
202.	Ellison Cobb	65	Farmer	S. C.
	Cynthia Cobb	65		S. C.
203.	John Roper	54	Farmer	S. C.
	Sarah C. Roper	51		S. C.
	Catherine S. Roper	26		S. C.
	Rose A. Roper	24		S. C.
	Rachel E. Roper	19		S. C.
	Malinda Roper	16		Ga.
	Harriet A. Roper	14		Ga.
	Andrew H. Roper	10		Ga.
	Hulda A. Roper	6		Ga.
204.	William Williams	60	Farmer	N. C.
	Jane Williams	60		N. C.
	Riller C. Williams (F)	22		N. C.
	Zachariah E. Williams	20	Farm hand	N. C.
205.	Thomas Williams	32	Farmer	N. C.
	Amanda Williams	22		Ga.
206.	Richard Williams	27	Farmer	N. C.
	Nancy J. Williams	24		Ga.
	Jane E. Williams	3		Ga.

Name	Age	Occupation	Born In
Mary E. Williams	2		Ga.
William H. Williams	1/12		Ga.
207. Simon Hambrick	28	Farmer	N. C.
Elizabeth H. Hambrick	23		S. C.
John A. Hambrick	6		Ga.
James L. Hambrick	3		Ga.
Robert T. Hambrick	1		Ga.
208. Joshua Moss	38	Farmer	S. C.
Hulda Moss	40		S. C.
Mary A. Moss	17		S. C.
Harrell Moss	15		S. C.
Elizabeth J. Moss	10		S. C.
Martha Moss	7		Ga.
209. Lewis Kilian	46	Carpenter	N. C.
Martha H. Kilian	39		N. C.
James A. Kilian	21	Farm hand	S. C.
George W. Kilian	18	Farm hand	Ga.
Lawson B. Kilian	13		Ga.
Mary E. Kilian	10		Ga.
William F. Kilian	7		Ga.
General S. Kilian	4		Ga.
John E. Kilian	1		Ga.
210. Hugh Briant	74	Farmer	N. C.
Elizabeth Briant	40		N. C.
Salina A. Briant	40		Ga.
Lucy Briant	35		Ga.
Virginia Briant	30		Ga.
Amanda Briant	25		Ga.
Martin V. Briant	20	Farm hand	Ga.
Herschel D. Briant	15	Farm hand	Ga.
211. Patrick Briant	47	Farmer	Ga.
Emma Briant	43		S. C.
Mary J. Briant	17		Ga.
Nancy E. Briant	12		Ga.
Emma F. Briant	10		Ga.
212. Anderson Martin	42	Farmer	S. C.
Susanna Martin	46		N. C.
Mary Collins	16		Ga.
Susan R. Collins	11		Ga.
213. Spencer Yancy	26	Farmer	Ga.
Delitha Yancy	23		S. C.
214. James Findley	54	Farmer	Va.
Sarah C. Findley	26		S. C.
John W. Findley	5		Ga.
William Findley	5		Ga.

	NAME	AGE	OCCUPATION	BORN IN
215.	Chester Corban	23	Farmer	S. C.
	Elizabeth Corban	24		Ga.
	Yerby C. Corban	5		Ga.
	Sarah A. Corban	3		Ga.
	Artilery L. Corban (F)	2		Ga.
216.	Joseph Stover	45	Farmer	N. C.
	Elizabeth Stover	50		S. C.
	Joseph Stover, Jr.	19	Farm hand	Ga.
	Jacob Stover	18	Farm hand	Ga.
	George W. Stover	12		Ga.
217.	John Erwin	34	Farmer	S. C.
	Jane Erwin	35		S. C.
	Martha A. Erwin	11		Ga.
	John W. Erwin	9		Ga.
	Amanda E. Erwin	7		Ga.
	Leander H. Erwin	5		Ga.
218.	James Chastain	38	Farmer	S. C.
	Jane A. Chastain	35		Ga.
	Nancy E. Chastain	13		Ga.
	Elizabeth Chastain	12		Ga.
	Loucinda Chastain	9		Ga.
	David Chastain	6		Ga.
	Jane Chastain	5		Ga.
	William B. Chastain	4		Ga.
	Miles T. Chastain	2		Ga.
	Benjamin Chastain	4/12		Ga.
219.	Reuben Partin	30	Farm hand	S. C.
	Nancy Partin	25		Ga.
	Richard Partin	2		Ga.
220.	Dudley Mulkey	23	Farmer	Ga.
	Evey Mulkey	20		Ga.
	William D. Mulkey	1		Ga.
221.	David Chastain	33	Farmer	Tenn.
	Lucinda Chastain	38		Ga.
	William Chastain	12		Ga.
	Obediah Chastain	8		Ga.
	Sarah A. Chastain	6		Ga.
	Mary J. Chastain	5		Ga.
	Samuel Chastain	2		Ga.
222.	William Stone	30	Farmer	S. C.
	Mary Stone	30		S. C.
	James H. Stone	4		Ga.
	John Stone	2		Ga.
223.	William Chastain	47	Farmer	S. C.
	Elizabeth Chastain	47		Ky.

Name	Age	Occupation	Born In
Rebecca Chastain	20		Ga.
Elizabeth Chastain, Jr.	18		Ga.
Jane Chastain	16		Ga.
John Chastain	14		Ga.
Harvey Chastain	12		Ga.
Marion Chastain	8		Ga.
Elijah Chastain	5		Ga.
Malinda Chastain	7		Ga.
Solomon Chastain	2		Ga.
Julia A. Chastain	6/12		Ga.
224. Daniel Powell	45	Farmer	Ga.
Mary A. Powell	35		Tenn.
Elizabeth Powell	10		Ga.
Abraham W. Powell	7		Ga.
Daniel P. Powell	4		Ga.
225. Pinkney Buckhannon	29	Farmer	S. C.
Mary A. Buckhannon	30		Ga.
Sarah J. Buckhannon	10		Ga.
William D. Buckhannon	6		Ga.
Frances R. Buckhannon	3		Ga.
226. Joseph Chastain	22	Farmer	Tenn.
Amanda Chastain	20		Ga.
Sarah E. Chastain	1		Ga.
227. George Evans	34	Farmer	S. C.
Lucy Evans	27		S. C.
Caroline Evans	10		Ga.
Lucy J. Evans	8		Ga.
Mary F. Evans	6		Ga.
Sarah E. Evans	4		Ga.
Joshua Evans	2		Ga.
George A. Evans	3/12		Ga.
228. Sidney Stover	26	Farmer	S. C.
Mary A. Stover	24		Ga.
Amanda Stover	2		Ga.
Isaac Stover	6/12		Ga.
229. Orval Davis	37	Farmer	S. C.
Margaret Davis	31		Ga.
Julette A. Davis	12		Ga.
Mary R. Davis	11		Ga.
Martha H. Davis	9		Ga.
Sarah F. Davis	6		Ga.
Robert T. Davis	4		Ga.
230. George Davis	27	Farmer	S. C.
Sarah A. Davis	18		Ga.
Amanda C. Davis	1		Ga.

	Name	Age	Occupation	Born In
231.	Alfred Milton	43	Farmer	S. C.
	Hulda Milton	39		S. C.
	Jordan Milton	18	Farm hand	Ga.
	Eliza M. Milton	16		Ga.
	William G. Milton	13		Ga.
	Caroline M. Milton	9		Ga.
	George Milton	7		Ga.
232.	Henry Findley	24	Farmer	Ga.
	Lucy Findley	23		Ga.
	Mondorah Findley	8/12		Ga.
233.	Hezekiah Findley	68	Farmer	S. C.
	Elizabeth Findley	65		S. C.
	Thomas Rutledge	28	Farm hand	S. C.
234.	Robert Cosby	26	Farmer	N. C.
	Julia A. Cosby	23		Ga.
	William C. Cosby	4		Ga.
	Margaret J. Cosby	4/12		Ga.
235.	Robert McCollum	28	Farmer	S. C.
	Elizabeth McCollum	62		S. C.
	Harmer McCollum	24	Farm hand	Ga.
	Mary McCollum	20		Ga.
	Stewart McCollum	21	Farm hand	Ga.
	Eliza McCollum	18		Ga.
236.	George Bunch	46	Farmer	S. C.
	Linda Bunch	40		S. C.
237.	Samuel Medling	60	Farmer	S. C.
	Hulda Medling	40		S. C.
	Bennett Medling	16	Farm hand	S. C.
	Susan Medling	15		S. C.
	Catherine Medling	11		S. C.
	Martha Medling	9		S. C.
	Mary A. Medling	7		S. C.
	Franklin Medling	5		S. C.
	Octava Medling	5/12		S. C.
	Sarah Corban	70		N. C.
238.	Samuel Davis	65	Farmer	S. C.
	Minerva Davis	60		S. C.
	Sarah P. Davis	24		S. C.
239.	Jeptha Dean	26	Farmer	S. C.
	Pressey Dean	18		Ga.
	Rhoda E. Dean	1		Ga.
240.	William Anderson	24	Farmer	Ga.
	Mossa C. Anderson	24		Ga.
	Licenia E. Anderson	2		Ga.

Name	Age	Occupation	Born In
Sarah A. Anderson	11/12		Ga.
Lucy Silvers	13		S. C.
241. Joseph Rutledge	70	Carpenter	S. C.
Canadas Rutledge	56		Ga.
Sarah A. Rutledge	20		Ga.
Caroline Rutledge	23		Ga.
Lacinnia J. Rutledge	8		Ga.
Spencer Rutledge	19	Farm hand	Ga.
Minor B. Rutledge	16	Farm hand	Ga.
242. William Julian	73	Farmer	N. C.
Lydia Julian	64		S. C.
243. Lawson Bowen	32	Farmer	S. C.
Caroline Bowen	29		S. C.
Thomas M. Bowen	5		Ga.
James M. Bowen	4		Ga.
Doctor R. Bowen	1		Ga.
Elisa Bowen	28		Ga.
244. George Highten	75	Farmer	Ga.
Margaret Highten	71		Tenn.
Francis Highten	21	Farm hand	S. C.
Frances Highten	20		Ga.
245. Davis Hightower	37	Farmer	S. C.
Elizabeth F. Hightower	25		Va.
William W. Hightower	9		Ga.
George H. Hightower	5		Ga.
John F. Hightower	3		Ga.
Margaret E. Hightower	2		Ga.
246. John Johnson	32	Farmer	N. C.
Aramissa Johnson	27		Ga.
Albert A. Johnson	3		Ga.
Georgeann E. Johnson	1		Ga.
247. Sarah Gravely	59	Domestic	Va.
Patton M. Gravely	30	Farm hand	Va.
Mary Gravely	20		Va.
Anderson Gravely	18	Farm hand	Va.
248. John Murphy	29	Farmer	N. C.
Narcissa Murphy	29		S. C.
Bertin E. Murphy	6		Ark.
William J. Murphy	5		S. C.
Augustus Murphy	2		S. C.
Mary F. Murphy	2/12		Ga.
249. Thomas Murphy	58	Farmer	N. C.
Margaret Murphy	47		N. C.
John Aster	1		Ga.

	Name	Age	Occupation	Born In
250.	Elijah Yancy	54	Farmer	S. C.
	Elizabeth Yancy	44		S. C.
	Elisha P. Yancy	22	Farm hand	Ga.
	Obadiah Yancy	20	Farm hand	Ga.
	Eliza J. Yancy	18		Ga.
	Mary E. Yancy	16		Ga.
251.	William Forester	41	Farmer	S. C.
	Zenith Forester (F)	32		S. C.
	Thala A. Forester	14		Ga.
	Mary A. Forester	11		Ga.
	Nancy M. Forester	5		Ga.
252.	Ezekiel Forester	32	Farmer	Ga.
	Nancy Forester	21		Ga.
	Allard Forester	6		Ga.
	Louisa T. Forester	4		Ga.
	Ellen A. Forester	2		Ga.
253.	Anna Brown	30	Domestic	Ga.
	Rachel L. Brown	16		Ga.
	Loucinda Brown	12		Ga.
	Henry T. Brown	18	Farm hand	Ga.
	Hetty A. Brown	4		Ga.
254.	William Craig	65	Farmer	N. C.
	Sarah Craig	59		N. C.
	Nancy M. Craig	21		N. C.
	Malina Craig	18		Ga.
	Peggy Craig	22		Ga.
	Rebecca Craig	13		Ga.
	Thomas Craig	23	Farm hand	Ga.
255.	Eda Craig	50	Domestic	S. C.
	Arminda Craig	18		Ga.
	Jackson Craig	16	Farm hand	Ga.
	Tilman Craig	13		Ga.
	Martha Craig	11		Ga.
256.	Asa Dinkins	37	Farmer	N. C.
	Nancy Dinkins	36		N. C.
	Elizabeth Dinkins	11		Ga.
257.	John Jones	23	Farmer	Ga.
	Mary Jones	20		Ga.
	Susanna J. Jones	11/12		Ga.
258.	David Silvey	44	Farmer	N. C.
	Nancy Silvey	40		N. C.
	Elizabeth Silvey	11		Ga.
	Marret Silvey	10		Ga.
	Ambrose Silvey	9		Ga.
	Martha Silvey	8		Ga.

Name	Age	Occupation	Born In
Thada C. Silvey	7		Ga.
Louvena Silvey	3		Ga.
Mary E. Silvey	4/12		Ga.
259. Russell Morris	35	Farmer	N. C.
Licena Morris	32		S. C.
Georgeann Morris	10		Ga.
Acha F. Morris (M)	1		Ga.
Vergil A. Morris	14		Ga.
James J. Morris	13		Ga.
Elizabeth Morris	10		Ga.
John Morris	10		Ga.
Mary A. Morris	7		Ga.
Singleton Morris	4		Ga.
260. Zachariah Smith	47	Farmer	Ga.
Sarah Smith	50		S. C.
Sarah E. Smith	18		Ga.
Milida Smith	16		Ga.
Jesse T. Smith	11		Ga.
Joseph C. Smith	10		Ga.
Lovis L. Smith	7		Ga.
Cassy K. Smith	4		Ga.
Mary Allen Smith	75		S. C.
261. John Hopson	47	Farmer	S. C.
Rachel Hopson	49		S. C.
Sarah L. Hopson	22		Ga.
Henry E. Hopson	17	Farm hand	Ga.
Rachel D. Hopson	10		Ga.
Elizabeth M. Hopson	9		Ga.
Fannie Stephens	75		S. C.
Tira C. Stephens (M)	4		Ga.
262. Francis Pedagru	23	Farmer	Ga.
Jane Pedagru	22		Ga.
William E. Pedagru	6/12		Ga.
Beriman Martin	12		Ga.
263. Levi Yancy	23	Farmer	Ga.
Martha A. Yancy	23		Ga.
Sophia E. Yancy	2		Ga.
Mary M. Yancy	3/12		Ga.
264. Elisha Yancy	55	Farmer	S. C.
Sophia Yancy	66		S. C.
Elizabeth Yancy	32		S. C.
Mary C. Yancy	15		Ga.
Louisa A. Yancy	12		Ga.
Jasper U. Yancy	3		Ga.
265. Levi Yancy, Sr.	57	Farmer	S. C.

	NAME	AGE	OCCUPATION	BORN IN
	Anna Yancy	50		Ga.
	Kiziah Yancy	30		Ga.
	Delaney Yancy	11		Ga.
	Nancy Yancy	9		Ga.
266.	James Silvey	28	Farmer	S. C.
	Mary Silvey	22		N. C.
	William Silvey	3		Ga.
	Nancy Silvey	4/12		Ga.
267.	Leander Childers	29	Farmer	N. C.
	Margaret Childers	27		N. C.
	Mary Childers	4		Ga.
	Martha Childers	3		Ga.
	Colony Childers (F)	2		Ga.
	Columbus Childers	8/12		Ga.
268.	William Thompson	65	Farmer	N. C.
	Nancy Thompson	62		N. C.
	Baylis Thompson	24	Farm hand	N. C.
269.	Louis Thompson	39	Farmer	N. C.
	Eliza Thompson	20		Ga.
	Mary J. Thompson	16		Ga.
	Clarke Thompson	14		Ga.
	Nancy A. Thompson	8		Ga.
	Caroline Thompson	6		Ga.
	John Thompson	5		Ga.
270.	Elijah Thompson	21	Farmer	Ga.
	Rebecca Thompson	20		Ga.
271.	Peter Kirkingdall	73	Bap. clergyman	Tenn.
	Sarah Kirkingdall	44		S. C.
	Peter Kirkingdall, Jr.	12		Ga.
	Abraham W. Kirkingdall	10		Ga.
	Jesse B. Kirkingdall	8		Ga.
	James D. Kirkingdall	6		Ga.
	Tilmon S. Kirkingdall	3		Ga.
	Rebecca K. Kirkingdall	1/12		Ga.
272.	Harry Williams	21	Farmer	N. C.
	Rosena Williams	14		Ga.
273.	James Cobb	28	Farmer	Ga.
	Martha Cobb	23		Ga.
	Laura Cobb	4		Ga.
	Nathan C. Cobb	3		Ga.
274.	Alfred Moor	60		N. C.
	Tempy Moor	60		S. C.
	Tempy Moor	19		N. C.
275.	Elias Allred	71	Farmer	N. C.
	Mary Allred	71		S. C.

	Name	Age	Occupation	Born In
276.	John Allred	26	Farmer	Ga.
	Martha Allred	29		N. C.
	Mary Allred	4		Ga.
	Elias J. Allred	3		Ga.
277.	Tilman Ingram	24	Farmer	Ga.
	Hannah Ingram	19		Ga.
	Elizabeth Ingram	1		Ga.
278.	Kinch Hines	45	Farmer	S. C.
	Catherine Hines	19		N. C.
	California Hines	2		Ga.
	Arkansas Hines	7/12		Ga.
279.	Thomas Taylor	68	Blacksmith	S. C.
	Elizabeth Taylor	62		S. C.
	Abraham Taylor	28	Farm hand	S. C.
	James Taylor	19	Farm hand	Ga.
	Martha Taylor	15		Ga.
	Amanda A. Taylor	9		Ga.
	Victoria M. Taylor	4		Ga.
280.	Jeremiah Warren	46	Farmer	S. C.
	Elizabeth J. Warren	35		S. C.
	Caroline Warren	16		Ga.
	Monroe T. Warren	13		Ga.
	Martha Warren	10		Ga.
	James C. Warren	7		Ga.
	William F. Warren	6		Ga.
	Ann E. Warren	5/12		N. C.
	Ann Garven	66		N. C.
281.	William Sawyers	44	Farmer	S. C.
	Martha Sawyers	24		N. C.
	Mary A. Sawyers	23		N. C.
	Sarah F. Sawyers	21		N. C.
	Charles M. Sawyers	20	Farm hand	Ga.
	Cynthia Sawyers	17		Ga.
	William B. Sawyers	14		Ga.
	Martha Sawyers, Jr.	12		Ga.
	Allen Sawyers	28	Farm hand	S. C.
282.	Thomas Cook	29	Farmer	S. C.
	Julia A. Cook	27		S. C.
	Martha A. Cook	6		Ga.
	John H. Cook	5		Ga.
	Samuel E. Cook	3		Ga.
	Joseph E. Cook	1		Ga.
283.	Richard Cook	28	Farmer	N. C.
	Sarah M. Cook	27		N. C.
	Joshua Cook	11		Ga.

	Name	Age	Occupation	Born In
	Martha B. Cook	8		Ga.
	John J. Cook	5		Ga.
	Isaac R. Cook	4		Ga.
	James J. Cook	3		Ga.
	Jasper Bowen	35	Farm hand	Ga.
284.	Cummings King	64	Farmer	N. C.
	Arpy King (F)	62		N. C.
	Louisa King	20		Ga.
	Loucida King	18		Ga.
285.	John King	26	Farmer	N. C.
	Malinda King	22		Ga.
	Arpy King (F)	1		Ga.
	Samuel Garner	8		Ga.
286.	James McCoy	42	Farmer	S. C.
	Simeon McCoy	13		Ga.
	Elijah McCoy	11		Ga.
	Rebecca A. McCoy	9		Ga.
	James McCoy	7		Ga.
	Sarah McCoy	5		Ga.
	John McCoy	3		Ga.
287.	Crawford Harper	60		Ga.
	Martha Harper	30		Ga.
	Nancy Harper	2		Ga.
288.	Robert Griffith	34	Farmer	N. C.
	Lavenia Griffith	31		N. C.
	Evans L. Griffith	9		Ga.
	Pence A. Griffith	7		Ga.
	Atha C. Griffith (F)	5		Ga.
	William E. Griffith	3		Ga.
	John M. Griffith	2		Ga.
289.	Jacob Holbert	33	Farmer	N. C.
	Nancy L. Holbert	27		N. C.
	Benjamin A. Holbert	8		Ga.
	Martha A. Holbert	5		Ga.
	Hiram M. Holbert	3		Ga.
290.	Benjamin Holbert	30	Farmer	N. C.
	Mary Holbert	27		Ga.
	Elizabeth Holbert	7		Ga.
	Stephen Holbert	5		Ga.
	Sarah Holbert	2		Ga.
291.	James Brown	30	Farmer	S. C.
	Sarah P. Brown	25		Ga.
	Martha A. Brown	10		Ga.
	Handsel Brown	7		Ga.
	Harrison Brown	5		Ga.
	Susan Brown	4		Ga.

	Name	Age	Occupation	Born In
292.	Latty Clayton	50	Domestic	N. C.
	Mariman Clayton	18	Farm hand	Ga.
293.	Robert Henderson	40	Farmer	N. C.
	Elizabeth Henderson	38		N. C.
	Sarah E. Henderson	17		Ga.
	William I. Henderson	15	Farm hand	Ga.
	Susan S. Henderson	12		Ga.
	John H. Henderson	10		Ga.
	James E. Henderson	8		Ga.
	Malissa A. Henderson	6		Ga.
	Jane Henderson	4		Ga.
	Berry R. Henderson	1		Ga.
294.	John Ray	46	Farmer	S. C.
	Mary Ray	45		Ga.
	Malinda Hix	25		Ga.
295.	James Loveless	50	Blacksmith	N. C.
	Sarah Loveless	43		S. C.
	Evans Loveless	19	Farm hand	Ga.
	Malinda Loveless	17		Ga.
	Samuel L. Loveless	15	Farm hand	Ga.
	Genette Loveless	13		Ga.
	Martha Loveless	11		Ga.
	James Loveless	9		Ga.
	Sarah E. Loveless	5		Ga.
	Adline Loveless	3		Ga.
296.	Horatio Talley	65	Farmer	N. C.
	Mary A. Talley	55		N. C.
	Ibby A. Talley	31		Ga.
	John Talley	3		Ga.
297.	Henry Snider	32	Farmer	N. C.
	Hester A. Snider	30		S. C.
	Samuel M. Snider	8		Ga.
	Thomas E. Snider	7		Ga.
	Nancy J. Snider	3		Ga.
298.	James McCutchen	29	Farmer	Ga.
	Mary McCutchen	25		Ga.
	Robert McCutchen	8		Ga.
	Josephine McCutchen	2		Ga.
	Maple McCutchen	2/12		Ga.
299.	Caleb Brown	23	Farmer	Ga.
	Elizabeth Brown	22		Ga.
	Levi Brown	1		Ga.
	Nancy Brown	3/12		Ga.
300.	William Nelson	45	Farmer	S. C.
	Elizabeth Nelson	40		S. C.

Name	Age	Occupation	Born In
Anna Nelson	16		Ga.
Emily F. Nelson	14		Ga.
Martha Nelson	10		Ga.
Mary Nelson	9		Ga.
Ary H. Nelson	2		Ga.
Lucinda Nelson	5/12		Ga.
Anna Bradley	66		Ky.
301. Samuel Brown	45	Farmer	S. C.
Rachel A. Brown	44		N. C.
Cynthia L. Brown	21		Ga.
Dicy J. Brown	16		Ga.
Mary E. Brown	11		Ga.
Joseph Brown	6		Ga.
302. Uriah Evans	46	Farmer	N. C.
Margaret Evans	40		N. C.
Marks Evans	21	Farm hand	N. C.
James Evans	18	Farm hand	N. C.
Mary A. Evans	15		N. C.
William R. Evans	13		N. C.
Edward Evans	6		Ga.
Francis J. Evans	2		Ga.
303. Alfred Moor, Jr.	22	Farmer	N. C.
Julia A. Moor	24		N. C.
Joel Moor	10/12		Ga.
304. Thomas Huskey	63	Miller	N. C.
Sarah Huskey	62		N. C.
305. James Bailey	38	Mechanic	S. C.
Mary Bailey	38		N. C.
Louisa J. Bailey	17		S. C.
Sophia F. Bailey	15		Ga.
William J. Bailey	11		Ga.
Susan Bailey	9		Ga.
Thomas A. Bailey	6		Ga.
Jesse Bailey	4		Ga.
Mary E. Bailey	1		Ga.
306. Robert Roblerds	34	Farmer	N. C.
Elizabeth Roblerds	32		Ga.
Nancy L. Roblerds	10		Ga.
Susanna E. Roblerds	8		Ga.
Anna P. Roblerds	6		Ga.
Mary E. Roblerds	4		Ga.
Robert H. Roblerds	3		Ga.
307. William Chambers	40	Farmer	S. C.
Elizabeth Chambers	26		S. C.
Charles Chambers	12		Ga.

	Name	Age	Occupation	Born In
	James Chambers	10		Ga.
	Lucy Chambers	1		Ga.
308.	Welkey McHan	30	Farmer	N. C.
	Lucinda McHan	29		Ga.
	Sarah C. McHan	6		Ga.
	James F. McHan	5		Ga.
	Martha M. McHan	3		Ga.
	Barney S. McHan	1		Ga.
309.	Isaac Shelton	28	Farmer	N. C.
	Sarah J. Shelton	21		Ga.
	Cynthia E. Shelton	4		Ga.
	Mary A. Shelton	2		Ga.
310.	Jeremiah Brown	46	Farmer	S. C.
	Susan Brown	42		S. C.
	William Brown	17	Farm hand	Ga.
	Samuel Brown	12		Ga.
	John Brown	11		Ga.
	Lemuel Brown	5		Ga.
311.	Quiller Reece	42	Farmer	S. C.
	Hulda Reece	37		S. C.
	Tempy C. Reece	17		Ga.
	Mary A. Reece	15		Ga.
	George W. Reece	13		Ga.
	Joshua Reece	10		Ga.
	John Reece	5		Ga.
312.	Thomas Johnson	46	Farmer	N. C.
	Mekey Johnson (F)	53		N. C.
	John J. Johnson	24	Farm hand	Ga.
	Henry B. Johnson	22	Farm hand	Ga.
	Jane Johnson	19		Ga.
	Albert W. Johnson	18	Farm hand	Ga.
	Mary C. Johnson	15		Ga.
	Mekey Johnson, Jr.	13		Ga.
313.	Isabella Loveless	55	Domestic	S. C.
	Samuel B. Loveless	14		Ga.
314.	Charles Madison	59	Farmer	C. F. (?)
	Sarah Madison	44		S. C.
	Joseph A. Madison	20	Farm hand	Ga.
315.	Abner Loveless	35	Farmer	Ga.
	Nancy Loveless	32		Ga.
	Barton Loveless	8		Ga.
	Catherine Loveless	6		Ga.
	Gid Roberts Loveless	4		Ga.
	Amanda Loveless	4		Ga.
	Benjamin Loveless	3		Ga.

Name	Age	Occupation	Born In
Josephine Loveless	1		Ga.
316. Isaac Padgett	47	Farmer	S. C.
Artilly Padgett	47		N. C.
Susan Padgett	18		Ga.
Jacob Padgett	17	Farm hand	Ga.
Harriett Padgett	16		Ga.
Scanzada Padgett	15		Ga.
John Padgett	13		Ga.
Missouri Padgett	12		Ga.
317. James Moseley	21	Farmer	S. C.
Cynthia Moseley	17		Ga.
Thomas B. Moseley	1		Ga.
318. Emsley O. Mann	31	Farmer	Ga.
Mary Mann	22		Ga.
Mary E. Mann	4		Ga.
Jane L. Mann	10		Ga.
319. Caswell Corban	36	Gentleman(!)	S. C.
Milly M. Corban	34		Ga.
Caswell M. Neal	8		Ga.
320. John Nix	25	Hotelkeeper	Ga.
Candis Nix	36		S. C.
Sarah J. Nix	6		Ga.
William D. Nix	5		Ga.
Elizabeth E. Nix	1		Ga.
Benjamin Dunegan	23	Grocer	Ga.
Joseph Wofford	26	Grocer	S. C.
James M. Hayes	28	Gentleman	S. C.
John F. Ketchisides	25	Tailor	Ga.
George Row	8		Ga.
321. Adin Keeter	38	Merchant	N. C.
Elizabeth Keeter	29		Ga.
Mary A. Keeter	6		Ga.
Benjamin H. Keeter	3		Ga.
322. Benjamin Hanie	49	Physician	S. C.
Elizabeth E. Hanie	39		Ga.
William H. Hanie	17	Farm hand	Ga.
John R. Hanie	16	Farm hand	Ga.
Nancy E. Hanie	13		Ga.
Thomas F. Hanie	12		Ga.
Elizabeth M. Hanie	11		Ga.
Mary A. Hanie	9		Ga.
Josephine L. Hanie	7		Ga.
Samuel T. Hanie	3		Ga.
323. John F. Lindsey	23	Farmer	S. C.
Sarah A. Lindsey	18		Ga.

Name		Age	Occupation	Born In
324.	Abraham Blackwell	48	Attorney	Ga.
	Rosella Blackwell	46		Ga.
	Berryman Holt	30	Carpenter	S. C.
	Nancy C. Holt	23		S. C.
	Virginia E. Holt	4		Ga.
	John F. Holt	2		Ga.
326.	James Rich	23	Blacksmith	Ga.
	Elizabeth Rich	19		Ga.
	Andrew Rich	2		Ga.
	Mary A. Rich	1/12		Ga.
327.	Thomas Gravit	50	Farmer	S. C.
	Lina Gravit	51		S. C.
	William Gravit	21	Farm hand	Ga.
	Caroline Gravit	18		Ga.
	Arenia Gravit	16		Ga.
328.	Newton McClain	31	Team driver	Ga.
	Mary McClain	31		Ga.
	Martha J. McClain	9		Ga.
	Cicero N. McClain	1		Ga.
329.	James Ferguson	56	Farmer	S. C.
	Malissa Ferguson	55		Ga.
	Cynthia M. Ferguson	18		S. C.
	Pascal T. Ferguson	24	Clk. of ordinary	S. C.
	Rhoda M. Ferguson	16		S. C.
	William Ferguson	14		S. C.
	Posey M. Ferguson	13		S. C.
	Willem Ferguson	10		S. C.
330.	Levi Ferguson	27	Farmer	S. C.
	Nancy B. Ferguson	26		Ga.
	James L. Ferguson	4		Ga.
331.	David Dobbs	25	Farmer	Ga.
	Cynthia A. Dobbs	23		Ga.
	Robert C. Dobbs	4		Ga.
	William P. Dobbs	11/12		Ga.
332.	Samuel McCutchen	70	Farmer	Ga.
	Cynthia McCutchen	67		Ga.
	Robert McCutchen	72	Farm hand	Ga.
	James Brown	20	Farm hand	Ga.
333.	Nancy Wilkins	64	Domestic	Ga.
	Josephine Miller	20		Ga.
334.	Joshua Wadkins	34	Farmer	S. C.
	Feroby Wadkins (F)	33		Tenn.
	Mary A. Wadkins	12		Ga.
	Henry O. Wadkins	9		Ga.
	Margaret E. Wadkins	7		Ga.

	Name	Age	Occupation	Born In
	John M. Wadkins	4		Ga.
	James M. Wadkins	1		Ga.
335.	Mary Tarbutton	60	Domestic	N. C.
	Jane Tarbutton	41		N. C.
	Reuben Tarbutton	16	Farm hand	Ga.
336.	Phoebe Padgett	60	Domestic	Ga.
337.	Jasper Padgett	30	Farmer	Ga.
	Lucy Padgett	26		Ga.
	Martha J. Padgett	6		Ga.
	Mary Padgett	4		Ga.
	Lemuel J. Padgett	2		Ga.
338.	Albert Moseley	25	Farmer	S. C.
	Julia A. Moseley	23		Ga.
	Harrison Moseley	2		Ga.
	John Mann	71	Farm hand	S. C.
	Elizabeth Mann	69		S. C.
339.	James M. Ferguson	31	Farmer	S. C.
	Cynthia A. Ferguson	32		S. C.
	Martha A. Ferguson	11		Ga.
	John A. Ferguson	9		Ga.
	Susan M. Ferguson	6		Ga.
340.	William Fowler	55	Farmer	N. C.
	Elizabeth Fowler	55		S. C.
	Rebecca Fowler	16		Ga.
	Demorcus Cantrell	29	Farm hand	Ga.
	Samuel Cantrell	21	Farm hand	Ga.
341.	Paten Heath	35	Farmer	Ga.
	Martha J. Heath	20		N. C.
	Elizabeth Heath	4/12		Ga.
342.	John Nelson	35	Blacksmith	S. C.
	Comfort I. Nelson	33		S. C.
	Chesterfield Nelson	11		Ga.
	John C. Nelson	10		Ga.
	Nancy E. Nelson	8		Ga.
	Sarah M. Nelson	7		Ga.
	Ellen J. Nelson	5		Ga.
	Catherine Nelson	3		Ga.
	Amanda Nelson	1		Ga.
343.	William H. Mann	40	Farmer	S. C.
	Mary A. Mann	30		Ga.
	James L. Mann	7		Ga.
	Harriett Mann	5		Ga.
	Cynthia A. Mann	3		Ga.
	Benjamin Mann	4/12		Ga.

	Name	Age	Occupation	Born In
344.	Hix Patterson	43	Farmer	S. C.
	Sarah Patterson	38		Ga.
	Ezekiel Patterson	20	Farm hand	Ga.
	Edward Patterson	18	Farm hand	Ga.
	Dred Patterson	15	Farm hand	Ga.
	Susan E. Patterson	13		Ga.
	Asa Patterson	10		Ga.
	Ary Patterson	11		Ga.
	Nancy Patterson	11		Ga.
	Kimsey Patterson	5		Ga.
	Amanda Patterson	2		Ga.
	Lawton Patterson	20	Farm hand	Ga.
345.	Hezekiah Poms	26	Farmer	S. C.
	Anna Poms	20		Ga.
	Ezekiel Poms	2		Ga.
	Anna C. Poms	3/12		Ga.
346.	Griffin Heath	48	Wagonmaker	N. C.
	Sarah Heath	28		Tenn.
	William B. Heath	10		Ga.
	Joseph Heath	6		Ga.
	Mary E. Heath	2		Ga.
347.	Jeremiah Lambert	59	Clk. Inf. Court	Ga.
	Sarah Lambert	61		N. C.
	Rebecca L. Lambert	23		Ga.
	Sarah J. Lambert	4		Ga.
348.	Davis Collins	47	Farmer	N. C.
	Martha A. Collins	45		N. C.
	Miles J. Collins	20	Farm hand	N. C.
	Margaret C. Collins	17		N. C.
	James C. Collins	15	Farm hand	N. C.
	Sarah Collins	13		Ga.
	Randell Collins	11		Ga.
	Amanda J. Collins	8		Ga.
	Alice Collins	2		Ga.
	Milton Collins	2		Ga.
349.	Hiram Polls	46	Farmer	S. C.
	Josey Polls	46		Ga.
	Jefferson Polls	19	Farm hand	Ga.
	Adeline Polls	17		Ga.
350.	William Murphey	22	Farmer	Ga.
	Elizabeth Murphey	18		Ga.
	Louisa Murphey	1		Ga.
351.	Hiram Reed	45	Farmer	S. C.
	Salenia Reed	41		S. C.
	Stephen Reed	18	Farm hand	S. C.
	Josephine Reed	8		Ga.

NAME	AGE	OCCUPATION	BORN IN
352. Thomas Taylor	44	Farmer	N. C.
Miranda Taylor	37		N. C.
Mary J. E. Taylor	17		Ga.
Vianna A. Taylor	15		Ga.
William H. Taylor	12		Ga.
Samuel L. Taylor	9		Ga.
Dicy A. Taylor (F)	7		Ga.
Martha Taylor	6		Ga.
George N. Taylor	4		Ga.
353. John Love	78	Farmer	Ireland
Elizabeth Love	65		Ireland
William H. Love	12		Ga.
Elizabeth C. Love	6		Ga.
Telitha Love	5		Ga.
354. Andrew Steel	56	Farmer	N. C.
James Steel	34	Distiller	N. C.
William Steel	23	Farm hand	N. C.
Darison Steel	18	Farm hand	N. C.
Martha Steel	20		N. C.
Margaret Steel	16		N. C.
Cynthia Steel	15		N. C.
Thomas Steel	11		N. C.
355. John M. Lang	27	Farmer	N. C.
356. John Bishop	22	Farmer	S. C.
Malinda Bishop	19		Ga.
Mary Bishop	8/12		Ga.
357. John Roland	28	Farm hand	Ga.
Elizabeth Roland	21		Ga.
Thomas Roland	1		Ga.
Robert Roland	16	Farm hand	Ga.
358. Hezekiah Campion	48	Farm hand	N. C.
Loucinda Campion	38		N. C.
Louisa Campion	20		N. C.
William Campion	18	Farm hand	N. C.
John M. Campion	15	Farm hand	Ga.
Thomas E. Campion	13		Ga.
Sarah E. Campion	11		Ga.
359. Griffin Cason	26	Farmer	Ga.
Hannah Cason	24		Ga.
John Cason	4		Ga.
Sarah J. Cason	3/12		Ga.
360. Jefferson Eubanks	29	Farmer	Ga.
Charlotte Eubanks	27		Ga.
Nancy C. Eubanks	12		Ga.
Mary A. Eubanks	9		Ga.

Name	Age	Occupation	Born In
Elinda Eubanks	7		Ga.
Susan E. Eubanks	3		Ga.
361. Robert Eubanks	26	Farmer	Ga.
Mary Eubanks	24		Ga.
John H. Eubanks	5		Ga.
Martha H. Eubanks	2		Ga.
362. Greenberry Wofford	56	Farmer	S. C.
Precious Wofford	57		S. C.
Elizabeth J. Wofford	29		S. C.
Benjamin Wofford	22	Farm hand	S. C.
Jacob Wofford	19		S. C.
Eber Wofford	16		S. C.
Mary A. Wofford	13		Ga.
363. Moses Anderson	19	Farmer	Ga.
John Anderson	16	Farm hand	Ga.
Amber Anderson (M)	14		Ga.
William Anderson	12		Ga.
Edward Anderson	9		Ga.
364. Rufus McKinney	37	Farmer	N. C.
Barbara McKinney	36		S. C.
Malissa V. McKinney	5		Ga.
James P. McKinney	3		Ga.
Sarah E. T. McKinney	5/12		Ga.
365. James Prather	50	Carpenter	Ky.
Parthenia Prather	43		S. C.
Martha Prather	21		Ga.
Mary Prather	19		Ga.
Caroline Prather	15		Ga.
Warren Prather	13		Ga.
Hester H. Prather	11		Ga.
Gideon R. Prather	9		Ga.
Unis C. Prather (F)	9		Ga.
James H. Prather	1		Ga.
Canzada Prather (F)	7		Ga.
366. Warren Wigington	29	Farmer	Ga.
Mariah Wigington	30		Ga.
Sarah A. Wigington	8		Ga.
James N. Wigington	6		Ga.
John H. Wigington	4		Ga.
367. Reuben Gravit	36	Farm hand	Ga.
Wilson Gravit	16	Farm hand	Ga.
Catherine Gravit	14		Ga.
368. Frederick Jackson	52	Attorney	N. C.
Nancy Jackson	24		Ga.
369. John Jackson	24	Marble rubber	S. C.

	Name	Age	Occupation	Born In
	Rebecca Jackson	21		S. C.
	Elizabeth J. Jackson	3		S. C.
370.	Miles Jackson	29	Farm hand	S. C.
	Frances Jackson	20		S. C.
	James H. Jackson	2		S. C.
	Ara Jackson	31		S. C.
371.	John Hale	26	Farm hand	Ga.
	Parthenia Hale	22		Ga.
	Cynthia J. Hale	4		Ga.
	John T. J. Hale	2		Ga.
372.	Joseph Chambers	28	Farm hand	Tenn.
	Elizabeth Chambers	24		Ga.
	Mary H. J. Chambers	3		Ga.
	Harriet E. J. Chambers	1		Ga.
373.	Berryman Wofford	31	Brickmason	S. C.
	Elizabeth Wofford	27		S. C.
	Quincy A. Wofford	8		Ga.
	Cicero Wofford	6		Ga.
	Tatem M. Wofford	4		Ga.
	Sarah Wofford	7/12		Ga.
374.	John H. Dorsey	44	Farmer	N. C.
	Sarah Dorsey	38		S. C.
	Mary J. Dorsey	18		S. C.
	Martha Dorsey	14		Ga.
	Benjamin F. Dorsey	12		Ga.
	Sarah M. Dorsey	10		Ga.
	Roxanna L. Dorsey	9		Ga.
	Elinda Dorsey	7		Ga.
	John R. Dorsey	5		Ga.
	James V. Dorsey	4		Ga.
	Andrew J. Dorsey	3		Ga.
	Amanda Dorsey	10/12		Ga.
375.	Brit Wadkins	30	Farmer	S. C.
	Elizabeth Wadkins	30		Ga.
	Rachel Wadkins	4		Ga.
	Joseph E. Wadkins	1/12		Ga.
376.	George Campmin	52	Farmer	N. C.
	Mary Campmin	53		S. C.
	George West	83		S. C.
376.	Warrick Hazlewood	48	Farmer	S. C.
	Jane Hazlewood	54		S. C.
	Emeline Hazlewood	13		Ga.
	Sarah Hayse	25		S. C.
377.	Peter C. Coward	42	Farmer	N. C.
	Olive Coward	43		S. C.

Name	Age	Occupation	Born In
Margaret S. Coward	19		N. C.
Stephen Coward	15	Farm hand	Ga.
Sophia Coward	9		Ga.
Caroline A. Coward	4		Ga.
Mary A. Coward	10/12		Ga.
378. John Varner	52	Farmer	S. C.
Ruth Varner	50		S. C.
William Varner	24	Farm hand	S. C.
Joseph Varner	22	Farm hand	S. C.
Viancey Varner (F)	19		S. C.
John R. Varner	15	Farm hand	S. C.
Mary F. Varner	11		S. C.
Perry D. Varner	10		S. C.
379. Edward Johnson	44	Farmer	N. C.
Edy Johnson	27		S. C.
Sarah E. Johnson	16		Ga.
Joseph Johnson	14		Ga.
Nancy L. Johnson	13		Ga.
Mary J. Evans	10		Ga.
John E. Johnson	8		Ga.
Mary J. Johnson	6		Ga.
Charlotte Johnson	1		Ga.
380. Joshua D. Dorsey	21	Farmer	S. C.
Rocilla Dorsey	18		Ga.
381. Eber West	43	Farmer	S. C.
Elizabeth West	41		N. C.
Julia A. West	11		Ga.
Missouri West	9		Ga.
Georgia West	6		Ga.
Sarah C. West	3		Ga.
Loucinda Hayse	17		S. C.
382. James B. Smith	31	Farmer	Ga.
Susan Smith	31		S. C.
James D. F. Smith	9		Ga.
George W. Smith	5		Ga.
Eber Smith	1		Ga.
Marick Smith	1		Ga.
383. Ezekiel Akins	50	Rockmason	N. C.
Jane Akins	49		S. C.
Lydia Akins	19		Ga.
Catherine Akins	15		Ga.
Esther Akins	13		Ga.
Mary Akins	11		Ga.
Barbara L. J. Akins	5		Ga.
Silas Akins	18	Farm hand	Ga.

	Name	Age	Occupation	Born In
	Amanda S. P. Akins	14		Ga.
	Thomas P. Thompson	4		Ga.
384.	William Swofford	24	Farmer	Ga.
	Julia A. J. Swofford	25		Ga.
	William L. Swofford	5		Ga.
	Sarah F. Swofford	4		Ga.
	Julia A. Swofford	.3		Ga.
	Sarah J. O. Swofford	3/12		Ga.
	John B. D. Swofford	10/12		Ga.
385.	Josiah Reese	44	Farmer	S. C.
	Lucinda Reese	43		S. C.
	Joseph W. Reese	20	Farm hand	Ga.
	John B. Reese	19	Farm hand	Ga.
	Zoufannie Reese	14		Ga.
	Martha C. Reese	11		Ga.
	Solomon M. Reese	8		Ga.
	Sarah A. E. Reese	4		Ga.
386.	William M. Reese	23	Farmer	Ga.
	Sarah Reese	20		Ga.
387.	Eber Tapp	25	Farmer	S. C.
	Sarah Tapp	22		Ga.
	Cicero Tapp	2		Ga.
388.	John H. Ammons	61	Farmer	S. C.
	Nancy Ammons	66		N. C.
	Philip Williams	25	Farm hand	N. C.
389.	John P. Wofford	30	Farmer	S. C.
	Martha Wofford	30		N. C.
	Cansada Wofford (F)	10		Ga.
	Lucy Wofford	5		Ga.
	Isabella Wofford	4		Ga.
	Augustus Wofford	3		Ga.
390.	Lawrence Bradley	55	Millwright	S. C.
	Jane Bradley	54		N. C.
	Jane Bradley	29		N. C.
	Virgil M. Bradley	18	Farm hand	N. C.
	Judson L. Bradley	15	Farm hand	Ga.
	Rebecca S. Bradley	13		Ga.
	Andrew J. H. Bradley	10		Ga.
391.	Samuel Hood	45	Farmer	S. C.
	Eleanor Hood	42		Ga.
	Dred P. Hood	16	Farm hand	Ga.
	Ezekiel Hood	12		Ga.
	Samuel T. Hood	10		Ga.
	Aster Hood (M)	7		Ga.
	Susan M. Hood	3		Ga.

	Name	Age	Occupation	Born In
	Martha M. Hood	1/12		Ga.
392.	John Hood	20	Farmer	Ga.
	Anna Hood	14		Ga.
393.	John Brock	22	Farmer	Ga.
	Anna Brock	18		Ga.
394.	Susan Howell	60		N. C.
395.	William Bishop	29	Farm hand	S. C.
	Elizabeth Bishop	34		S. C.
	James M. Bishop	10		S. C.
	Louvinia Bishop	7		S. C.
	William H. Bishop	4		Ga.
396.	William Ray Bishop	26	Farmer	S. C.
	Mary A. Bishop	21		S. C.
397.	Samuel Tate	63	Farmer	Ga.
	Mary Tate	56		Ga.
	Caleb Tate	34	Farm hand	Ga.
	Farish C. Tate	25	Farm hand	Ga.
398.	Stephen Griffith	54	Farmer	Ga.
	Julia A. Griffith	82		N. C.
399.	Jesse Pendley	44	Miller	N. C.
	Mary H. Pendley	36		Ga.
	Mary L. Pendley	14		Ga.
	Thomas T. Pendley	12		Ga.
	Rufus C. Pendley	11		Ga.
	Samuel T. Pendley	8		Ga.
	William Pendley	6		Ga.
	Barbara M. Pendley	3		Ga.
	Samuel M. Pendley	11/12		Ga.
400.	Lewis Quinton	40	Farmer	N. C.
	Nancy Quinton	43		S. C.
	Berton Quinton	21	Farm hand	N. C.
	Henry Quinton	19	Farm hand	N. C.
	Mary Quinton	18		Ga.
	Sarah Quinton	15		Ga.
	Elizabeth Quinton	14		Ga.
	John Quinton	12		Ga.
	Martha Quinton	9		Ga.
401.	Lewis Holtsclaw	41	Farmer	S. C.
	Catherine Holtsclaw	41		S. C.
	Jane Holtsclaw	13		S. C.
	Mary Holtsclaw	10		S. C.
	Elias Holtsclaw	6		Ga.
	Elijah Holtsclaw	6		Ga.
	Columbus Holtsclaw	2		Ga.

	Name	Age	Occupation	Born In
402.	Berryman Brooks	27	Farmer	S. C.
	Esther Brooks	65		N. C.
	Harriet Brooks	28		S. C.
403.	Larkin Moss	65	Farmer	N. C.
	Margaret Moss	40		S. C.
	Margaret Moss, Jr.	16		S. C.
	Nancy Moss	12		S. C.
	Warren Moss	9		S. C.
	Elias A. Moss	5		S. C.
404.	Jasper White	28	Farmer	Ga.
	Sarah White	29		N. C.
	Elias White	4		Ga.
405.	Francis Coward	23	Farmer	N. C.
	Jane Coward	24		N. C.
	Malinda Coward	3		Ga.
	John Coward	1		Ga.
406.	Rhoda Padgett	45	Domestic	N. C.
	John L. Padgett	16	Farm hand	Ga.
	Alfred Padgett	20	Farm hand	Ga.
	Matilda Padgett	20		Ga.
407.	Elisha Whitemore	45	Farmer	S. C.
	Ann Whitemore	40		N. C.
	James Whitemore	16	Farm hand	Ga.
	Lafayette Whitemore	14		Ga.
	Martha Whitemore	12		Ga.
	Julia A. Whitemore	4		Ga.
	Sarah Whitemore	2		Ga.
	Permelinda Whitemore	65		N. C.
408.	Ary Mayfield (F)	25		S. C.
	Leroy Mayfield	10		Ga.
	John Mayfield	8		Ga.
	Josephine Mayfield	5		Ga.
	Cena Mayfield	3		Ga.
	Richmond Mayfield	2/12		Ga.
409.	Joshua Swanson	47	Miller	N. C.
	Elizabeth Swanson	47		S. C.
	Margaret Swanson	22		S. C.
	Mary Swanson	19		S. C.
	Mahala Swanson	16		S. C.
	Edwin Swanson	15	Farm hand	Ga.
	Nathaniel Swanson	11		Ga.
410.	John G. Coffee	20	Farmer	Ga.
	Mary A. Coffee	20		N. C.
	Winnie Coffee	58		N. C.
	John L. Coffee	16	Farm hand	N. C.

Name	Age	Occupation	Born In
411. Hiram Harris	31	Farmer	N. C.
Mary Harris	29		S. C.
Alfred Harris	11		S. C.
Sarah L. Harris	8		Ga.
Hesterann Harris	5		Ga.
Samantha Harris	3		Ga.
Mary S. Harris	11/12		Ga.
412. Thomas J. Fields	23	Farmer	Ga.
Salina Fields	21		Ga.
413. James McCaa	35	Farmer	N. C.
Margaret McCaa	29		N. C.
James A. McCaa	10		Ga.
Alfred McCaa	7		Ga.
Sarah McCaa	6		Ga.
Martha L. McCaa	4		Ga.
John E. McCaa	1		Ga.
414. John Pettit	55	Farmer	S. C.
Elmer Pettit	54		N. C.
Susan Pettit	25		N. C.
Henry Pettit	17	Farm hand	Ga.
Amanda Pettit	15		Ga.
John Pettit	11		Ga.
415. Joshua Darnell	28	Farmer	S. C.
Mary Darnell	24		Ga.
Elias L. Darnell	4		Ga.
James Darnell	1		Ga.
Mary Darnell	3/12		Ga.
Joshua Darnell, Sr.	65		N. C.
416. Able Honea	49	Farmer	S. C.
Nancy Honea	47		S. C.
Robert Honea	17	Farm hand	Ga.
William Honea	14		Ga.
Celia Honea	12		Ga.
James Honea	10		Ga.
417. Miles Bramlet	50	Farmer	Va.
Anna Bramlet	44		Ga.
Sarah Bramlet	19		Ga.
Pacia Bramlet	17		Ga.
Malinda Bramlet	15		Ga.
Sampson Bramlet	12		Ga.
William Bramlet	11		Ga.
James Bramlet	5		Ga.
418. Elizabeth Worley	48	Domestic	N. C.
419. Thomas Ray	22	Farmer	Ga.
Julia A. Ray	17		Ga.

	Name	Age	Occupation	Born In
420.	William Cowart	48	Farmer	Ga.
	Abigail Cowart	38		Ga.
	Mary Cowart	14		Ga.
	Jane M. Cowart	13		Ga.
	John L. Cowart	8		Ga.
	Juda Cowart (F)	6		Ga.
	Josephine Cowart	2		Ga.
	Caroline Cowart	2		Ga.
421.	John Hayse	40	Farmer	S. C.
	Elizabeth Hayse	50		S. C.
	Winnie Hayse	30		S. C.
	Celia Hayse	20		S. C.
	Sarah Hayse	18		S. C.
	James Hayse	16		S. C.
	Rebecca Hayse	14		S. C.
	Lydia Hayse	13		S. C.
422.	Thomas Hayse	28	Farmer	S. C.
	Mima Hayse	30		Ga.
	Thomas Hayse, Jr.	7		Ga.
	Landrum Hayse	1		Ga.
423.	William Hayse	27	Farmer	S. C.
	Sarah Hayse	27		Ga.
	Elizabeth Hayse	6		Ga.
	John Hayse	4		Ga.
	James Hayse	2		Ga.
424.	Elias Wadkins	50	Farmer	S. C.
	Mary Wadkins	50		S. C.
	Franklin Wadkins	19	Farm hand	Ga.
	Thomas Wadkins	18	Farm hand	Ga.
	Joseph Wadkins	14		Ga.
	Margaret Wadkins	17		Ga.
	Elizabeth Wadkins	9		Ga.
425.	Thomas Wadkins	25	Farmer	Ga.
	Malissa Wadkins	18		Ga.
426.	Mason Stanfield	30	Farmer	N. C.
	Malinda Stanfield	20		Ga.
	Dicy Stanfield (F)	4		Ga.
	Adolphus Stanfield	1		Ga.
427.	Carrie A. Neal	55	Domestic	N. C.
	Merida Neal	21	Farm hand	N. C.
	Sarah Neal	23		N. C.
	William Neal	6		Ga.
428.	Alex Graham	37	Farmer	Ga.
	Jane Graham	27		N. C.
	Alfred Graham	12		Ga.

NAME	AGE	OCCUPATION	BORN IN
Cynthia Graham	9		Ga.
Carrie A. Graham	1		Ga.
429. Richard McGaah	30	Farmer	Ga.
Rebecca McGaah	25		N. C.
William P. McGaah	1		Ala.
Rhoda A. McGaah	11/12		Ga.
Milly A. McGaah	27		N. C.
Lucinda J. Crow	7		Ga.
430. Josiah McGaah	60	Farmer	N. C.
Delilah McGaah	60		N. C.
William McGaah	24	Farm hand	Ga.
George McGaah	21	Farm hand	Ga.
Benjamin McGaah	19	Farm hand	Ga.
431. Thomas Champion	23	Farmer	N. C.
Elizabeth Champion	27		Ga.
432. Wilson Cowart	37	Farmer	N. C.
Mary Cowart	36		Ga.
Sarah A. Cowart	16		Ga.
George M. Cowart	14		Ga.
Lucy Cowart	11		Ga.
Jacob Cowart	8		Ga.
Mary Cowart	6		Ga.
Susan Cowart	4		Ga.
William Cowart	1		Ga.
433. Virginia Briant	44	Domestic	Ga.
Russell Briant	21	Farm hand	Ga.
Elizabeth Briant	17		Ga.
Licena Briant	14		Ga.
John Briant	11		Ga.
Frances Briant	8		Ga.
Cynthia Briant	5		Ga.
Elias Briant	3		Ga.
434. Samuel Hamby	70	Farmer	S. C.
Catherine Hamby	60		N. C.
Stephen Hamby	21	Farm hand	Ga.
435. John Hamby	23	Farmer	Ga.
Nancy Hamby	19		N. C.
Samuel T. Hamby	1		Ga.
436. John Hambrick	30	Farmer	Ga.
Sarah Hambrick	27		Ga.
Sarah Hambrick	5		Ga.
Hannah Hambrick	2		Ga.
437. Barbara Good	50	Midwife	N. C.
Silome Good	18	Farm hand	N. C.
Joseph Good	16	Farm hand	N. C.

	Name	Age	Occupation	Born In
	Alfred Good	14		Ga.
	William Good	11		Ga.
	Ada Woods	40		S. C.
438.	William Swofford	23	Farmer	Ga.
	Elizabeth Swofford	23		Ga.
	Frances Swofford	4		Ga.
	Mary Swofford	1		Ga.
	Sarah Swofford	6/12		Ga.
	Martha Strickling	37		Ga.
	John Strickling	8		Ga.
439.	Miles Darnell	21	Farmer	Ga.
	Elizabeth Darnell	18		Ga.
440.	James Paxton	24	Farmer	Ga.
441.	Martin Paxton	54	School teacher	Ga.
	Elizabeth Paxton	30		Ga.
	Rhoda Paxton	48		Ga.
	George Paxton	16	Farm hand	Ga.
	Lucy Paxton	11		Ga.
	Emeline Paxton	4		Ga.
442.	Jonathan Pendley	95		Va.
	Milly Pendley	55		S. C.
	Benjamin Pendley	17	Farm hand	Ga.
443.	John Padgett	37	Farmer	Ga.
	Sarah Padgett	27		Ga.
	Elisha Padgett	11		Ga.
	Sebron Padgett	9		Ga.
	Rial Padgett	7		Ga.
	Leroy Padgett	4		Ga.
444.	Doctor Padgett	25	Farmer	Ga.
	Christina Padgett	17		Ga.
445.	John Miller	20	Farm hand	S. C.
	Leanna Miller	24		Ga.
446.	William Elrod	60	Farmer	S. C.
	Nancy Elrod	52		S. C.
	Mary C. Elrod	18		S. C.
	Sarah Elrod	14		S. C.
	Lucinda Elrod	12		S. C.
	Nancy Elrod	22		S. C.
447.	Jeremiah Barnett	58	Farmer	S. C.
	Pacia Barnett	60		S. C.
	Falanie Barnett	30		S. C.
	Nancy Barnett	26		S. C.
	Sarah Barnett	24		S. C.
	Agnes Barnett	22		S. C.
	Araminta Barnett	16		S. C.

	Name	Age	Occupation	Born In
448.	William Barnett	27	Farmer	S. C.
	Milly Barnett	20		S. C.
449.	Jack Jackson	30	Farmer	S. C.
	Caroline Jackson	32		N. C.
	Thomas Jackson	14		Ga.
	Hester A. Jackson	5		Ga.
	Columbus Jackson	2		Ga.
450.	Thomas Jackson	45	Farmer	S. C.
	Lucenia Jackson	30		S. C.
	Frances Jackson	16		S. C.
	William Jackson	14		S. C.
	Nancy Jackson	12		S. C.
	Andrew Jackson	10		S. C.
451.	John Weaver	20	Farmer	Ga.
	Mary Weaver	24		S. C.
	Milsada Weaver	1		Ga.
452.	Nathan Shirley	25	Farmer	Ga.
	Rhoda Shirley	23		Ga.
	Mary Shirley	3		Ga.
	Martha Shirley	1		Ga.
453.	Isaac Disheroon	36	Farmer	Ga.
	Margaret Disheroon	66		N. C.
	Lucinda Paxton	27		Ga.
	Thomas J. Paxton	22	Farm hand	Ga.
454.	Samuel Weaver	45	Farmer	Ga.
	Harriet Weaver	40		Ga.
	Jasper M. Weaver	20	Farm hand	Ga.
	Peter Weaver	16	Farm hand	Ga.
	Hazly Weaver (F)	9		Ga.
	Elizabeth Weaver	6		Ga.
	Daniel Weaver	4/12		Ga.
455.	Benjamin Goss	37	Farmer	Ga.
	Jemima Goss	35		S. C.
	Cara L. Goss	11		Ga.
	John Goss	5		Ga.
	William Goss	3		Ga.
	Joseph Goss	8/12		Ga.
456.	John McElroy	28	Farmer	Ga.
	Delila McElroy	25		Ga.
	Mary McElroy	3		Ga.
	William McElroy	2		Ga.
	John H. McElroy	3/12		Ga.
	John McElroy, Sr.	69	Farm hand	Ga.
	Mary McElroy	70		S. C.
	Greenberry Goss	16	Farm hand	Ga.

	NAME	AGE	OCCUPATION	BORN IN
457.	William Mills	33	Farmer	N. C.
	Anna Mills	36		N. C.
	Corida Mills	8		Ga.
	Susan Mills	4		Ga.
	Joseph Mills	6/12		Ga.
	John Ledbetter	10		Ga.
458.	Joushia M. Good	32	Farmer	Ga.
	Margaret Good	27		N. C.
	Martha Good	5		Ga.
	Margaret Good, Jr.	1		Ga.
459.	John Woodall	47	Farmer	S. C.
	Ann Woodall	40		Ga.
	Russell Woodall	20	Farm hand	Ga.
	Sarah Woodall	18		Ga.
	Sabina Woodall	14		Ga.
	Harriett Woodall	12		Ga.
	Thomas Woodall	10		Ga.
	John Woodall	7		Ga.
	Ruth Woodall	2		Ga.
460.	James Carver	35	Farmer	N. C.
	Frances Carver	34		S. C.
	Julia A. Carver	10		Ga.
	Robert Carver	9		Ga.
	Christina Carver	8		Ga.
	Mary Carver	7		Ga.
	Elouisa Carver	6		Ga.
	Frederick Carver	4		Ga.
	Silas Carver	1		Ga.
461.	William Wadkins	27	Farm hand	S. C.
	Angeline Wadkins	27		Ga.
	Arminda Wadkins	7		Ga.
	Lucinda Wadkins	7/12		Ga.
462.	Thomas Kuykingdall	50	Miller	N. C.
	Matilda Kuykingdall	50		S. C.
	Arpha Ann Kuykingdall	16		Ga.
	Athret Kuykingdall (F)	13		Ga.
	Louisa M. Kuykingdall	11		Ga.
463.	Thomas Harris	70	Mechanic	N. C.
	Lucinda Harris	45		S. C.
	Eliza Harris	16		Ga.
	Lucinda Harris	12		Ga.
	James Harris	7		Ga.
464.	Riley Davis	35	Farm hand	N. C.
	Eliza A. Davis	30		Ga.
	Mary Ann Davis	3		Ga.

Name	Age	Occupation	Born In
Kirlis Newman	25	Carpenter	Ga.
Elizabeth Newman	21		Ga.
Narcissa Hutchison	18		Ga.
James R. Hutchison	13		Ga.
Emeline Hutchison	14		Ga.
465. Albert Fossett	27	Farmer	S. C.
Luvinia Fossett	26		N. C.
Elizabeth Fossett	4		Ga.
Pascal P. Fossett	1		Ga.
Turner Hutchison	65	Farm hand	S. C.
466. James M. Herrington	32	Farmer	S. C.
Elizabeth Herrington	32		S. C.
William Herrington	7		Ga.
Joshua Herrington	5		Ga.
Nancy C. Herrington	3		Ga.
Decatur Herrington	5/12		Ga.
467. Augustus Fossett	30	Farmer	S. C.
Jane C. Fossett	30		S. C.
Mary Fossett	8		Ga.
James Fossett	6		Ga.
Caroline Fossett	3		Ga.
468. Mary Fossett	68	Domestic	Va.
469. William Glover	27	Farm hand	Ga.
Elizabeth Glover	23		S. C.
Lucinda Glover	2		Ga.
470. John Hanie	22	Farmer	S. C.
Permina Hanie	18		S. C.
William Hanie	1		Ga.
Newton Hanie	17	Shoemaker	S. C.
471. William Padgett	35	Farmer	Ga.
Martha Padgett	29		S. C.
Mary Padgett	9		Ga.
Albert Padgett	8		Ga.
472. Ephraim Scruggs	20	Farmer	Ga.
Tabitha Scruggs	19		Ga.
John Scruggs	2/12		Ga.
Mehala Scruggs	60		S. C.
473. William Chumler	29	Farmer	Ga.
Samantha Chumler	35		Ga.
Isabella Chumler	2		Ga.
474. Berry V. Padgett	37	Farmer	N. C.
Malinda Padgett	35		Ga.
Cicero Padgett	14		Ga.
Eliza Padgett	9		Ga.
Levi Padgett	5		Ga.

	NAME	AGE	OCCUPATION	BORN IN
	Alvin Padgett	7		Ga.
	Jesse Padgett	2		Ga.
475.	Vivalva Barnett	38	Farmer	S. C.
	Mary Barnett	33		S. C.
	Ruthenia Barnett	14		Ga.
	Luther Barnett	11		Ga.
	Mary G. Barnett	9		Ga.
	Jeremiah M. Barnett	7		Ga.
	William Barnett	4		Ga.
	Joel Barnett	5/12		Ga.
476.	Alfred Pendley	22	Farmer	Ga.
	Eda Pendley	24		Ga.
477.	Jesse Padgett	57	Bap. clergyman	N. C.
	Eda Padgett	57		N. C.
	John Hogan	22	Farm hand	N. C.
	Nancy Hogan	22		Ga.
478.	Cary S. Padgett	30	Farmer	Ga.
	Mary H. Padgett	18		Ga.
	Malindy V. Padgett	1		Ga.
479.	Stephen Smith	20	Farmer	Ga.
	Samantha Smith	18		Ga.
480.	Robert Evans	40	Farmer	N. C.
	Emeline Evans	38		Ala.
	Joseph W. Evans	14		Ga.
	Salina Evans	11		Ga.
	Martha Evans	10		Ga.
	James W. Evans	6		Ga.
	Emily C. Evans	1		Ga.
	Susan Evans	4		Ga.
481.	Thomas Honea	33	Farmer	S. C.
	Maiden Honea	27		S. C.
	Sarah E. Honea	11		Ga.
	Mary C. Honea	8		Ga.
	Thomas H. Honea	6		Ga.
	Amanda J. Honea	4		Ga.
482.	Greenberry Page	45	Farmer	S. C.
	William L. Page	19	Farm hand	Ga.
	Minerva C. Page	17		Ga.
	James F. Page	15	Farm hand	Ga.
	Susanna E. Page	13		Ga.
483.	Thomas W. Elrod	26	Farmer	S. C.
	Manva Elrod	18		Ga.
	Anna Murphy	60		Ga.
	Martha Garner	31		Ga.
	Malissa Garner	7		Ga.

Name	Age	Occupation	Born In
484. James Dobson	29	Farmer	Ga.
Elizabeth Dobson	20		Ga.
Margaret Dobson	3		Ga.
William Dobson	1		Ga.
485. John Harge	30	Farmer	N. C.
Lucinda Harge	40		Tenn.
Sarah Harge	10		Ga.
Miranda Harge	3		Ga.
486. Andrew Lovelady	44	Farmer	S. C.
Sarah Lovelady	39		Ga.
Silas R. Lovelady	14		Ga.
Martha L. Lovelady	13		Ga.
Mary L. Lovelady	12		Ga.
Sarah A. L. Lovelady	10		Ga.
Jesse M. L. Lovelady	9		Ga.
John P. Lovelady	7		Ga.
Elizabeth G. Lovelady	5		Ga.
Thomas J. Lovelady	3		Ga.
Andrew J. Lovelady	5/12		Ga.
487. Reuben J. Bowlin	25	Farmer	Ga.
Margaret E. Bowlin	34		Ga.
Mary S. Bowlin	5		Ga.
James M. Bowlin	4		Ga.
William J. Bowlin	2		Ga.
Henry F. Bowlin	2		Ga.
488. James Huggins	25	Farmer	Ga.
Elizabeth Huggins	30		Ga.
Rachel Huggins	22		Ga.
Frances Huggins	19		Ga.
Mary Huggins	17		Ga.
489. Casuel Hall	18	Farmer	S. C.
Martha Hall	18		N. C.
Sarah P. Hall	10/12		Ga.
490. Wilder Anders	48	Farm hand	Ga.
Elizabeth Anders	48		Ga.
Malissa Anders	2		Ga.
Christopher Anders	17	Farm hand	Ga.
James A. Anders	15	Farm hand	Ga.
Mary E. Anders	10		Ga.
John Jinkins	8		Ga.
491. James P. Grover	33	Farmer	Ga.
Prudence Grover	26		Ga.
Miller T. Grover	10		Ga.
Nancy E. Grover	8		Ga.
Joel Grover	6		Ga.

Name	Age	Occupation	Born In
Susan C. Grover	4		Ga.
John W. Grover	10/12		Ga.
492. David Hall	60	Hatter	S. C.
Elizabeth Hall	28		S. C.
Lillia Hall	50		S. C.
Caroline Hall	22		S. C.
Martissa A. Hall	16		S. C.
Nathaniel Hall	14		Ga.
Roswell Hall	7		Ga.
493. Elizabeth Hall	54	Domestic	S. C.
Moses M. Hall	17	Farm hand	Ga.
494. William Cantrell	25	Farmer	Ga.
Mary E. Cantrell	22		N. C.
Demarkus Cantrell	7		Ga.
Elizabeth Cantrell	5		Ga.
Amanda Cantrell	4		Ga.
James Cantrell	2		Ga.
Henry Cantrell	6/12		Ga.
495. Sarah Davis	30	Domestic	N. C.
Mary Davis	5		Ga.
496. Christopher Cook	37	Farmer	Tenn.
Susan Cook	29		Ga.
George Cook	2		Ga.
Laura Richards	18		S. C.
William Wilkins	2		Ga.
497. John Ridings	40	Farmer	S. C.
Lucinda Ridings	28		S. C.
Jeptha Ridings	9		Ga.
Harvey Ridings	8		Ga.
Charles Ridings	3		Ga.
Sarah Ridings	84		S. C.
William Sims	45	Bap. clergyman	S. C.
498. David Stone	40	School teacher	S. C.
Margaret Stone	27		Ga.
John P. Stone	5		Ga.
David A. Stone	4/12		Ga.
499. Elizabeth Chitwood	65	Domestic	S. C.
Elizabeth Chitwood	36		Ga.
Lucinda Loving	56		Ga.
500. Thomas Wilson	33	Farmer	S. C.
Serviva Wilson	44		N. C.
Hannah O. Wilson	9		Ga.
James H. Wilson	5		Ga.
Jeptha Wilson	3		Ga.

Name	Age	Occupation	Born In
Malana Carver	12		Ga.
Samuel Carver	14		Ga.
501. John Bosman	27	Farmer	Ga.
Sarah C. Bosman	24		Ga.
James C. Bosman	3		Ga.
Samuel C. Bosman	4/12		Ga.
502. Samuel Brown	20	Farmer	Ga.
Nancy C. Brown	23		Ga.
Mary M. Brown	3/12		Ga.
503. William Wilson	48	Farmer	S. C.
Mary Wilson	47		S. C.
Cardana Wilson	17		S. C.
Mary S. Wilson	9		Ga.
Mary A. Spears	25		Ga.
William T. Spears	3		Ga.
504. James Faulkner	49	Farmer	Ireland
Lydia A. Faulkner	37		Ga.
John J. Faulkner	13		Ga.
Joseph D. Faulkner	12		Ga.
James F. Faulkner	9		Ga.
Stephen N. Faulkner	7		Ga.
Samuel A. Faulkner	6		Ga.
Charles J. Faulkner	4		Ga.
Thomas B. Faulkner	3		Ga.
Margaret Faulkner	2/12		Ga.
505. John Humphrey	21	Farmer	Tenn.
Eveline Humphrey	22		S. C.
Mary G. Humphrey	2/12		Ga.
506. William E. Biles	22	Farmer	Ga.
Nancy Biles	20		Tenn.
507. John Brooks	40	Farmer	S. C.
Louisa Brooks	40		N. C.
Mathew Brooks	13		Ga.
Alfred H. Brooks	9		Ga.
Joseph M. Brooks	5		Ga.
Noah J. Brooks	3		Ga.
James B. Brooks	8/12		Ga.
Anna Hampton	25		S. C.
508. Elizabeth Mears	47	Domestic	N. C.
Sarah N. Mears	18		Ga.
509. James Standfield	30	Farmer	N. C.
Eliza A. Standfield	26		N. C.
Eleanor Standfield	7		Ga.
James A. Standfield	5		Ga.

	NAME	AGE	OCCUPATION	BORN IN
510.	Allen Standfield	26	Farmer	N. C.
	Mary Standfield	27		N. C.
	Columbus N. Standfield	10/12		Ga.
511.	Abner Dunnegan	32	Farmer	Ga.
	Lucinda Dunnegan	25		Ga.
	Andrew J. Dunnegan	3		Ga.
512.	William G. Hales	53	Miller	Tenn.
	Arabella Hales	18		Ga.
	Warren A. Hales	16	Farm hand	Ga.
	Joseph E. Hales	13		Ga.
	Richard V. Hales	10		Ga.
	Jasper A. Hales	8		Ga.
	Isaac Hales	6		Ga.
513.	Samuel Collins	55	Blacksmith	N. C.
	Jane Collins	50		N. C.
	Amantha A. Collins	26		N. C.
	Elizabeth A. Collins	25		N. C.
	Eliza S. Collins	17		N. C.
	Mary A. Collins	16		N. C.
	Margaret Collins	14		Ga.
	Joseph N. Collins	11		Ga.
	Lucy B. Collins	5		Ga.
514.	Robert Wilkins	28	Farmer	Ga.
	Sarah Wilkins	32		N. C.
	Andrew J. Wilkins	6		Ga.
	Lucy J. Wilkins	4		Ga.
	Eleanor K. Wilkins	2		Ga.
515.	George Medling	39	Farmer	S. C.
	Sefrania Medling	28		N. C.
	Sefrania C. Medling	8		Ga.
	Kipy S. Medling (F)	7		Ga.
	James A. Medling	5		Ga.
	Tema W. Medling (M)	3		Ga.
	Mary C. Medling	2/12		Ga.
	Delila Carver	19		Ga.
	Julius A. Carver	6/12		Ga.
516.	Alfred Holcomb	46	Farmer	Ga.
	Millie Holcomb	30		Ga.
	William W. Holcomb	18	Farm hand	Ga.
	McDaniel Holcomb	13		Ga.
	James J. Holcomb	10		Ga.
	Thomas F. Holcomb	9		Ga.
	Sarah F. Holcomb	8		Ga.
	Sherard H. Holcomb	3		Ga.
	Cicero C. Holcomb	1		Ga.

Name	Age	Occupation	Born In
517. George W. Moss	22	Farmer	S. C.
Martha A. Moss	23		N. C.
Mary J. Moss	6/12		Ga.
Joseph Hazlewood	22	Farm hand	S. C.
518. Daniel Caylor	49	Mechanic	N. C.
Sarah Caylor	38		S. C.
Alford Caylor	15	Farm hand	Ga.
Malissa J. Caylor	13		Ga.
Lovadia Caylor	11		Ga.
Kizeann L. Caylor (F)	8		Ga.
Sarah B. Caylor	6		Ga.
William H. Caylor	4		Ga.
Mary C. Caylor	1		Ga.
Francis M. Caylor	1/12		Ga.
519. Abel Caylor	39	Farmer	N. C.
Camilla Caylor	29		S. C.
Newton Caylor	11		Ga.
Mary C. Caylor	8		Ga.
Andrew J. Caylor	4		Tenn.
Sarah A. Caylor	3		Tenn.
Rebecca E. Caylor	1		Tenn.
520. Willy Moss	25	Farmer	S. C.
Frances Moss	27		N. C.
Love Moss	7		S. C.
George E. Moss	5		S. C.
Nancy D. Moss	1		Ga.
Lewis Moss	60	Farm hand	S. C.
Nancy Moss	67		S. C.
521. John Mullens	62	Farmer	S. C.
Frances Mullens	60		S. C.
Margaret Mullens	35		Ga.
Mary C. Mullens	23		Ga.
Alfred W. Mullins	19	Farm hand	Ga.
Martha J. Mullens	16		Ga.
James F. Mullens	7		Ga.
522. Nancy Williamson	28	Domestic	Ga.
Francis Williamson	6		Ga.
John J. Williamson	4		Ga.
Mary L. Williamson	?		Ga.
Samantha A. Williamson	1		Ga.
523. William Paul	68	Farmer	Va.
Malissa Paul	60		Va.
Rebecca Paul	19		N. C.
Newah Paul	15		N. C.
524. William Voss	27	Brickmason	Ga.

Name	Age	Occupation	Born In
Lucy Voss	27		N. C.
Alfred G. Voss	10/12		Ga.
525. Joseph Paul	21	Farmer	N. C.
Rhoda J. Paul	19		Ga.
526. Isaac Hazlewood	47	Farmer	S. C.
Jane Hazlewood	45		S. C.
John H. Hazlewood	17	Farm hand	Ga.
Jane T. Hazlewood	16		Ga.
Moses H. Hazlewood	10		Ga.
Arlin L. Hazlewood	7		Ga.
527. Benjamin Hazlewood	25	Farmer	S. C.
Lucy Hazlewood	22		S. C.
Sarah T. Hazlewood	1		Ga.
528. Robert Derring	45	Farmer	Ga.
Mary Derring	42		Ga.
Sarah Q. Derring	21		Ga.
John B. Derring	19	Farm hand	Ga.
Mary D. Derring	14		Ga.
Reuben L. Derring	13		Ga.
Elizabeth C. Derring	11		Ga.
Rebecca D. Derring	8		Ga.
Jeremiah Derring	6		Ga.
Joseph Derring	2		Ga.
529. Ira Dunnegan	55	Farmer	Ga.
Elizabeth Dunnegan	53		S. C.
Martha A. Dunnegan	33		Ga.
Elizabeth Dunnegan, Jr.	12		Ga.
530. Robert Reid	28	Farmer	S. C.
Rosa A. Reid	19		S. C.
Albert M. C. Reid	11/12		Ga.
531. Wiley Carver	33	Farmer	N. C.
Mary A. Carver	26		Ga.
Louisa C. Carver	11		Ga.
Sarah J. Carver	10		Ga.
Mary A. Carver	8		Ga.
Sarah Carver	6		Ga.
Aaron Carver	5		Ga.
Henry H. Carver	3		Ga.
532. John H. Reaves	24	Farmer	S. C.
Hannah Reaves	21		N. C.
Margaret A. Reaves	3		S. C.
Martha J. Reaves	1		Ga.
533. Elizabeth Simmons	48	Domestic	N. C.
Elias W. Simmons	21	Farm hand	Ga.
Samuel H. Simmons	18	Farm hand	Ga.

NAME	AGE	OCCUPATION	BORN IN
Emily J. Simmons	14		Ga.
Rosida Simmons	4		Ga.
James Right	10		Ga.
534. George Mullens	39	Farmer	S. C.
Mary Mullens	41		N. C.
Griffin F. Mullens	16	Farm hand	Ga.
Martin B. Mullens	14		Ga.
535. Samuel Tatem	20	Farmer	N. C.
Elizabeth Tatem	18		Ga.
Missouri Tatem	2		Ga.
Amanda Tatem	4/12		Ga.
Hugh Tatem	14		Ala.
536. William C. Rippy	36	Blacksmith	N. C.
Martha Rippy	33		N. C.
Mary L. Rippy	8		Ga.
Anonamous J. Rippy	5		Ga.
Andrew P. Rippy	5		Ga.
William L. Rippy	3		Ga.
Susan A. Rippy	9/12		Ga.
Sarah M. Knox	27		S. C.
537. James Mullens	38	Farmer	S. C.
Melvina Mullens	26		S. C.
William F. Mullens	12		Ga.
Susanna Mullens	9		Ga.
John A. Mullens	7		Ga.
Andrew J. Mullens	5		Ga.
Frances P. Mullens	1		Ga.
538. Green Mullins	27	Farmer	Ga.
Elizabeth Mullins	24		Ga.
Doctor B. Mullins	6		Ga.
Christopher C. Mullins	4		Ga.
Elias M. Mullins	2		Ga.
539. Calvin King	19	Farmer	N. C.
Margaret King	30		N. C.
Martha A. King	40		N. C.
540. William Knox	63	Farmer	S. C.
Agnes Knox	50		N. C.
Louisa E. Knox	15		Ga.
Frances Knox	12		Ga.
Lewis B. Knox	8		Ga.
Jane Riley Knox	73		S. C.
541. John R. West	27	Farmer	S. C.
Dicy M. West	23		S. C.
James West	1		Ga.
Mary West	1/12		Ga.

	Name	Age	Occupation	Born In
542.	John Hazlewood	57	Cooper	S. C.
	Agnes Hazlewood	50		S. C.
	Dorcas Hazlewood	22		S. C.
	Mary A. Hazlewood	16		S. C.
	Elizabeth C. Hazlewood	14		S. C.
	Lancaster Hazlewood	13		S. C.
	Nancy C. Hazlewood	11		S. C.
	John F. Hazlewood	9		S. C.
543.	Benjamin Coward	56	Bap. clergyman	N. C.
	Catherine Coward	49		N. C.
	Harriet Coward	23		Ga.
	Alfred W. Coward	21	Farm hand	Ga.
	Thomas Coward	19	Farm hand	Ga.
	Benjamin M. Coward	17	Farm hand	Ga.
	Joseph L. Coward	16	Farm hand	Ga.
	Catherine Coward	14		Ga.
	Mary L. Coward	10		Ga.
	Jesse P. Coward	8		Ga.
	Drucilla Coward	6		Ga.
	Rachel Coward	4		Ga.
544.	Andrew B. Coward	34	Farmer	N. C.
	Nancy J. Coward	27		N. C.
	Merritt R. Coward	9		Ga.
	Susanna Coward	6		Ga.
	Sarah M. Coward	3		Ga.
545.	Robert Swofford	21	Farmer	Ga.
	Sarah C. Swofford	22		N. C.
546.	Elizabeth Payne	33	Domestic	Tenn.
	Livia A. Payne	15		Ga.
	James M. Payne	12		Ga.
	Lidy C. Payne	10		Ga.
	Mary A. Payne	8		Ga.
547.	Allison Colwell	22	Farmer	Ga.
	Frances Colwell	20		Ga.
	Elizabeth Colwell	61		N. C.
	William Colwell	25	Farm hand	S. C.
	Lester Colwell	5/12		Ga.
548.	Elijah Morrison	33	Farmer	N. C.
	Esther Morrison	29		N. C.
	Julia Morrison	10		Ga.
	Emily Morrison	8		Ga.
	Montgomery Morrison	5		Ga.
	Eleanor Morrison	8/12		Ga.
549.	Hiram Forester	63	Farmer	S. C.
	Millie Forester	40		Ga.

Name	Age	Occupation	Born In
Thomas Forester	24	Farm hand	Ga.
Mary T. Forester	20		Ga.
Sarah E. Forester	16		Ga.
William E. Forester	12		Ga.
John B. Forester	10		Ga.
550. James Mooney	70		S. C.
Vina Mooney	42		S. C.
Rachel Mooney	38		Ga.
Caroline Mooney	16		Ga.
Henry Mooney	14		Ga.
Jackson Mooney	12		Ga.
Miranda Mooney	2		Ga.
551. Joseph Simmons	33	Farmer	N. C.
Matilda A. Simmons	30		Ga.
Mary L. Simmons	10		Ga.
Martha J. Simmons	9		Ga.
Squire D. Simmons	8		Ga.
Robert K. Simmons	6		Ga.
Nancy L. Simmons	5		Ga.
Rachel L. Simmons	4/12		Ga.
552. Thomas Ray	50	Farmer	Ga.
Mary Ray	31		Ga.
Sarah Ray	12		Ga.
Aaron Ray	10		Ga.
Thomas Ray	4		Ga.
John Ray	2		Ga.
553. Jesse Rippy	65	Farmer	N. C.
Sarah Rippy	61		N. C.
Thomas E. Rippy	19	Farm hand	S. C.
554. James W. Fowler	28	Farmer	S. C.
Anna C. Fowler	26		N. C.
Mary Fowler	5		Ga.
Demima Fowler	4		Ga.
Sarah G. Reed	10		Ga.
555. Anonimous Rippy	32	Farmer	N. C.
Charlotte Rippy	28		S. C.
William A. Rippy	10		Ga.
556. Lewis Willis	45	Farmer	S. C.
Anna Willis	37		Ga.
Mary E. Willis	14		Ga.
William W. Willis	12		Ga.
Daniel Willis	10		Ga.
Elizabeth Willis	4		Ga.
Mittimore Willis (M)	2		Ga.
557. Thomas Briant	28	Grocer	Ga.

Name	Age	Occupation	Born In
Amous Briant (F)	23		Ga.
James M. Briant	5		Ga.
Robert R. Briant	3		Ga.
Sarah J. Briant	4/12		Ga.
558. John Roe	30	Farmer	S. C.
Mary Roe	35		Ga.
Lagenia Roe	7		Ga.
Solomon Roe	5		Ga.
Mary A. Roe	2		Ga.
559. James Crump	28	Farm hand	N. C.
Mary Crump	20		N. C.
560. Doctor Gipson	30	Farm hand	N. C.
Minnie Gipson	30		N. C.
Dugin Gipson	7		Ga.
John Gipson	3		Ga.
561. Robert Bell	25	Farmer	N. C.
Mary Bell	25		N. C.
562. Elsa King	30	Domestic	N. C.
Mary A. King	5		Tenn.
William R. King	3		Tenn.
563. William C. Atherton	39	Miller	England
Catherine Atherton	38		N. Y.
Edward Atherton	13		N. J.
Malissa Atherton	9		Ala.
James T. Atherton	1		Ga.
Mary Atherton	70		England
William Garner	19	Farm hand	Ga.
564. Millard Huskey	26	Farm hand	Tenn.
Malinda Huskey	22		Ga.
566. Zepheniah Dover	60	Farmer	S. C.
Nancy Dover	56		S. C.
Green Dover	28	Farm hand	S. C.
Louisa Dover	26		S. C.
Martin M. Dover	20	Farm hand	S. C.
Martha Dover	6		Ga.
Sarah Dover	5		Ga.
Nancy Dover	2/12		Ga.
567. Julian Parker	50	Farmer	S. C.
Celia Parker	40		S. C.
Rufus Parker	18	Farm hand	Ga.
Jane Parker	15		Ga.
Aaron Parker	13		Ga.
Marion Parker	4		Ga.
568. William B. Swan	51	Farmer	Tenn.
Mary A. Swan	46		Tenn.

Name	Age	Occupation	Born In
Martha A. Swan	20		Ga.
Sarah M. Swan	16		Ga.
Sarmita T. Swan	13		Ga.
Margaret L. Swan	10		Ga.
James M. Swan	7		Ga.
Love N. Swan	4		Ga.
569. Clark Holmes	39	Farmer	Ga.
Catherine Holmes	38		S. C.
Frances M. Holmes	16		Ga.
John M. Holmes	14		Ga.
Arminda Holmes	10		Ga.
David Holmes	7		Ga.
Camellia Holmes	5		Ga.
Francis M. Holmes	3		Ga.
Edney Holmes	9/12		Ga.
570. William Temple	21	Farmer	N. C.
Fannie Temple	21		N. C.
John E. Temple	1		Ga.
571. Amos White	50	Farmer	S. C.
Rhoda White	55		S. C.
572. John Bolen	50	Farmer	N. C.
Mary Bolen	50		N. C.
Agnes Bolen	20		N. C.
John W. Bolen	18	Farm hand	N. C.
Angbon Bolen	15	Farm hand	N. C.
Margaret Bolen	13		N. C.
Mary Bolen	11		N. C.
Joseph Bolen	9		N. C.
Roxanna Bolen	6		Ga.
Demarcus Bolen	3		Ga.
Martha Bolen	2		Ga.
573. William Smith	65	Farmer	N. C.
Drusilla Smith	35		N. C.
Avoid Smith	19	Farm hand	N. C.
Solomon Smith	14		N. C.
Margaret Smith	7		N. C.
574. Green Gillaspie	59	Mechanic	S. C.
Rebecca Gillaspie	52		S. C.
Sophia J. Gillaspie	21		Ga.
Sarah A. Gillaspie	18		Ga.
Green D. Gillaspie	13		Ga.
Mary T. Gillaspie	12		Ga.
Malissa S. Gillaspie	10		Ga.
Amanda E. Gillaspie	7		Ga.
575. Josiah C. Hailey	26	Farmer	Ga.

Name	Age	Occupation	Born In
Margaret Hailey	24		S. C.
Robert Hailey	4		Ga.
Mary T. Hailey	1		Ga.
576. Squire R. Kiley	50	Carpenter	Ala.
Mary Kiley	54		Ala.
George W. Kiley	19	Farm hand	Ga.
Sarah C. Kiley	16		Ga.
Lucius T. Kiley	13		Ga.
577. Stephen Kelley	23	Farmer	Tenn.
Mary Kelley	20		Ga.
Sarah A. Kelley	3		Ga.
Lorine Kelley	9/12		Ga.
Josephine Kelley	10		Ga.
578. John Ferguson	27	Farmer	S. C.
Malenia Ferguson	27		N. C.
Barbara M. A. Ferguson	3		Ga.
Eliza C. Ferguson	2/12		Ga.
579. Carr Hudgens	40	Farmer	Ga.
Sarah Hudgens	50		Ga.
Tall Hudgens	12		Ga.
Hester Hudgens	9		Ga.
Sarah Hudgens	7		Ga.
Mary Hudgens	5		Ga.
Virginia Hudgens	3		Ga.
580. Sarah Young	60	Domestic	S. C.
Martha Young	31		Ga.
Ibbis Young (F)	28		Ga.
Malissa Young	25		Ga.
Frances Young	23		Ga.
Samuel Young	20	Farm hand	Ga.
581. Isaac Young	35	Farmer	S. C.
Nancy Young	30		Ga.
Louisa Young	10		Ga.
Samuel Young	9		Ga.
Rebecca S. Young	7		Ga.
William Young	5		Ga.
582. Alcy Kelley (F)	40	Domestic	S. C.
Martha Kelley	22		S. C.
Demetrius Kelley	1		Ga.
583. Thomas Haley	22	Farmer	Ga.
Frances Haley	19		S. C.
Christopher C. Haley	1		Ga.
Garrison Moss	28	Farm hand	S. C.
Pinkney E. Moss	30	Farm hand	S. C.
584. Francis Mauldin	70	Miller	S. C.

	Name	Age	Occupation	Born In
	Catherine Mauldin	64		Ga.
	Matilda Mauldin	26		S. C.
585.	Joseph Wilkey	47	Farmer	S. C.
	Annice Wilkey	37		N. C.
	Margaret Wilkey	24		S. C.
	Edward M. Wilkey	19	Farm hand	S. C.
	Elizabeth Wilkey	16		Ga.
	Sarah F. Wilkey	10		Ga.
	Nancy M. Wilkey	3		Ga.
	Harvey Blalock	19	Farm hand	Ga.
	Rebecca Blalock	17		Ga.
	Safrana Blalock	15		Ga.
	Minda Blalock	13		Ga.
	Russell Blalock	11		Ga.
	Agnes Blalock	9		Ga.
586.	Jesse Wilkey	55	Farmer	S. C.
	Catherine Wilkey	48		S. C.
	William M. Wilkey	16	Farm hand	S. C.
	Mason Wilkey	14		Ga.
	Sarah O. Wilkey	10		Ga.
587.	Briant Bradley	54	Farmer	N. C.
	Malinda Bradley	56		S. C.
	Sarah J. Bradley	27		Ga.
	Stephen B. Bradley	25	Farm hand	Ga.
	James J. Bradley	21	Farm hand	Ga.
	Emily M. Bradley	16		Ga.
	Josephine M. Bradley	12		Ga.
588.	Lorenzo Smith	55	Clockmaker	Vt.
	Matilda Smith	35		N. C.
	Americus L. Smith	12		Ga.
	Mary J. Smith	9		Ga.
589.	Wade Moss	39	Farmer	S. C.
	Martha Moss	40		S. C.
	Silas Moss	17	Farm hand	S. C.
	Mary Moss	15		S. C.
	Anderson Moss	12		Ga.
	Celia L. Moss	10		Ga.
	Lorenzo Moss	8		Ga.
	James M. Moss	6		Ga.
	Aaron Moss	4		Ga.
	Rhoda A. Moss	1		Ga.
590.	Lawson Dover	38	Farmer	S. C.
	Harriet Dover	25		Ga.
591.	William H. McClure	27	Farmer	S. C.
	Dezenius McClure (F)	30		N C.

	Name	Age	Occupation	Born In
	John S. H. McClure	5		Ga.
	Milton H. McClure	3		Ga.
	Joseph H. McClure	3/12		Ga.
592.	Green Moss, Jr.	26	Farmer	S. C.
	Elva Moss	22		N. C.
	Amanda Moss	2		Ga.
	Emeline Collins	21		N. C.
593.	Northel Bradley	38	Farmer	N. C.
	Isabella Bradley	37		Ga.
	Emily S. Bradley	14		Ga.
	Thomas J. Bradley	12		Ga.
	Adolphus M. Bradley	10		Ga.
	Augustus Bradley	7		Ga.
594.	Eldridge Kinney	47	Farmer	Ga.
	Jane Kinney	39		N. C.
	Abigail Kinney	13		Ga.
	Celia A. Kinney	10		Ga.
	Teletha E. Kinney	9		Ga.
	Martha M. Kinney	7		Ga.
	Samuel F. Kinney	5		Ga.
	Cynthia N. Kinney	2		Ga.
595.	James Eaton	36	Farmer	Ga.
	Mary Eaton	39		N. C.
	Emma E. Eaton	13		Ga.
	Sarah L. Eaton	10		Ga.
	Margaret R. Eaton	3		Ga.
	Zinnus Eaton	6		Ga.
	Julius T. Eaton	3		Ga.
	Millard F. Eaton	2		Ga.
596.	John Ingram	38	Farmer	N. C.
	Louisa Ingram	29		Ga.
	Permelia A. Ingram	12		Ga.
	William Ingram	11		Ga.
	Richard G. Ingram	9		Ga.
	Joel M. Ingram	6		Ga.
	Lafayette Pinson	8		Ga.
	Permelia J. Pinson	6		Ga.
	Harriet R. Pinson	3		Ga.
	Mary C. Pinson	10/12		Ga.
597.	James H. Williams	28	Farmer	N. C.
	Margaret C. Williams	28		N. C.
	Robert E. Williams	2		Ga.
	Buenavista Williams	9/12		Ga.
598.	Julius Collins	25	Farmer	N. C.
	Thalanda Collins	19		Ga.

	Name	Age	Occupation	Born In
	John D. Collins	1		Ga.
599.	Henry Kilby	41	Farmer	N. C.
	Harriet Kilby	42		S. C.
	Isaac Kilby	17	Farm hand	Ga.
	Arch Kilby	15	Farm hand	Ga.
	James H. Kilby	13		Ga.
	Louisa C. Kilby	11		Ga.
	Jeremiah W. Kilby	5		Ga.
	Jane Dilard	35	Domestic	N. C.
	Mary H. Dilard	9		Ga.
600.	Sarah N. Norrell	27	Domestic	S. C.
	Augustus D. Norrell	14		Ga.
	Georgia A. Norrell	12		Ga.
	Henry W. Norrell	10		Ga.
	Winnie Williams	45		S. C.
	Harriet Williams	40		S. C.
601.	Robert Childers	64	Farmer	S. C.
	Pacia Childers	54		S. C.
	Cynthia Childers	33		Ga.
	Jane Childers	25		S. C.
	Robert Childers	23	Farm hand	S. C.
	Reuben Childers	19	Farm hand	S. C.
	Jacob Childers	17	Farm hand	S. C.
	Mary Childers	17		S. C.
	Adeline Childers	13		S. C.
602.	Andrew Knight	28	Merchant	S. C.
	Eliza C. Knight	22		N. C.
603.	Chany Carver	60	Domestic	S. C.
	Nancy Carver	18		Ga.
604.	Martin Talley	21	Farmer	Ga.
	Sarah Talley	26		Ga.
	Canada A. Talley	10/12		Ga.
	Sarah Chambers	22		S. C.
	James Roe	14		S. C.
605.	Solomon C. Talmore	46	Farmer	S. C.
	Mary A. Talmore	23		Ga.
	Aaron B. Talmore	21	Farm hand	Ga.
	Joseph S. Talmore	12		Ga.
	Cynthia M. Talmore	11		Ga.
	Augustus F. Talmore	7		Ga.
	Rhoda S. Talmore	66		S. C.
606.	Ancel Rowe	37	Carpenter	S. C.
	Ara A. Rowe	28		S. C.
	Ibba A. Rowe	13		Ga.
	Charles Rowe	12		Ga.

NAME	AGE	OCCUPATION	BORN IN
Hannah Rowe	10		Ga.
Ancel Rowe, Jr.	8		Ga.
Mary J. Rowe	5		Ga.
Nancy Neighbors	24		Ga.
607. Nathan Talley	60	Merchant	S. C.
Mary Talley	50		S. C.
608. Elisha Bennett	25	Farmer	Ga.
Sarah J. Bennett	22		S. C.
Albert E. Bennett	11		Ga.
Thomas J. Bennett	10		Ga.
Alonzo H. Bennett	8		Ga.
609. Ransom Bennett	30	Farmer	Ga.
Matilda Bennett	31		S. C.
Louisa J. Bennett	12		Ga.
Mary E. Bennett	8		Ga.
William W. Bennett	6		Ga.
John S. Bennett	4		Ga.
610. Alfred Smith	21	Farmer	Ga.
Cassandra Smith	54		Ireland
Andrew J. Smith	19	Farm hand	Ga.
Ophir Smith (F)	17		Ga.
Ephraim C. Smith	14		Ga.
Fendley C. Smith	11		Ga.
James M. Smith	9		Ga.
Martha Davis	9		Miss.
611. Martha Corban	51	Domestic	S. C.
Andrew J. Corban	19	Farm hand	Ga.
James H. Corban	9		Ga.
612. George W. Findley	22	Farmer	Ga.
Margaret Findley	23		S. C.
Erwin Findley	10/12		Ga.
Milda Davis	18		Ga.
613. Alexander Findley	48	Farmer	S. C.
Hulda Findley	47		S. C.
Harrison Findley	21	Farm hand	Ga.
Elizabeth Findley	14		Ga.
Wiley Dean	20	Farm hand	Ga.
614. Nathan Findley	24	Farmer	S. C.
Amanda Findley	29		Ga.
James O. Findley	4		Ga.
Mary I. Findley	6/12		Ga.
615. Lemuel Hood	28	Farmer	Ga.
Malissa Hood	16		Ga.
James M. Hood	5/12		Ga.

	NAME	AGE	OCCUPATION	BORN IN
616.	Samuel Young	30	Farmer	Tenn.
	Narcissus Young	28		S. C.
	George W. Young	5		Ga.
	Martha M. Young	3		Ga.
	Rebecca Young	1		Ga.
	Alvin McCollum	24	Farm hand	Ga.
617.	John J. Dean	24	Farmer	Ga.
	Terissa Dean	16		Ga.
	Rhoda C. Dean	8/12		Ga.
618.	Mansel Findley	26	Farmer	N. C.
	Perlina Findley	31		Va.
	John E. Findley	4		Ga.
	Elizabeth Findley	2		Ga.
	Moses Findley	1		Ga.
	Harrison Findley	1/12		Ga.
619.	William Corban	40	Farmer	S. C.
	Rosanna Corban	30		S. C.
	Rial Corban	17	Farm hand	S. C.
	Yerby Corban	16	Farm hand	S. C.
	Hulda C. Corban	14		S. C.
	Martha A. Corban	13		S. C.
	Mary J. Corban	9		Ga.
	Merida L. Corban (M)	8		Ga.
	Susan Corban	6		Ga.
	Calvin B. Corban	3		Ga.
	Julia A. Corban	1		Ga.
	Sarah Towers	26		Ga.
	Moses M. Towers	9/12		Ga.
	Martha Coward	11		Ga.
	Rebecca Moon	12		Ga.
620.	Sarah Young	49	Domestic	N. C.
	Thomas Young	24	Farm hand	N. C.
	Buren Young	22	Farm hand	Ga.
	Mary A. Young	14		Ga.
	Drewery Young	12		Ga.
621.	Benjamin Striplin	39	Farmer	S. C.
	Mary Striplin	35		S. C.
	Mary E. Striplin	16		Ga.
	William A. Striplin	14		Ga.
	John A. Striplin	12		Ga.
	Lucinda C. Striplin	11		Ga.
	Susan E. Striplin	10		Ga.
	Alfred L. Striplin	7		Ga.
	Martha J. Striplin	4		Ga.
	Joseph B. Striplin	3		Ga.
	Moses A. Striplin	4/12		Ga.

NAME	AGE	OCCUPATION	BORN IN
622. Francis Pool	26	Farmer	N. C.
Matilda A. Pool	25		S. C.
William W. Pool	6		Ga.
Leander D. Pool	4		Ga.
Fassa Jane Pool	3		Ga.
623. Patrick H. Temples	25	Farmer	N. C.
Mary A. Temples	24		Tenn.
Thomas A. Temples	5		Ga.
Martha S. Temples	2		Ga.
624. Larkin Temples	50	Farmer	N. C.
Susan Temples	50		N. C.
Millie C. Temples	22		N. C.
Mary E. Temples	16		N. C.
Rutha G. Temples	14		N. C.
Anna L. Temples	13		N. C.
Manda W. Temples	12		S. C.
Narcissa P. Temples	11		S. C.
John Temples	10		S. C.
George W. Temples	9		Ga.
625. Edward Clark	35	Farmer	N. C.
Sarah Clark	35		N. C.
Margaret M. Clark	16		N. C.
Andrew J. Clark	14		Ga.
Mary E. Clark	14		Ga.
Harvey Clark	11		Ga.
Susan C. Clark	8		Ga.
Henry Clark	7		Ga.
John Clark	6		Ga.
Edward Clark	4		Ga.
Elias W. Clark	3		Ga.
626. Henry Clark	49	Farmer	N. C.
Elizabeth Clark	40		N. C.
627. Henry Talley	32	Farmer	S. C.
Mary E. Talley	30		Ga.
Eliza A. Talley	12		Ga.
Morgan N. Talley	10		Ga.
James J. Talley	9		Ga.
Sarah C. Talley	8		Ga.
Mary E. Talley, Jr.	3		Ga.
John O. Talley	1		Ga.
628. Gilland Davis	26	Farmer	N. C.
Abby A. Davis	19		Ga.
Amanda C. Davis	1		Ga.
629. William West	30	Farmer	S. C.
Malinda West	32		Ga.

Name	Age	Occupation	Born In
Stephen C. West	19	Farm hand	Ga.
Jesse F. West	14		Ga.
Doctor F. West	10		Ga.
Eliza M. West	12		Ga.
Alfred E. West	6		Ga.
Marion C. West	9/12		Ga.
630. Alexander Harris	47	Farmer	Va.
Ary J. Harris	24		S. C.
Master A. Harris	20	Farm hand	S. C.
Ase A. Harris	16	Farm hand	Ga.
Henry P. Harris	15	Farm hand	Ga.
Mary E. Harris	13		Ga.
631. Madison Bruce	23	Farmer	Ga.
Eliza Bruce	19		Ga.
Martha J. Bruce	1		Ga.
632. David Caylor	35	Farmer	N. C.
Permelia Caylor	31		N. C.
Martha A. Caylor	13		Ga.
George Caylor	12		Ga.
Lucinda Caylor	8		Ga.
Minerva Caylor	7		Ga.
William W. Caylor	5		Ga.
Amanda Caylor	4		Ga.
633. Joseph Thomas	37	Farmer	N. C.
Mary Thomas	27		N. C.
Elizabeth Thomas	10		Ga.
Rhoda C. Thomas	7		Ga.
William T. Thomas	2		Ga.
Thomas Thomas	60	Farmer	N. C.
Adeline Thomas	18		N. C.
634. William Agin	37	Farmer	S. C.
Nancy Agin	36		Ga.
William H. Agin	17	Farm hand	Ga.
John F. Agin	14		Ga.
James A. Agin	13		Ga.
Greenberry Agin	11		Ga.
Thomas M. Agin	8		Ga.
Andrew J. Agin	6		Ga.
Nancy A. Agin	1		Ga.
Mary Roe	19		Ga.
James Roe	1		Ga.
635. James Simmons	57	Farmer	S. C.
Elizabeth Simmons	50		N. C.
Philip R. Simmons	26	Attorney	Ga.
Richard L. Simmons	24	Millwright	Ga.

	Name	Age	Occupation	Born In
	Adelaide E. Simmons	18		Ala.
	Leander A. Simmons	23	Gentleman	Ga.
	Henry R. Simmons	20	Farm hand	Ga.
	Franklin Simmons	16	Farm hand	Ga.
	Julia A. Simmons	14		Ga.
	Burrill Key	25	School teacher	Ga.
636.	Hezekiah Wilkins	40	Miller	N. C.
	Mary Wilkins	39		N. C.
	Cynthia A. Wilkins	18		Ga.
	Judge T. Wilkins	14		Ga.
	Cicero H. Wilkins	11		Ga.
	Sarah A. Wilkins	5		Ga.
	James H. F. Wilkins	2		Ga.
637.	Cynthia Mullinax	39	Domestic	S. C.
	James J. Mullinax	19	Farm hand	S. C.
	Hezekiah Mullinax	17	Farm hand	S. C.
	Benson Mullinax	15	Farm hand	S. C.
	Francis M. Mullinax	11		S. C.
	Doctor W. Mullinax	8		Ga.
	Margaret J. Mullinax	6		Ga.
	Madison A. Mullinax	4		Ga.
	Rosanna C. Mullinax	1		Ga.
638.	Jasper Fowler	19	Farmer	Ga.
	Sarah Fowler	20		S. C.
	Pascal L. Fowler	1		Ga.
639.	William Gaines	23		S. C.
	Lydia Gaines	24		Ga.
	Rial T. Gaines	4		Ga.
	William A. Gaines	8/12		Ga.
	Wilson Roe	59	Farm hand	S. C.
	Ruth A. Roe	10		S. C.
	Keziah Roe	8		Ga.
640.	Henry Haney	37	Farmer	S. C.
	Margaret Haney	36		S. C.
	Thomas J. Haney	16	Farm hand	Ga.
	William R. Haney	13		Ga.
	James F. Haney	10		Ga.
	Benjamin F. Haney	6		Ga.
	Alfred Martin	19	Farm hand	S. C.
641.	Put Hopkins	75		S. C.
	Eveline Hopkins	39	Domestic	S. C.
	Arenia Hopkins	19	Domestic	Ga.
	Lucinda Hopkins	16		Ga.
	Louisa Hopkins	16		Ga.
642.	Allen Freeman (F)	58	Domestic	S. C.

NAME	AGE	OCCUPATION	BORN IN
Harriet E. Freeman	17		S. C.
John W. Freeman	14		S. C.
Frances M. Yancey	25	Domestic	S. C.
John N. Yancey	5		Ga.
Lewis F. Yancey	3		Ga.
James W. Yancey	2		Ga.
643. Floyd Yancey	23	Farmer	Ga.
Eleanor E. Yancey	20		S. C.
Nicy A. Yancey	8/12		Ga.
Malinda Yancey	20	Domestic	Ga.
646. Lewis Larnin	32	Farmer	Ga.
Mary Larnin	30		S. C.
Martin B. Larnin	11		Ga.
Lucy A. Larnin	9		Ga.
Martha A. Larnin	6		Ga.
Mary A. Larnin	5		Ga.
Lewis W. Larnin	3		Ga.
George W. Larnin	11/12		Ga.
647. George Sturgis	62	Farm hand	N. C.
Eliza Sturgis	59		S. C.
James Sturgis	14		Ga.
Jane Sturgis	13		Ga.
Rebecca Sturgis	10		Ga.
Dean Sturgis	2		Ga.
648. Nathan Yancey	35	Farm hand	Ga.
Julia A. Yancey	30		Ga.
Elizabeth Yancey	6		Ga.
John Yancey	4		Ga.
Floyd Yancey	4/12		Ga.
649. Allison Sexton	61	Blacksmith	S. C.
Sarah Sexton	46		S. C.
Sarah E. Sexton	6		Ga.
Asa S. Sexton	4		Ga.
650. Elijah Thomas	25	Farmer	S. C.
Canty Thomas	21		S. C.
Joseph A. Thomas	3		Ga.
Mary F. Thomas	1		Ga.
651. James Parker	25	Farm hand	S. C.
Rosanna Parker	25		S. C.
Martin Parker	3		Ga.
William Parker	11/12		Ga.
652. John Turner	34	Farmer	S. C.
Elizabeth Turner	31		S. C.
William E. Turner	9		Ga.
George M. Turner	8		Tenn.

NAME	AGE	OCCUPATION	BORN IN
Thomas G. Turner	6		Ga.
Rosanna Turner	5		Ga.
James Turner	4		Ga.
Amos Turner	3		Ga.
Elizabeth J. Turner	2/12		Ga.
Alfred W. Grover	23	Farm hand	Ga.
653. John Talley	27	Farmer	N. C.
Sarah Talley	27		S. C.
Hester A. J. Talley	6		Ga.
Amanda C. Talley	5		Ga.
Eliza A. Talley	1		Ga.
654. John McCollum	43	Farm hand	Ga.
Mary McCollum	33		N. C.
William J. McCollum	12		Ga.
Sarah A. McCollum	8		Ga.
Ira McCollum	7		Ga.
Tempy E. McCollum	1		Ga.
655. Lawson Qualls	19	Farmer	Ga.
Susan E. Qualls	17		Ga.
Eliza H. Qualls	4/12		Ga.
656. George Varner	15	Farmer	Ga.
657. Jeremiah Holcomb	40	Farmer	S. C.
Jane Holcomb	2)		Ga.
James E. Holcomb	6		Ga.
John H. Holcomb	5		Ga.
Millie C. Holcomb	4		Ga.
Lewis F. Holcomb	3		Ga.
Susan E. Holcomb	2		Ga.
Elias F. Holcomb	4/12		Ga.
658. Samuel C. Stover	27	Farmer	S. C.
Jeremiah J. Stover	1		Ga.
Julia A. Stover	25		Ga.
659. Jeremiah Stover	25	Farmer	S. C.
Mary Stover	25		Ga.
660. Henry D. Holcomb	65		Ga.
Hester A. Holcomb	64		S. C.
Martha A. Holcomb	28		Ga.
William A. Holcomb	25	Gentleman	Ga.
Hester Holcomb	24		Ga.
Dalina A. Holcomb	5		Ga.
661. Elizabeth Lenning	62	Domestic	N. C.
Mary Chapman	34		Tenn.
John Chapman	14		Ga.
Philip L. Chapman	12		Ga.

	NAME	AGE	OCCUPATION	BORN IN
662.	Jacob Stover	50	Farmer	N. C.
	Lydia Stover	47		S. C.
	Sarah H. Stover	14		Ga.
	Columbus G. Stover	13		Ga.
	Amanda E. Stover	11		Ga.
	Lydia L. Stover	9		Ga.
663.	James Turner	33	Farmer	S. C.
	Sarah E. Turner	27		N. C.
	Martha A. Turner	7		Ga.
	Sarah E. Turner	6/12		Ga.
664.	Alfred Moon	57	Farm hand	N. C.
	Tempy Moon	50		N. C.
	Julia A. Moon	14		Ga.
665.	Joseph Griffin	37	Farmer	S. C.
	Harriet Griffin	37		S. C.
	Nancy A. Griffin	16		S. C.
	John Griffin	14		Ala.
	Margaret Griffin	12		Ala.
	Georgia A. Griffin	10		Ga.
	Marion Griffin	6		Ga.
	Mary Griffin	1/12		Ga.
666.	Jordan Presley	31	Farmer	Ga.
	Harriet Presley	39		S. C.
	William B. Presley	9		Ga.
	Hester A. Presley	8		Ga.
	George L. Presley	1		Ga.
	James H. Roper	16	Farm hand	Ga.
	Benjamin F. Roper	13		Ga.
667.	Henry Forester	27	Farm hand	Ga.
	Louisa Forester	21		Ga.
	Martha J. Forester	2		Ga.
	John L. Forester	6/12		Ga.
668.	Cicero Taylor	33	Farmer	Ga.
	Sarah Taylor	23		Ga.
	Malinda A. Taylor	6		Ga.
	Laura J. Taylor	3		Ga.
	William Culver	19	Farm hand	Ga.
669.	Solomon Taylor	66	Farmer	N. C.
	Sarah Taylor	60		S. C.
	James Taylor	23	Farm hand	Ga.
	Washington J. Taylor	21	Farm hand	Ga.
670.	James H. Embrey	31	Farmer	S. C.
	Martha Embrey	28		Tenn.
	Fannie Embrey	12		S. C.
	James H. Embrey	8		S. C.

	Name	Age	Occupation	Born In
	Nancy A. Embrey	2		S. C.
671.	Joshua Denney	82	Farmer	N. C.
	Adeline Denney	62		Va.
	Ennice A. Denney	23	Farm hand	S. C.
	Stephen Morrel	13		S. C.
	Mary A. Morrel	11		S. C.
672.	James Cantrell	36	Distiller	S. C.
	Eliza Cantrell	45		S. C.
	Martha Bayley	21		S. C.
	John Bayley	16	Farm hand	S. C.
	Benister Bayley	14		S. C.
	William O. Bayley	2		Ga.
673.	Henry Johnson	45	Farmer	S. C.
	Nancy Johnson	31		S. C.
	Martha Johnson	8		S. C.
	Elizabeth Johnson	7		Ga.
	Frances Johnson	4		Ga.
674.	Thomas E. Cantrell	28	Farmer	S. C.
	Elizabeth Cantrell	21		S. C.
	Eveline Cantrell	3		Ga.
	James Cantrell	1		Ga.
	Mary Turner	36	Domestic	S. C.
	Sarah Turner	14		Ga.
	Fielder Turner	13		Ga.
	Memory Turner (M)	11		Ga.
	Margaret Turner	9		Ga.
	John Turner	8		Ga.
	Martha J. Turner	5		Ga.
	Roland Taylor	16	Farm hand	Ala.
	John Taylor	15	Farm hand	Ala.
	Tharanna Taylor	13		Ala.
	Ann Taylor	12		Ala.
	Cassey Taylor	11		Ga.
	Susan Taylor	10		Ga.
	James Taylor	7		Ga.
	George M. Taylor	4		Ga.
675.	Middleton Turner	62	Farmer	S. C.
	Elizabeth Turner	49		S. C.
	Thomas McCoy	49	Farm hand	S. C.
676.	David Turner	31	Farmer	S. C.
	Margaret A. Turner	25		S. C.
	Ellen J. Turner	6		Ga.
	Margaret A. Turner	5		Ga.
	George T. Turner	1		Ga.
677.	James McHan	52	Farmer	Va.

	Name	Age	Occupation	Born In
	Rebecca McHan	51		N. C.
	Jeremiah McHan	5		Ga.
678.	Abraham Presley	37	Miller	Ga.
	Demias Presley (F)	29		Ga.
	Martha A. Presley	13		Ga.
	Sarah J. Presley	12		Ga.
	Jackson A. Presley	8		Ga.
	Robert T. Presley	6		Ga.
	Mary Presley	4		Ga.
	John H. Presley	8/12		Ga.
678.	Stephen Brown	40	Farmer	S. C.
	Susanna Brown	29		N. C.
	Benjamin Brown	9		Ga.
	Manda E. Brown	7		Ga.
	Mancil A. Brown	6		Ga.
	Nancy Brown	3		Ga.
	John H. Brown	7/12		Ga.
679.	Ephraim Presley	58	Farmer	Ga.
	Mary Presley	37		Ga.
	Nancy J. Presley	16		Ga.
	Joseph M. Presley	13		Ga.
	Taylor Presley	12		Ga.
	Cicero Presley	9		Ga.
	Amanda Presley	7		Ga.
	DeKalb Presley	5		Ga.
	Jeremiah Presley	2		Ga.
680.	Rebecca Anderson	49	Domestic	S. C.
	Agnes A. Anderson	10		Ga.
	Nancy J. Anderson	7		Ga.
	Julia A. Anderson	6		Ga.
681.	David Landsdown	58	Farmer	N. C.
	Julia A. Landsdown	39		Ga.
	Jackson E. Landsdown	18	Farm hand	Ga.
	David A. Landsdown, Jr.	16	Farm hand	Ga.
	Billy A. Landsdown	3		Ga.
	Calvin Dooly	24	Farm hand	Ga.
682.	John Collet	46	Farmer	Ga.
	Virginia Collet	35		S. C.
	Alonzo W. Collet	17	Farm hand	Ga.
	Permissa A. Collet	16		Ga.
	Archer B. Collet	14		Ga.
	Harriet Collet	12		Ga.
	Sarah Collet	6		Ga.
	John Collet	5		Ga.
	Martha A. Collet	1		Ga.

	Name	Age	Occupation	Born In
683.	Eric Collet	21	Farmer	Ga.
	Cynthia Collet	18		Ga.
	Amantha J. Collet	1		Ga.
684.	Evin C. Disharoon	38	Farmer	Ga.
	Martha J. Disharoon	34		Ga.
	James M. Disharoon	13		Ga.
	Mary A. Disharoon	12		Ga.
	Martha J. Disharoon	10		Ga.
	Major J. Disharoon	5		Ga.
	Irvin C. Disharoon	3		Ga.
685.	Bethel Q. Disharoon	26	Farmer	Ga.
	Roxanna Disharoon	16		Ga.
	Margaret E. Disharoon	6/12		Ga.
686.	Nancy Brown	50	Domestic	N. C.
	Mary Brown	48		N. C.
	Sarah Brown	47		N. C.
	Elizabeth A. Brown	34		Ga.
	Malissa Brown	7		Ga.
	Esther Brown	5		Ga.
687.	Samuel Norton	32	Farmer	Ga.
	Rhoda Norton	32		Ga.
	William T. Norton	12		Ga.
	Jeremiah B. Norton	11		Ga.
	Margaret A. Norton	9		Ga.
	Sarah A. Norton	5		Ga.
	Mary C. Norton	4		Ga.
	Jasper A. Norton	1		Ga.
688.	Thomas Norton	55	Farmer	S. C.
	Margaret Norton	49		Tenn.
	Sarah Parker	25		Ga.
	Thomas Parker	8		Ga.
	Samuel M. Norton	6		Ga.
	Adolphus E. Norton	4		Ga.
	Margaret A. Norton	2		Ga.
689.	Mary Jones	38	Domestic	Tenn.
	Charles A. Jones	13		Ga.
	Caleb Jones	10		Ga.
690.	Levi Warren	45	Farmer	N. C.
	Caldonia Warren	34		N. C.
	Wilson Warren	14		N. C.
	William Warren	12		N. C.
	Martin Warren	10		Ga.
	Sarah J. Warren	8		Ga.
	Champion Warren	6		Ga.
	Robert Warren	4		Ga.

Name	Age	Occupation	Born In
Henry Warren	1		Ga.
691. Jesse Hammontree	65	Distiller	N. C.
Deopy A. Hammontree	50		Tenn.
Stephen H. Hammontree	21	Farm hand	Ga.
Samuel T. Hammontree	19	Farm hand	Ga.
Sylvestus E. Hammontree	17	Farm hand	Ga.
Nelson P. Hammontree	14	Farm hand	Ga.
692. John E. Eubanks	50	Farm hand	S. C.
Mary E. Eubanks	30		N. C.
Joseph Eubanks	18	Farm hand	Ga.
William Eubanks	8		Ga.
Susanna Eubanks	6		Ga.
Thomas Eubanks	4		Ga.
Jane Fields	16		Ga.
693. James Bradford	48	Marble rubber	Ga.
Miranda Bradford	46		Ga.
Lucinda Bradford	20		Ga.
Sarah A. Bradford	16		Ga.
Giles E. Bradford	14		Ga.
Ransom I. Bradford	12		Ga.
James M. Bradford	10		Ga.
Mary Bradford	8		Ga.
Martha J. Bradford	6		Ga.
John N. Bradford	4		Ga.
694. William Brown	38	Farmer	N. C.
Martha Brown	29		N. C.
Lafayette Brown	6		Ga.
George W. Brown	4		Ga.
Mary Brown	2		Ga.
Martha S. Brown	8/12		Ga.
695. James Bruce	32	Farmer	S. C.
Lucinda Bruce	30		S. C.
John A. Bruce	13		Ga.
Julia A. Bruce	9		Ga.
Caroline Bruce	6		Ga.
Matilda M. Bruce	3		Ga.
696. Thomas J. Chapler	61	Farmer	Ga.
Frances Chapler	52		S. C.
Thomas J. Chapler	19	Farm hand	Ga.
Benjamin F. Chapler	16	Farm hand	Ga.
Julia A. Chapler	13		Ga.
697. Toliver Wadkins	29	Farmer	Ga.
Elizabeth Wadkins	32		S. C.
Rachel L. Wadkins	2		Ga.
Joseph F. Wadkins	1/12		Ga.

	NAME	AGE	OCCUPATION	BORN IN
698.	William Fuller	44	Clergyman	Ky.
	Jane Fuller	31		Ga.
699.	Isabella Bottoms	25	Domestic	Ga.
	Mary Bottoms	2		Ga.
700.	David Young	48	Farmer	N. C.
	Susan Young	49		Ga.
	Sarah M. Young.	13		Ga.
	William G. Young	12		Ga.
	Nancy A. Young	11		Ga.
	Anna C. Young	10		Ga.
	James R. Young	8		Ga.
701.	Thomas Grover	34	Farmer	Ga.
	Lorenna Grover	37		Ga.
	Mary A. Grover	22		Ga.
	William Grover	21	Farm hand	Ga.
	David Grover	19	Farm hand	Ga.
	Ezekiel Grover	16	Farm hand	Ga.
	Kimsey Grover	12		Ga.
	Anna Grover	9		Ga.
	Sarah J. Grover	5		Ga.
	Millie Grover	3		Ga.
	Susanna Grover	3/12		Ga.
702.	John Mann	44	Farmer	S. C.
	Malinda Mann	39		Ga.
	Mary Mann	18		Ga.
	James Mann	16	Farm hand	Ga.
	Elizabeth Mann	14		Ga.
	Nancy Mann	12		Ga.
	Thomas Mann	4		Ga.
	Malinda Mann	1		Ga.
703.	Levi Hall	35	Tailor	S. C.
	Kiskah Hall	33		Ga.
	William J. Hall	12		Ga.
	Joel J. Hall	6		Ga.
	John L. Hall	5		Ga.
	Sarah E. Hall	2		Ga.
704.	Merrick West	39	Farmer	S. C.
	Sarah West	34		N. C.
	Columbus West	13		Ga.
	Hester A. West	11		Ga.
	Louisa A. West	9		Ga.
	Augustus West	7		Ga.
	Theanotia West	2		Ga.
705.	Bayless Bruce	32	Merchant	Ga.
	Fannie Bruce	25		Ga.

	Name	Age	Occupation	Born In
	Franklin Bruce	7		Ga.
	Cunningham Bruce	6		Ga.
	James Bruce	4		Ga.
	William Bruce	2		Ga.
	Robert Kelley	25	Clerk	Ga.
	Drayton Cunningham	28	Physician	Ga.
	Henrietta Cunningham	40	School teacher	S. C.
706.	Absalom Wheeler	52	Farmer	N. C.
	Elizabeth Wheeler	47		N. C.
	Alfred L. Wheeler	19	Farm hand	S. C.
	Laura A. Wheeler	21		N. C.
	Mary A. Wheeler	17		Tenn.
	Justine Wheeler	15		Tenn.
	Clementine Wheeler	13		Ga.
	David C. Wheeler	11		Ga.
	Julia A. Wheeler	8		Ga.
	Betha A. Wheeler	6		Ga.
	Alonzo Wheeler	4		Ga.
	Robert C. Wheeler	7/12		Ga.
	Amanda Wheeler	17		Ga.
707.	Thomas Ketherside	33	Carpenter	Tenn.
	Sarah A. Ketherside	26		N. C.
	Mary E. Ketherside	4		N. C.
	John W. Ketherside	2		N. C.
	Elizabeth Carter	27		N. C.
708.	William C. Thompson	44	Farmer	Ga.
	Elizabeth Thompson	43		S. C.
	Hudge Thompson	18	Farm hand	Ga.
	Asberry Thompson	16	Farm hand	Ga.
	Samuel Thompson	14		Ga.
	Greenberry Thompson	12		Ga.
	Martha Thompson	10		Ga.
	Sarah J. Thompson	8		Ga.
709.	Miles Berry	40	Farmer	Ga.
	Nancy L. Berry	40		N. C.
	William J. Berry	17	Farm hand	Ga.
	Jesse P. Berry	14		Ga.
	Margaret E. Berry	12		Ga.
	Mary S. Berry	11		Ga.
	Cynthia A. Berry	8		Ga.
	Samuel M. Berry	6		Ga.
	John H. Berry	4		Ga.
710.	Reuben Hopkins	32	Farmer	S. C.
	Artemissa Hopkins	24		Ga.
	Mary Hopkins	5		Ga.

Name	Age	Occupation	Born In
William Hopkins	4		Ga.
Anna E. Hopkins	2		Ga.
Martha Hopkins	2/12		Ga.
711. Henry Bozeman	37	Farmer	Ga.
Jane C. Bozeman	35		Ga.
William A. Bozeman	15	Farm hand	Ga.
Cynthia C. Bozeman	14		Ga.
Nancy E. Bozeman	12		Ga.
Martha E. Bozeman	11		Ga.
David E. Bozeman	5		Ga.
Samuel A. Bozeman	4		Ga.
712. Jeremiah Brown	25	Farmer	Ga.
Mary Brown	22		Ga.
Nancy L. Brown	1		Ga.
713. Thomas Brown	57	Farmer	S. C.
Nancy A. Brown	60		S. C.
714. Susan Lenning	31	Domestic	Ga.
Zachariah Lenning	10		Ga.
John Lenning	8		Ga.
Joseph E. Lenning	5		Ga.
715. Rachel Eaton	50	Domestic	S. C.
716. Cynthia Cunningham	43	Domestic	S. C.
Elizabeth Cunningham	15		S. C.
Robert J. Cunningham	13		S. C.
Marvel J. Cunningham (M)	7		Ga.
Virginia M. Cunningham	5		Ga.
717. Rachel Moseley	42	Domestic	S. C.
Elizabeth Moseley	12		Ga.
Samuel L. Moseley	10		Ga.
Nancy C. Moseley	7		Ga.
Sarah J. Moseley	4		Ga.
Hannah L. Moseley	2		Ga.
718. Hosea Hopkins	42	Farmer	S. C.
Susan Hopkins	39		S. C.
William T. Hopkins	15	Farm hand	Ga.
Mary E. Hopkins	14		Ga.
Reuben R. Hopkins	13		Ga.
Susan Hopkins	13		Ga.
Nancy R. Hopkins	11		Ga.
Emery H. Hopkins	9		Ga.
Margaret Hopkins	8		Ga.
Joseph M. Hopkins	7		Ga.
Sarah Hopkins	6		Ga.
719. Stuart Wigington	52	Farmer	S. C.
Nancy Wigington	47		S. C.

Name	Age	Occupation	Born In
Martha Wigington	7		Ga.
720. Abner Honea	44	Farmer	S. C.
Sarah Honea	50		S. C.
Mary E. Honea	20		S. C.
Nancy M. Honea	16		S. C.
George M. Honea	13		S. C.
Martha A. Honea	10		S. C.
721. John Lyon	65	Blacksmith	Tenn.
Diana Lyon	66		S. C.
722. Dred Patterson	46	Farmer	Ga.
Sarah Patterson	42		Ga.
Nancy Patterson	20		Ga.
Mossa Patterson	17		Ga.
Nella Patterson	15		Ga.
Martha Patterson	13		Ga.
Lucy Patterson	10		Ga.
Caroline Patterson	8		Ga.
Elizabeth Patterson	4		Ga.
William Patterson	2		Ga.
Jane Lawson	17		Ga.
723. John Jordan	22	Farmer	S. C.
Martha Jordan	22		S. C.
724. Thomas Turner	35	Farmer	S. C.
Mary E. Turner	32		Ga.
James E. Turner	9		Ga.
William B. Turner	2		Ga.
Sarah E. Turner	2/12		Ga.
725. Benjamin Davis	47	Farmer	N. C.
Nancy C. Davis	33		Ga.
Martha C. Davis	9		Ga.
Ancel Davis	7		Ga.
Rial C. Davis	3		Ga.
726. Joseph Morris	47	Farmer	S. C.
Mahalia Morris	45		N. C.
Elizabeth Morris	20		S. C.
Pinkney Morris	19		S. C.
Martha E. Morris	16		S. C.
Sarah A. Morris	15		Ga.
Susan C. Morris	13		Ga.
Mary Morris	10		Ga.
Misry E. Morris	9		Ga.
Lafrana Morris	7		Ga.
Tennessee Morris	3		Ga.
727. Joseph Morris, Jr.	25	Farmer	S. C.
Vina Morris	23		Ga.

	Name	Age	Occupation	Born In
	James F. Morris	1		Ga.
728.	Joel Keeter	31	Farmer	S. C.
	Catherine Keeter	21		Ga.
	John A. Keeter	2		Ga.
	Cansada Keeter	1		Ga. ⸱
	Susanna Keeter	72		S. C.
	John C. Keeter	34	Farm hand	N. C.
729.	William Morris	60	Farmer	S. C.
	Mary A. Morris	51		S. C.
	Perry H. Morris	17	Farm hand	S. C.
	Emery C. Morris	12		S. C.
730.	Margaret McKinney	70	Domestic	N. C.
	Jane McKinney	29		N. C.
731.	Asberry Young	21	Farmer	Ga.
	Cynthia Young	22		Ga.
	Henry Young	3		Ga.
	Albert Young	1		Ala.
732.	Asa Holcomb	30	Farmer	Ga.
	Mary A. Holcomb	30		Ga.
	Anna A. Holcomb	12		Ga.
	Henry J. Holcomb	9		Ga.
	Nelly A. Holcomb	6		Ga.
	Hix Holcomb	2		Ga.
	Thomas Holcomb	5/12		Ga.
733.	Levi Parker	50	Carpenter	N. C.
	Elinda Parker	50		S. C.
	Martin Parker	21	Farm hand	N. C.
734.	Greenwood Holcomb	43	Farmer	Ga.
	Elizabeth Holcomb	42		Ga.
	Joel J. Holcomb	16	Farm hand	Ga.
	John M. Holcomb	15	Farm hand	Ga.
	James R. Holcomb	13		Ga.
	Charles D. Holcomb	19		Ga.
	Rebecca A. Holcomb	7		Ga.
	Sophia Holcomb	6		Ga.
	Shem C. Holcomb	1		Ga.
735.	William Ray	65	Farmer	S. C.
	Jane Ray	63		S. C.
	Sando Ray	30	Farm hand	S. C.
736.	George Clark	60	Carpenter	N. C.
	Eliza Clark	32		Tenn.
	John Clark	16	Farm hand	Ala.
	William J. Clark	14		Ala.
	Benjamin Clark	10		Ala.

	Name	Age	Occupation	Born In
	Martha V. Clark	8		Ga.
	Jasper Clark	4		Ga.
	Frances M. Clark	2		Ga.
	Margaret C. Clark	4/12		Ga.
737.	David Black	41	Farmer	S. C.
	Jane Black	40		Ga.
	Franklin A. Black	15	Farm hand	Ga.
	John J. Black	10		Ga.
	Andrew J. Black	6		Ga.
	Sarah E. Black	11/12		Ga.
738.	Nancy Cox	42	Domestic	Ga.
	Rhoda A. Cox	18		Ga.
	Susan A. Cox	16		Ga.
	Jesse Cox	14		Ga.
	James R. Cox	12		Ga.
	Samuel T. Cox	8		Ga.
	Martha Cox	10		Ga.
	Thomas D. Cox	5		Ga.
	William Cox	3		Ga.
	John A. Cox	4		Ga.
739.	John Oaks	43	Farmer	N. C.
	Julia A. Oaks	36		Ga.
	William A. Oaks	14		Ga.
	Mary A. Oaks	7		Ga.
	Julia A. Oaks	5		Ga.
	Martha L. Oaks	2		Ga.
	Sarah Holcomb	40		S. C.
740.	Francis Bradford	24	Farmer	Ga.
	Sarah Bradford	26		S. C.
	Mary A. Bradford	8		Ga.
	Martha J. Bradford	6		Ga.
	Sarah A. Bradford	4		Ga.
	Samantha Bradford	1		Ga.
741.	Asa Baggett	69	Farmer	N. C.
742.	Isabella Tarbutton	44	Domestic	S. C.
	Isabella J. Tarbutton	21		Ga.
	Phoebe A. Tarbutton	19		Ga.
	Nancy Tarbutton	16		Ga.
	Frances M. Tarbutton	13		Ga.
	James C. Tarbutton	9		Ga.
743.	Seth Russell	64	Farmer	N. C.
	Sarah Russell	46		N. C.
	Garland Green	40	Carpenter	N. C.
744.	Perry McKinney	38	Farmer	N. C.
	Eliza McKinney	27		N. C.

	Name	Age	Occupation	Born In
745.	Abram Crow	48	Farmer	N. C.
	Phoebe A. Crow	46		Ga.
	Anna Crow	27		Ga.
	Susan Crow	26		Ga.
	Malinda A. Crow	24		Ga.
	Diana Crow	22		Ga.
	Henry Crow	17	Farm hand	Ga.
	Kimsey Crow	14		Ga.
	John M. Crow	12		Ga.
	James A. Crow	9		Ga.
	Elizabeth Crow	9		Ga.
	Thomas A. Crow	5		Ga.
	Ezekiel Crow	6		Ga.
	Abner Townsend	40	Farm hand	Ga.
	Thomas Townsend	35	Farm hand	Ga.
	Washington Townsend	30	Farm hand	Ga.
746.	Edward Townsend	40	Farmer	Ga.
	Mary A. Townsend	26		S. C.
	Nancy Townsend	18		Ga.
	Edward Townsend, Jr.	16	Farm hand	Ga.
	Samuel H. Townsend	14		Ga.
	Elias C. Townsend	12		Ga.
	Kimsey Townsend	9		Ga.
	William S. Townsend	5		Ga.
	John H. Townsend	3		Ga.
	Thomas H. Townsend	9/12		Ga.
747.	Joseph Corban	25	Farmer	S. C.
	Malinda Corban	18		Ga.
	John Corban	3		Ga.
	Amanda Corban	9/12		Ga.
748.	Dannie Taylor	24	Farmer	Ga.
	Mary N. Taylor	21		Ga.
749.	Martin Holtsclaw	65	Farmer	S. C.
	Elizabeth Holtsclaw	33		S. C.
	Benjamin Holtsclaw	19	Farm hand	S. C.
	Martha Holtsclaw	17		S. C.
	William Holtsclaw	9		S. C.
750.	Sanford Ray	29	Farmer	S. C.
	Rachel Ray	25		S. C.
	Hurlit Ray	6		Ga.
	Martha J. Ray	5		Ga.
	Delilah V. Ray	3		Ga.
	William H. Ray	2		Ga.
	Thomas B. Ray	1		Ga.
751.	Delila Corbin	56	Domestic	S. C.

	Name	Age	Occupation	Born In
	Benjamin Corbin	22	Farm hand	S. C.
	Abigail Corbin	21		Ga.
	Susanna Corbin	17		Ga.
	Jasper Corbin	15	Farm hand	Ga.
	John N. Corbin	14		Ga.
	Malinda Corbin	12		Ga.
752.	William Neal	26	Farmer	N. C.
	Mary Neal	23		N. C.
	Nancy C. Neal	8		Ga.
	Sarah D. Neal	6		Ga.
	John Neal	4		Ga.
	California Neal	2		Ga.
753.	Richard Fulton	39	Farmer	Ga.
	Martha J. Fulton	29		Va.
	Nancy Fulton	14		S. C.
	Thomas Fulton	13		S. C.
	Andrew M. Fulton	10		Ga.
	William F. Fulton	8		Ga.
	Sarah A. Fulton	2		Ga.
	Benjamin Fulton	3/12		Ga.
754.	White Lindsey	20	Farmer	Ga.
	Lorenia Lindsey	23		Ga.
	William E. Lindsey	3		Ga.
	Phebia J. Lindsey	4/12		Ga.
755.	Moses Anderson	28	Farmer	Ga.
	John Anderson	16	Farmer	Ga.
	Woodville Anderson	16		Ga.
	William Anderson	14		Ga.
	Edward Anderson	10		Ga.
756.	John Hopkin	62	Farmer	S. C.
	Malinda Hopkin	42		N. C.
	Frances Hopkin	17		Ga.
	James Hopkin	14		Ga.
	Lucinda Hopkin	5		Ga.
757.	Martin Morris	22	Farmer	N. C.
	Sarah E. Morris	18		Ga.
	Mary A. Morris	5		Ga.
	Martha R. Morris	1		Ga.
758.	William Whitfield	47	Farmer	N. C.
	Anna Whitfield	47		N. C.
	Martha Whitfield	18		Ga.
	John C. Whitfield	15	Farm hand	Ga.
	Samuel T. Whitfield	14		Ga.
	Mary Whitfield	12		Ga.
	Julia A. Whitfield	11		Ga.

Name	Age	Occupation	Born In
Caleb Whitfield	7		Ga.
Narcissus Whitfield	9		Ga.
Licena Whitfield	5		Ga.
Thomas Whitfield	4		Ga.
Stephen G. Whitfield	2		Ga.
759. James Lenning	29	Farmer	Ala.
Margaret Lenning	26		Ga.
John E. Lenning	2		Ga.
George L. Lenning	4/12		Ga.
760. Elbert Caneda	56	Farmer	S. C.
Anna F. Caneda	41		S. C.
Sarah A. Caneda	15		S. C.
Mary J. Caneda	13		S. C.
Miranda Caneda	11		S. C.
Margaret E. Caneda	8		S. C.
Dorah A. Caneda	6		S. C.
Carrie A. Caneda	2		S. C.
761. William Hale	27	Farmer	Ga.
Nancy Hale	19		Ga.
Mary Hale	2		Ga.
762. William McCroy	55	Farmer	S. C.
Catherine McCroy	49		S. C.
Andrew McCroy	24	Farm hand	S. C.
William McCroy, Jr.	12		Ga.
Emily McCroy	10		Ga.
James McCroy	7		Ga.
Margaret McCroy	6		Ga.
763. John Lambert	34	Farmer	Ga.
Catherine Lambert	29		Ga.
Mary J. Lambert	10		Ga.
David M. Lambert	9		Ga.
Adeline R. Lambert	5		Ga.
John H. Lambert	4		Ga.
Joseph M. Lambert	2		Ga.
Sarah M. Lambert	1/12		Ga.
764. Sampson Lambert	20	Farmer	Ga.
Lucinda C. Lambert	21		Ga.
765. James O. Owens	29	Farm hand	Ga.
Mary A. Owens	29		S. C.
William F. Owens	7		S. C.
John W. Owens	2		S. C.
766. Silas Nicholson	31	Farmer	S. C.
Mary Nicholson	23		S. C.
Malinda Nicholson	9		S. C.
Jane Nicholson	6		S. C.

Name	Age	Occupation	Born In
Miranda Nicholson	1		Ga.
767. Lemuel Padgett	34	Miller	Ga.
Mary N. Padgett	31		Ga.
Absalom A. Padgett	11		Ga.
Mahalia A. Padgett	9		Ga.
William M. Padgett	8		Ga.
Martha A. Padgett	5		Ga.
Pleasant M. Padgett	3		Ga.
John L. Padgett	1		Ga.
768. Jasper Compton	38	Farmer	Ga.
Eliza Compton	28		S. C.
Harriet S. Compton	7		Ga.
Thomas J. Compton	5		Ga.
John D. Compton	3		Ga.
Doctor L. Compton	2		Ga.
769. William Whitfield	23	Farmer	Ga.
Charity H. Whitfield	20		Ga.
770. Stephen Coward	41	Farmer	N. C.
Sophia Coward	42		N. C.
Lewis E. Coward	13		Ga.
Mary Coward	10		Ga.
Benjamin Coward	8		Ga.
Louisa O. Coward	5		Ga.
Hesterann L. Coward	2		Ga.
771. William Hazlewood	35	Farm hand	S. C.
Elizabeth Hazlewood	35		S. C.
Georgia A. Hazlewood	7		Ga.
Mary B. Hazlewood	4		Ga.
John M. Hazlewood	1/12		Ga.
William H. Hazlewood	1/12		Ga.
772. Samuel Waldrop	30	Farmer	S. C.
Nancy Waldrop	30		S. C.
Julia A. Waldrop	7		Ga.
Priscilla Waldrop	1		Ga.
773. Allen McCutchen	39	Farmer	Ga.
Harriet McCutchen	28		Ga.
Violett McCutchen	6		Ga.
Julia McCutchen	4		Ga.
774. Zachariah Glasscock	35	Shoemaker	Va.
Susan Glasscock	30		N. C.
Pastillia A. Glasscock	6		Ga.
Andrew J. Glasscock	4		Ga.
James M. Glasscock	4		Ga.
775. John Berry	44	Gentleman	N. C.
Mary E. Berry	23		Ga.

Name	Age	Occupation	Born In
William C. Berry	1		Ga.
776. Jeremiah Sosebee	29	Carpenter	Ga.
Catherine Sosebee	40		N. C.
William G. Sosebee	5		Ga.
John W. Sosebee	3		Ga.
James H. Sosebee	5/12		Ga.
777. Nancy Sosebee	60	Domestic	S. C.
Wilbern Sosebee	23	Farm hand	Ga.
Martha Sosebee	18		Ga.
Henry J. Sosebee	21	Farm hand	Ga.
James L. Sosebee	15	Farm hand	Ga.
778. Grafton Adair	39	Blacksmith	S. C.
Eliza Adair	35		S. C.
James P. Adair	9		S. C.
Alfred Adair	6		Ga.
William Adair	4		Ga.
Susan M. Adair	1		Ga.
779. Alfred McArthur	32	Farmer	S. C.
Alpha J. McArthur	23		N. C.
William P. McArthur	2		Ga.
John McArthur	1/12		Ga.
780. Elias W. Allred	36	Hotelkeeper	Ga.
Martha Allred	35		Ga.
William T. Day	30	Attorney	Ga.
John W. Heath	25	Attorney	Ga.
781. Lemuel J. Allred	45	Farmer	S. C.
Nancy Allred	43		Ga.
Samuel D. Allred	20	Farm hand	Ga.
Elias Allred	16	Farm hand	Ga.
Martha Allred	12		Ga.
Josephine Allred	9		Ga.
James Allred	6		Ga.
Cicero Peeples	20	Farm hand	Ga.
782. Caleb Griffin	50	Farmer	Ga.
Mary Griffin	45		Ga.
Sarah A. Griffin	24		Ga.
Stephen Griffin	22	Farm hand	Ga.
Nelly Griffin	16		Ga.
John W. Griffin	14		Ga.
Mary Griffin	10		Ga.
Caleb Griffin	6		Ga.
783. James Swofford	45	Farmer	S. C.
Miles Swofford	19	Farm hand	Ga.
Emily Swofford	17		Ga.
Jane Swofford	15		Ga.

Name	Age	Occupation	Born In
Eda Swofford	13		Ga.
James J. Swofford	10		Ga.
John Swofford	8		Ga.
Mary Swofford	4		Ga.
Amanda Swofford	3/12		Ga.
784. William Parker	35	Farmer	N. C.
Malinda Parker	31		N. C.
Champion Parker	13		N. C.
James Parker	10		N. C.
William Parker	4		N. C.
Samuel P. Parker	1		N. C.
785. Marcus Hasty	75	Farmer	S. C.
Nancy Hasty	55		Ga.
Oliver Fitts	32	Farm hand	Ga.
Emeline Fitts	23		S. C.
James Fitts	7		Ga.
George Fitts	3/12		Ga.
786. Andrew Kuykingdall	27	Farm hand	Ga.
Sarah Kuykingdall	28		Ga.
James A. Kuykingdall	9		Ga.
John Kuykingdall	8		Ga.
Thomas Kuykingdall	6		Ga.
Martha Kuykingdall	3		Ga.
Richard Landsdown	26	Farmer	Ga.
787. William Pinion	68	Farmer	S. C.
Caroline Pinion	36		S. C.
Franklin Pinion	23	Farm hand	Ga.
Thomas Pinion	19	Farm hand	Ga.
Harrison Pinion	11		Ga.
Margaret Pinion	9		Ga.
Malinda Pinion	4		Ga.
Thomas Pinion	7		Ga.
788. John Darnel, Jr.	26	Farmer	S. C.
Martha Darnel	26		Tenn.
Mary Darnel	11/12		Ga.
789. Isam Brooks	22	Farmer	S. C.
Martha Brooks	26		N. C.
790. Robert Coward	65	Farmer	N. C.
Emily Coward	66		N. C.
Misery Coward	30		N. C.
Wesley Coward	6		Ga.
791. Samuel B. Coward	28	Farmer	N. C.
Rebecca Coward	22		Ga.
George Coward	5		Ga.
Margaret Coward	3		Ga.

	NAME	AGE	OCCUPATION	BORN IN
	Martha Coward	2/12		Ga.
	James M. Coward	26	Farmer	N. C.
792.	Jeptha Pinion	38	Farmer	Ga.
	Nancy Pinion	29		Ga.
	Elias Pinion	10		Ga.
	James Pinion	8		Ga.
	Miles Pinion	3		Ga.
	Mary Darnell	70		Ga.
793.	Frances Cantrell	70	Domestic	Ga.
	Martha Cantrell	23	Domestic	Ga.
	Stephen Cantrell	5		Ga.
794.	Samuel Shipman	29	Farm hand	N. C.
	Drucilla Shipman	31		N. C.
	Mary Shipman	11		N. C.
	Lucy Shipman	6		N. C.
795.	Hiram Coward	24	Farmer	Ga.
	Sarah Coward	20		S. C.
	Stephen Coward	1		Ga.
796.	Michael Good	24	Farmer	N. C.
	Julia A. Good	18		Ga.
	Mary Good	1		Ga.
	Reuben Fields	35	Carpenter	Ga.
797.	Andrew Good	27	Farmer	N. C.
	Rachel Good	22		N. C.
	James M. Good	7/12		Ga.
798.	Sarah Blackstock	31	Domestic	Ga.
	Matilda Blackstock	33	Domestic	Ga.
	Cynthia Blackstock	9		Ga.
	Frances Blackstock	7		Ga.
799.	Richard Blackstock	25	Farmer	Ga.
	Mary Blackstock	23		Ga.
	John Blackstock	2		Ga.
	Elizabeth Blackstock	1/2		Ga.
800.	Van Kirkingdall	25	Farmer	Ga.
	Caroline Kirkingdall	24		Ga.
	William Kirkingdall	3/12		Ga.
801.	William Tate	33	Farmer	Ga.
	Mary M. Tate	21		Ga.
	William B. Tate	1		Ga.
	Farish C. Tate	2		Ga.
802.	John A. Lyon	35	Physician	S. C.
	Elizabeth Lyon	33		Tenn.
	John A. Lyon, Jr.	9		Ga.
	James A. Lyon	8		Ga.

Name	Age	Occupation	Born In
Thomas H. Lyon	6		Ga.
William F. Lyon	2		Ga.
Freland W. Lyon	3/12		Ga.
803. John Hendricks	38	Farmer	Ga.
Leanna Hendricks	38		N. C.
Malinda Hendricks	14		Ga.
Thomas Hendricks	12		Ga.
Jane Hendricks	9		Ga.
Nancy Hendricks	6		Ga.
Andrew Hendricks	4		Ga.
George Hendricks	2		Ga.
804. William Manus	50	Farmer	N. C.
Mary A. Manus	33		N. C.
Elias Manus	2		Ga.
805. James Coward	75	Farmer	N. C.
Mary Coward	65		N. C.
Carson Coward	12		Ga.
Scott Coward	13		Ga.
Narcissa Coward	16		Ga.
Matilda White	3		Ga.
806. William Darnell	50	Farmer	N. C.
Martha Darnell	45		N. C.
Hiram Darnell	18	Farm hand	Ga.
Sarah Darnell	16		Ga.
Jasper Darnell	14		Ga.
Harriet Darnell	12		Ga.
Martha Darnell	10		Ga.
Nancy Darnell	7		Ga.
Emily Darnell	5		Ga.
Susan Darnell	10/12		Ga.
807. Harvey Coward	40	Farmer	N. C.
Lucinda Coward	38		N. C.
James Coward	13		Ga.
Mary Coward	10		Ga.
Silas Coward	8		Ga.
808. John Forester	34	Miller	S. C.
Jane Forester	26		S. C.
John Forester	10		S. C.
William Forester	2/12		Ga.
Amanda Forester	2/12		Ga.
809. Alexander Brooks	23	Farmer	S. C.
Rhoda Brooks	45		S. C.
Mary Brooks	13		N. C.
810. John Darnell	41	Farmer	N. C.
Elizabeth Darnell	30		N. C.

Name	Age	Occupation	Born In
Sion Darnell	14		Ga.
William Darnell	12		Ga.
Mary Darnell	10		Ga.
Absalom Darnell	7		Ga.
Thomas Darnell	4		Ga.
John Darnell	2		Ga.
811. Alfred Pendley	48	Farmer	N. C.
Elizabeth Pendley	30		Ga.
Harvey Pendley	18	Farm hand	Ga.
Bertha Pendley	13		Ga.
William Pendley	12		Ga.
Nancy Pendley	10		Ga.
Malissa Pendley	6		Ga.
Barbara Pendley	3		Ga.
Thomas Pendley	2/12		Ga.
812. Joseph Wilkins	40	Farmer	Va.
Elizabeth Wilkins	37		S. C.
Martin Wilkins	17	Farm hand	Ga.
Andrew Wilkins	15	Farm hand	Ga.
Thomas Wilkins	13		Ga.
Abram Wilkins	10		Ga.
Caroline Wilkins	9		Ga.
John Wilkins	7		Ga.
William Wilkins	5		Ga.
813. Thomas Pendley	63	Farmer	N. C.
Mahalia Pendley	49		N. C.
John L. Pendley	39	Farm hand	N. C.
Sarah Pendley	35		N. C.
Celia Pendley	33		N. C.
Adline Pendley	18		Ga.
Martha Pendley	16		Ga.
Parthenia Pendley	14		Ga.
Jesse Pendley	13		Ga.
Thomas Pendley	11		Ga.
Isaac Pendley	9		Ga.
Elias Pendley	2		Ga.
814. John Pendley	20	Farmer	Ga.
Caroline Pendley	28		Ga.
815. Abram Goode	25	Farmer	N. C.
Carrie Goode	19		Ga.
Caleb G. Goode	2		Ga.
Stephen Goode	9/12		Ga.
816. Van Coffee	26	Farmer	Ga.
Frances Coffee	22		N. C.
John Coffee	1		Ga.

Name	Age	Occupation	Born In
817. Elbert Coffee	34	Farmer	Ga.
Hetta Coffee	26		Ga.
Evaline Coffee	9		Ga.
William Coffee	7		Ga.
Mary Coffee	5		Ga.
Winnie Coffee	3		Ga.
Solenia Coffee	1		Ga.
818. Glenn Coward	26	Farmer	N. C.
Jane Coward	26		Ga.
Martin Coward	2		Ga.
John Coward	2/12		Ga.
819. Isaac Burlison	43	Farmer	N. C.
Matilda Burlison	41		N. C.
William Burlison	16	Farm hand	Ga.
James Burlison	12		Ga.
Elizabeth Burlison	10		Ga.
Daniel Burlison	7		Ga.
Martha Burlison	5		Ga.
820. Thomas Fields	60	Farmer	N. C.
Susan Fields	54		N. C.
William Fields	17	Farm hand	Ga.
Nancy Fields	12		Ga.
Evaline Fields	10		Ga.
John Fields	8		Ga.
James Fields	6		Ga.
821. John Fann	25	Farmer	Tenn.
Jane Fann	19		S. C.
George Fann	3		Ga.
Wesley Fann	1		Ga.
822. William Weaver	31	Farmer	Ga.
Nancy Weaver	32		Ga.
Harriet Weaver	3		Ga.
David Weaver	2		Ga.
823. James Bramlet	25	Farmer	Ga.
Mary Bramlet	29		Ga.
Emeline Bramlet	8		Ga.
Robert Bramlet	6		Ga.
Caroline Bramlet	4		Ga.
Elizabeth Bramlet	2		Ga.
824. Elisha Russell	75	Farmer	N. C.
Nancy Russell	72		N. C.
825. Joseph Hayes	50	Farmer	S. C.
Nancy Hayes	40		S. C.
Joshua Hayes	20	Farm hand	S. C.
Sarah Hayes	19		S. C.

	Name	Age	Occupation	Born In
	John Hayes	18	Farm hand	S. C.
	Mary Hayes	14		S. C.
	Nancy Hayes, Jr.	6		S. C.
826.	John Russell	25	Farmer	Ga.
	Cynthia Russell	20		Ga.
	Jackson Russell	6		Ga.
	Sarah Russell	4		Ga.
	David Russell	2		Ga.
827.	Ancel Wigington	45	Farmer	S. C.
	Rachel Wigington	38		S. C.
	Robert Wigington	18	Farm hand	Ga.
	Elizabeth Wigington	16		Ga.
	Joseph Wigington	13		Ga.
	Margaret Wigington	10		Ga.
	Mary Wigington	4		Ga.
	Walter Wigington	2		Ga.
828.	George Tomlin	65	Farmer	N. C.
	Nancy Tomlin	36		N. C.
	Thomas Tomlin	14		Ga.
	Harvey Tomlin	11		Ga.
	John Tomlin	9		Ga.
	William Tomlin	6		Ga.
829.	Sion A. Darnell	28	Farmer	Ga.
	Emily Darnell	33		Ga.
	Elizabeth Darnell	13		Ga.
	Levi Darnell	5		Ga.
	Mary Darnell	3		Ga.
	Cicero Darnell	1		Ga.
830.	William Partin	38	Farmer	S. C.
	Nancy Partin	36		S. C.
	Mary Partin	15		Ga.
	Frances Partin	13		Ga.
	Malissa Partin	11		Ga.
	James Partin	8		Ga.
	Henry Partin	6		Ga.
	Thomas Partin	2		Ga.
831.	Francis Whelchel	26	Farmer	Ga.
	Emeline Whelchel	25		N. C.
	William Whelchel	7		Ga.
	Sarah Whelchel	4		Ga.
	James Whelchel	2/12		Ga.
832.	Francis Godfrey	35	Farmer	S. C.
	Rebecca Godfrey	33		N. C.
	Calaway Godfrey (M)	9		Ga.
	Mary Godfrey	7		Ga.

Name	Age	Occupation	Born In
Martha Godfrey	6		Ga.
Julia Godfrey	5		Ga.
Lafayette Godfrey	3		Ga.
Lucius Godfrey	8/12		Ga.
833. Leander Neal	31	Blacksmith	S. C.
Susanna Neal	34		S. C.
James Neal	11		Ga.
Eli Neal	5		Ga.
Leander Neal, Jr.	9		Ga.
834. William Pendley	28	Farmer	Ga.
Saleda Pendley	19		Ga.
Mary Pendley	4/12		Ga.
835. William McNara	80	Stonemason	Scotland
Elizabeth McNara	25		Ga.
Harriet McNara	4		Ga.
James McNara	2		Ga.
836. Silveo Taberaux	52	Farmer	France
Dilly Taberaux (F)	22		Ga.
Adeline Taberaux	15		France
Alfrasie Taberaux (F)	14		France
Mary Taberaux	1		Ga.
Jelang Taberaux	24	Farm hand	France
837. Batus Taberaux	26	Farmer	France
Frances Taberaux	21		Ga.
838. Thomas Gordon	37	Farmer	Ga.
Sobitha Gordon	30		Tenn.
William Gordon	13		Ga.
Jane Gordon	6		Ga.
Elias Gordon	2		Ga.
Julia Gordon	7/12		Ga.
839. Minor W. Cox	48	Blacksmith	S. C.
Lucinda Cox	56		S. C.
George Cox	14		N. C.
840. John McTaylor	55	Farm hand	N. C.
Sarah McTaylor	55		N. C.
Jemima McTaylor	17		Ga.
Lucinda McTaylor	19		Ga.
William McTaylor	13		Ga.
Talley McTaylor	11		Ga.
Sarah McTaylor	2		Ga.
841. Marshall McClure	32	Merchant	S. C.
Piety K. McClure	32		S. C.
Sarah E. McClure	11		Ga.
Adolphus M. McClure	9		Ga.
Georgia A. McClure	2		Ga.

	Name	Age	Occupation	Born In
	Martha McClure	34		S. C.
	Jane McClure	11		Ga.
842.	William Gordon	40	Merchant	Ala.
	Sarah C. Gordon	20		N. C.
	Joseph E. Gordon	2		Ga.
	William A. Gordon	1		Ga.
	James Morrison	14		Ga.
843.	Allison McHan	48	Farmer	Va.
	Catharine McHan	37		N. C.
	William D. McHan	17	Clk., Merchant	N. C.
	James L. McHan	16	College student	N. C.
	Henry M. McHan	14		N. C.
	Alfred W. McHan	11		Ga.
	Allison McHan (M)	8		Ca.
	Catherine McHan	6		Ga.
	Martha McHan	4		Ga.
	Joseph B. McHan	2		Ga.
844.	Celia A. Dyks	38	Domestic	S. C.
	John W. F. Dyks	11		S. C.
	Mary E. Dyks	3		Ga.
845.	John E. Price	55	Farmer	N. C.
	Elizabeth Price	48		S. C.
	Ervin Price	19	Farm hand	Ga.
	Louisa E. Price	16		Ga.
	William W. Price	13		Ga.
	Gelassa A. Price (F)	11		Ga.
	Mary L. Price	7		Ga.
846.	Jonathan Taylor	48	Blacksmith	N. C.
	Patient Taylor	48		N. C.
	Joseph Taylor	20	Marble rubber	N. C.
	Malinda Taylor	16		N. C.
	Martha C. Taylor	14		N. C.
	Laura A. Taylor	15		N. C.
	Stephen Taylor	10		N. C.
	William Taylor	4/12		Ga.
847.	John Pool	37	Marble rubber	S. C.
	Susanna Pool	35		Ga.
	Seth Pool	16	Farm hand	Ga.
	Samuel T. Pool	14		Ga.
	Elizabeth Pool	12		Ga.
	Warren W. Pool	10		Ga.
	Mary M. Pool	2/12		Ga.
	John H. Pool	2/12		Ga.
848.	Elizabeth Pool	35	Domestic	Ga.
	John Pool	16	Farm hand	Ga.

NAME	AGE	OCCUPATION	BORN IN
Jasper Pool	12		Ga.
Susan Pool	11		Ga.
Dred Pool	8		Ga.
Mary M. Pool	5		Ga.
Calvin Poole	2		Ga.
849. Ephraim Sosebee	40	Blacksmith	Ga.
Sarah Sosebee	39		Ga.
Nelson Sosebee	22	Miller	Ga.
Rhoda A. Sosebee	18		Ga.
William T. Sosebee	16	Farm hand	Ga.
John W. Sosebee	14		Ga.
Nancy Q. Sosebee	10		Ga.
Mary J. Sosebee	9		Ga.
Jeremiah M. Sosebee	6		Ga.
Julia A. Sosebee	6		Ga.
Jasper Sosebee	4		Ga.
Benjamin Sosebee	7/12		Ga.
850. Henry Talmer	25	Farmer	S. C.
Martha Talmer	23		S. C.
Benjamin Talmer	4		Ga.
Elizabeth Talmer	2		Ga.
851. George Summey	34	Marble dealer	N. C.
Anna W. Summey	33		N. C.
Elizabeth Summey	14		N. C.
Fannie L. Summey	13		N. C.
Johnny C. Summey (F)	11		N. C.
Sarah A. Summey	9		N. C.
Charles L. Summey	3		Ga.
Lilly M. Summey	1		Ga.
Joseph A. Besaner	22	Marble agent	N. C.
John R. Howell	30	Stonecutter	S. C.
James M. Cox	22	Stonecutter	S. C.
John Dykes	18	Stonecutter	Ga.
Edward J. Prather	22	Stonecutter	Ga.
852. William Hurlick	44	Master mason	Pa.
Catherine Hurlick	28		England
Susan G. Hurlick	4		Ga.
Eli Coffee	29	Stonecutter	Ga.
Stephen Cox	25	Stonecutter	Ga.
Caleb Cox	22	Marble rubber	Ga.
John Turner	24	Apprentice	N. C.
853. Mary Mann	42	Domestic	Ga.
William Mann	22	Farm hand	Ga.
Rial J. Mann	18	Farm hand	Ga.
Littleton M. Ma...	16	Farm hand	Ga.

Name	Age	Occupation	Born In
Lucinda Mann	14		Ga.
John Mann	11		Ga.
James Mann	10		Ga.
Robert Mann	8		Ga.
Sarah Mann	4		Ga.
854. William Simmons	35	Attorney	Ga.
Adeline Simmons	38		Ga.
Thomas G. Simmons	11		Ga.
Roxanna Simmons	9		Ga.
William Simmons	7		Ga.
Maddox M. Simmons	5		Ga.
John F. Simmons	3		Ga.
Benjamin H. Simmons	1		Ga.
855. Ortha Watts	22	Domestic	Ga.
Sarah J. Watts	4		Ga.
Martha C. Watts	2		Ga.
856. John L. Hall	20	Farmer	Ga.
Phoebe A. Hall	20		Ga.
857. Carian Ward	69	Domestic	Va.
Susan R. Ward	27	Domestic	Ga.
George P. Ward	5		Ga.

GEORGIA—PICKENS COUNTY.

I, William Tate, Assistant Marshal, do solemnly swear that the foregoing was made out according to my oath and the instructions to the best of my knowledge and belief, so help me God.

Sworn to and subscribed before me this 28th day of July, 1860.

(Signed) WILLIAM TATE,
Assistant Marshal.

(Signed) P. R. SIMMONS,
Judge Inferior Court.

Chapter IV ★ ★ ★ ★ ★
MILITARY HISTORY

●

DURING THE period since the creation of Pickens County, three of the nation's wars have been fought.

The second of these, the Spanish-American War, drew comparatively few enlistments from North Georgia and by its nature needs little space in the present account.*

The third of these conflicts, the World War, found Pickens County ready and eager to do her part and to furnish her quota of men and money for the nation's defense. More than three hundred soldiers enlisted from Pickens County (names will be found at end of this chapter), and the county's people were glad to respond whole-heartedly to every measure designed for the welfare of their country, in common with all other patriotic Americans. Twelve of the soldiers from Pickens County lost their lives in this great conflict.

It is the War Between the States, of course, that furnishes the distinctive part of Pickens County's military history, because this was the only war to reach and ravage home soil. Every Southern county has its own fund of lore to add to Civil War tradition; Pickens is no exception, and not only is her story a most interesting one but it is a story whose true

---

*Mention should be made, however. of the notable record of a Pickens County soldier who lost his life in the Spanish-American War. The following account is from the Pickens County Progress for October 13, 1899:

"NAVAL CADET WOOD.—In the little time that was his to live, Naval Cadet Welborn Cicero Wood, of Jerusalem, Pickens County, Ga., lived gloriously. He was killed at Orani, near Manila, September 26 [1899]. It was he who first spied Cervera's fleet escaping from the mouth of Santiago Harbor, and he who hoisted the famous '250' signal—'The enemy are escaping.' He was on the Texas then, under the gallant Phillip."

recital would seem indeed, from the standpoint of her citizens, to be highly desirable. The author has been at some pains, therefore, to collect as many facts as possible, and they are here presented.

PICKENS COUNTY IN THE CIVIL WAR

We express our earnest hope that . . . if a call is made upon our county for troops, the company will take its place in the gallant ranks of the Army of the Southern Confederacy and do valiant battle in the cause of our beloved South and in defense of the dearest rights of freemen against the encroachments of the wicked and dangerous black republican administration.

These words, written at the opening of the Civil War, did not come from slave-owning South Georgians or Virginians, or from fiery, impetuous Carolinians. They were merely the official expression of the attitude of a North Georgia county that many people, to this good day, think was "Union in sentiment" during the War Between the States. The words quoted are from the official presentments of the April 1861 grand jury of Pickens County, Georgia.

It is at this point in our story that we come to one of the least understood periods in the history of Pickens County. Impressions of the role which Pickens played during the Civil War run all the way from that of an "all-white" county justifiably hesitant to fight the slave-owners' battles, to that of an entire section of people uniformly disloyal to the Southern cause. The last picture, of course, is imaginary and without the slightest claim on truth; the first is nearer to the facts; but none of the commentators seems to have thought of the possibility that, officially and as a whole, Pickens County might have been devotedly patriotic to the Confederacy from the Secession to Appomattox!

Let us look at the reasons for the criticism the county has received. The chief ones are that the people here were in the main opposed to Secession; that the Union flag was allowed to float from the courthouse at Jasper for some time after Georgia had seceded; that a portion of the county's population retained their Union sympathies during the war.

These things all appear to have been quite true. But if the reader, after a fair and impartial consideration of the facts, should arrive at the conclusion that Pickens County has been unjustly maligned for its part in the Civil War—I think he will do so with good reason.

It is now generally accepted that the War Between the States was primarily the result, not of the slavery dispute, but of the economic pressure of high tariffs on the agricultural South, the attendant dispute over states' rights, and the attempt of the South to preserve a civilization fundamentally different, because largely based on slavery, from that of the North.

Under this interpretation of affairs, it becomes less easy to say with certainty that the people of Pickens and other mountain counties, even though they owned but few slaves, actually dissented from the opinions held against the North by the people of the plantation sections. That they did dissent in any alarming degree seems only to have been taken for granted, under the theory that slavery was the prime issue of the war. The high tariffs of the time, protecting Northern industry but raising the prices which Southern farmers had to pay on manufactured goods, were as damaging to the small farmer of North Georgia as they were to the planter of the lower state. Add to this the fact that states' rights were one of the fetishes of the liberty-loving mountaineers, and it is evident that their hearts were, in the main, against their Northern oppressors.

Against the North—but not against the Union. Here we have an apparent inconsistency, which is in reality not an inconsistency at all; and the explanation sheds light on the actions of the mountaineers. The North was not, to their minds, exemplifying the doctrines on which the Union had been founded. The North was not the Union they loved. They were not confusing the two—it is their critics who have done that. They regarded Georgia—one of the "original thirteen" —as being no less a part of the Union than any other state or section, which was certainly true; and their love for the Union reflected their love for Georgia, not for the North.

I think it was this feeling that accounted for the things for which Pickens County is criticized in connection with the Civil War. It explains the sentiment against Secession, the episode of the Union flag, and even the refusal of some of the county's good people to turn against the Union after the war began. For those citizens who may have given aid and comfort to the enemy, and especially for those few who acted as spies and informers against their neighbors, there seems to be no legitimate excuse and none is offered. But that the great majority of the county's people should have given their support, after Secession became a fact, to the cause of the South, despite their affection for the Union and despite the fact that they did not own slaves, seems to argue a greater and even more creditable patriotism, if anything, than that displayed in the plantation regions.

And it appears from the historical evidence—which includes the rosters of six companies sent by Pickens County to the Confederate Army—that the majority *did* give their unstinted support to the Southern cause. But let us begin at the beginning.

In 1860 a fourth of Georgia's population was black, while Pickens County in that year contained almost no negroes. Only a few well-to-do families here kept slaves, the county being unsuited for large plantations of the type that made slave labor essential. It does not appear that there was any great amount of bitterness in North Georgia against the institution of slavery, or against the slave-owning sections on principle; but there was enough difference in the types of civilization here and in those sections to leave Mountain Georgians rather unsympathetic to the viewpoint of downstate planters insofar as the slave question was concerned. As for the tariff and states' rights problems, the other causes of the Civil War, citizens of North Georgia were largely of the opinion that these matters could be settled without recourse to Secession. And to Secession they were, in great measure, strongly opposed—in which they differed not at all from the outstanding patriot of the Confederacy, Robert E. Lee.

The attitude of Pickens County seems to have been exactly expressed by its representative to the historic Secession Convention of January 1861, James Simmons. Mr. Simmons was one of those voting against Secession, but he and the other dissenters signed the ordinance after its passage, in the interest of unity. Mr. Simmons was also one of six representatives to sign a document protesting against the course taken by the convention but expressing their patriotism in these words: "Yet as good citizens, we yield to the will of a majority of her people as expressed by their representatives, and we hereby pledge 'our lives, our fortunes and our sacred honor' to the defense of Georgia, if necessary, against hostile invasion from any source whatsoever."

It was soon after the adjournment of the Secession Convention that the startling fact became known all over the state that Pickens County was still flying the Union flag from her courthouse at Jasper. This is one of the events for which the county is noted, or "notorious," and it has led to such statements as the one that Pickens "practically seceded from the Confederacy."

It is not recorded or known with certainty who was responsible for this happening, though there are several versions linking the names of prominent citizens of the county to the incident. It is fairly certain that this was the last Union flag to fly below the Mason and Dixon line after the Secession, up until the Surrender, but it is equally certain that the flag was removed within a short time, probably a month at the most, and by the people themselves. The following account of the incident is given by Col. I. W. Avery in his *History of Georgia* (p. 187):

At Jasper, Pickens County, where the Union loyalty was very ardent, a United States flag was raised upon a pole soon after secession and kept afloat in bold open defiance of Confederate authority for several weeks. The provocation was very irritating to the people after we had seceded, to have the flag of the repudiated Union floating defiantly, the insulting emblem of a hostile power seeking our subjection. Appeals upon appeals were made to Governor Brown to send troops to cut it down. To all of these the astute Executive was wisely deaf. He preferred to let the Union ebullition spend its force. There were very few slaves in that section, and in consequence the slavery sentiment was not strong, while the devotion to the government was very ardent. The veneration for the United States flag was especially earnest. Governor Brown declined to have the flag cut down. He said:

"By no means; let it float. It floated over our fathers, and we all love the flag now. We have only been compelled to lay it aside by the injustice that has been practiced under its folds. If the people of Pickens desire to hang it out, and keep it there, let them do so. I will send no troops to interfere with it."

The flag continued to float for a while, until the people became ashamed of this sort of action, and took it down themselves without any disturbance whatever; and the county soon after came in with its troops, and did good service in the Confederate cause.

The words of the governor, as recorded above, were of course extremely well-chosen and tactful; but if we remember that Governor Brown had gone to his high position direct from the bench of the Blue Ridge Circuit, and that he knew the innermost hearts of the mountain people, being one of them, then we may believe that his words were also entirely sincere. There is, in fact, no reason to doubt that the flag-raisers had acted out of the exact motives expressed in Governor Brown's statement. In its true light, the flag episode is seen as less damning to Pickens County; but its unique historical flavor will make it remembered for many years to come.

Whether, in the final analysis, the Jasper flag-raisers were justified on the grounds given, or whether they were not, we know that the majority of the citizens of Pickens County during the Civil War period needed no justification for their words or acts because both were unmistakably Southern in spirit. The grand jury presentments of the time leave no room for doubt on this point, and by their official nature we may regard them as conclusive evidence. There is no hearsay or guesswork about the document quoted at the beginning of this chapter, and it was written at about the same time that the flag-raising incident happened.

Another presentment of a Pickens grand jury, that of September 1861, further illustrates the true spirit of the county's people and in addition gives us an interesting glimpse of life in the county during the first year of the war. It is quoted here:

We are glad to report that since the last term of this court our county has sent two companies of Volunteers to meet the Invader and they are now in the service of the Confederate States. In addition to this over 100 volunteers have gone from this county in companies from the adjoining counties, and if we mistake not the spirit of our people there are hundreds of others ready and willing should necessity require it, to offer their bosoms to the shafts of battle in defense of our altars and our firesides.

And whereas many of those who have gone to the war have left

families in destitute condition and whereas the inferior court did
at the request of the citizens in a public meeting assess a tax upon
our citizens to supply the wants of said families, and whereas the
inferior court have thought proper in view of the high taxes our
citizens have to pay, to discontinue the jury tax for the present and
give it to the destitute families of our brave soldiers, we avail ourselves of this opportunity to give an expression of our approbation
to the wise, firm and patriotic course pursued by our inferior court
in this noble cause.

We would respectfully urge upon all our citizens the necessity of
union of sentiment and concert of action in repelling the invader
from our soil and by furnishing our brave soldiers on the tented
field with everything necessary for their efficiency and comfort and
in supplying the wants and protecting from insult and injury their
wives and little ones left behind.

. . . In taking leave of His Honor, George D. Rice, we tender to
him the thanks of this body for the able and dignified manner in
which he has presided over this court and the strong sympathy he
manifest for our troubled country by protecting the rights of our
citizens who are in the service of our country.

The spirited observations of the two grand juries already
quoted are matched by those of still a third—the jury of
September 1862, which felt confident that the boys from
Pickens would help to "include the territories of the enemy"
if necessary. This presentment is also given:

We congratulate the country on the recent victory achieved by
our noble army on the battlefield of Manassas, and feel confident
that the citizens of Pickens will in the future as they have in the past
sustain the Confederate Government by furnishing men and money,
and will assist in driving the last Yankee from our soil and if need
be to include the territories of the enemy to obtain an honorable
peace.

The tone of other presentments on the subject of the War
is the same; and it will be borne in mind that the opinions
expressed were those of the best and most representative
citizens of Pickens County, who were, furthermore, speaking
officially for the people of the county as a whole.

As explained by the autumn grand jury of 1861, not only had two companies of volunteers to the Southern Army enlisted from Pickens up to that time, but over one hundred citizens of the county had enlisted in companies sent by adjoining counties. Since there is no accurate way to obtain the names or total number of those who went outside the county to enlist, the only names given in the roster of Confederate soldiers in the latter part of this chapter are those of the men actually enlisting in Pickens County. Even without counting the others, this roster shows more than 550 Confederate soldiers from Pickens, or approximately one-eighth of the county's entire population in 1860; and this proportion was likely raised to a sixth or even more by the other enlistments. This would have been a creditable showing for any county in the entire Confederacy.

Though it is hardly necessary, let me say here that there were no "Union companies from Pickens County."

The first company leaving Pickens County to join the Army of the South was Company E of the 23rd Regiment of Georgia Volunteers, under the captaincy of Samuel Tate, whose son, Carter Tate, drilled the company at Big Shanty. The commanding officer of the 23rd Regiment was Colonel Thomas Hutcherson, of Salacoa in Cherokee County; and the entire regiment had been recruited from the counties of Cherokee Georgia. All of its 1500 men were mustered into service at Camp McDonald (now Kennesaw, Ga.) on August 31, 1861.

It was evidently Company E to which the grand jurors of April 1861 referred, in one of their presentments, as being then in the process of organization; the jury expressing the hope that the company would soon be ready to take its place "in the gallant ranks of the Army of the Southern Confederacy." In the same presentment, the jurors also took note of the interesting fact that a Confederate flag had been made and presented to the company by Miss Henrietta Cunningham, a school teacher at Jasper.

After Captain Tate's men left for the front, other companies of volunteers organized themselves in Pickens and followed Company E as Governor Brown called them out. The other five companies from Pickens County were: Company L of the 36th Regiment; Company C—known as the "Pickens Volunteers"—of the 43rd Regiment; Company L of the 43d; Company I—the "Pickens Raid Repellers"—of the Cherokee Legion of Volunteer Infantry; and Company I of the 8th Regiment, 3d Brigade, 1st Division of Georgia State Troops. These companies, which were commanded respectively by Captains Thomas Williams, Benjamin F. Hanie, Merrick H. West, James Bruce, and William T. Day, all did valiant service in the cause of the Confederacy. The names of all officers and soldiers who enlisted from Cherokee County are given at the end of this chapter.

Pickens County was out of the main path of destruction when Sherman's army passed through Georgia in the spring of 1864 on its famous "march to the sea"; nor were there any extensive military operations in the county at any other time during the Civil War. As in all the mountainous sections, a good deal of guerrilla fighting occurred within the bounds of Pickens; and raiding parties from the Union Army were also sent here at various times, as well as scouting troops sent by the Confederates to hold them in check. A detachment of Wheeler's Cavalry camped near Hinton for part of one winter, and a detachment from Wilder's Brigade camped for a short period in Long Swamp Valley near the Tate homestead.

Of such nature were the military activities that took place within the county's boundaries. But while there were no major engagements in Pickens, the county's people nevertheless felt in no uncertain manner the heavy hand of War, through those privations and hardships which are common to a people fighting in their own territory and which are, in their way, even more bitter and disheartening than the ravages of actual warfare. This condition not only prevailed here during the aftermath, when the entire South was economically prostrate, but began in Pickens County during the first year of the struggle.

Something of the hardships that early beset the people of this county may be inferred from the 1861 jury presentments already quoted, in which the destitute families of absent soldiers are mentioned, as well as the burdensome nature of the taxes which had to be paid. With considerably less wealth than the counties of Lower Georgia, Pickens and the other mountain counties were among the first in the state to feel the economic pressure of the war. Notwithstanding this fact, the spirit of the county remained firmly with the South; there was no hint that the people of Pickens wanted other than an honorable—and victorious—peace. Cheerfully the moneyed citizens contributed of their means to the cause of the South, and to the support of their impoverished neighbors. As early as September 1861, jurors renounced their pay and turned it into the fund for soldiers' families. Officials of the county gave part of their salaries. Every possible means was taken to insure the welfare of the war-stricken as well as to aid the Confederate cause.

Anent the hardships suffered by the Southern people during the Civil War, there is much historical mention of the scarcity of salt—a commodity which arouses little attention when you can get it, but a great deal of concern when you can't. As in many other districts of the South, salt became so scarce in Pickens County that barrels which had contained meat were boiled to get the salt out of them, and dirt from under smokehouses was washed to dissolve the salt from it. The situation was relieved to some extent when Governor

Brown succeeded in obtaining a large quantity of salt in Atlanta, and distributed it to the people of the state. An interesting incident from the records of Pickens County is the appropriation of twenty-five dollars, by the inferior court on January 3, 1863, to W. H. Simmons "for carrying the citizens' names and money to Atlanta for salt."

GUERRILLA BANDS IN PICKENS

One of the by-products of the peculiar situation existing in the mountain region of Georgia during the Civil War was the growth of a body of outlaws, or renegades, who formed themselves into gangs, either Northern or Southern in sympathy, and made a business of robbing and killing people of opposite sympathies and of preying on the country-side generally.

In Pickens County, and in the adjoining county of Cherokee, there operated two such gangs: McCollum's Scouts and the Jordan Gang, as they were known. The former was headed by Benjamin F. McCollum, of a prominent Cherokee County family; the latter, by Benjamin F. Jordan, who also came from another county. A detailed and interesting account of the activities of McCollum's Scouts, written by Judge W. A. Covington, is given in Rev. L. G. Marlin's *History of Cherokee County*. This account gives several instances, obtained by Judge Covington through personal information, in which the crimes of murder and robbery were committed by outlaw bands—apparently without any authority but their own inclinations and the will of their leader. One noted case was the killing of two men named Covington (distantly related to the above mentioned writer) who were taken by a guerrilla band in Dawson County and brought to Pickens. One of them was hanged; the other, attempting to get away, was shot and killed in the yard of a resident at

Four Mile, on the Old Federal Road. The location of this double slaying is still known as "Covington Hang."

The reasons for this particular act are unknown, but most of the killings and robberies done by the two gangs were directed against people who had aided the Union forces in some way. It was during the year 1864 that the two above mentioned bands flourished, the same year in which Sherman invaded and despoiled the state. In the course of his march Sherman was given information by some of the citizens sympathetic to the Union as to which of their neighbors should be raided, and informers of this sort constituted the chief class of victims of McCollum and Jordan. On the other hand, some of the actions of these gangs seemed to be in total disregard of the victim's affiliations.

There seems to be some question as to the authority, if any, under which McCollum's Scouts, and possibly Jordan's Gang also (since the two groups are shown by court records to have overlapped to some degree), committed their various acts of depredation and retaliation. While the county records of Pickens and Cherokee, and the state records so far as known, offer no light on the subject, I am informed by certain of McCollum's descendants now living in the state that there is in existence a document showing that the leader of the "Scouts" was commissioned by Governor Brown to carry out a sort of "sub rosa" warfare against Union sympathizers and Union outlaw gangs. State history does not seem to record any such official condonement, not to say authorization, of acts like those charged to the McCollum and Jordan gangs; it is possible, on the other hand, that military necessity may have prompted Governor Brown to take some such step. It is a matter of history that during the war the mountains of North Georgia harbored a large number of slackers and deserters from the Southern Army who had fled thence to escape service. These fugitives turned outlaw, ravaging and terrorizing the countryside, and made it necessary for Governor Brown to send troops against them. According to Avery—*

Governor Brown issued his proclamation outlawing these men and sent Major Galt and Major Wynn, commanding detachments of reserve infantry and cavalry, to break up the mischief. These officers seized some fifty of the ringleaders, headed by a deserter named Jeff Anderson, returned some two hundred men directly to their commands, and hustled out fully two thousand absentees.

But this happened in 1863 and the activities of the McCollum and Jordan bands did not get under good headway until the following year. Of course, it may have been that the "mischief" was not entirely broken up by the troops.

Viewing the record of the two gangs, most people would probably conclude that if they did have any official authority, they overstepped it considerably. This is to be gathered from the court records of Pickens County for the years of 1865 and 1866, during which a large number of true bills for murder and robbery were found by the grand jury against Benjamin F. McCollum, Benjamin F. Jordan, and various members of their gangs, both collectively and individually. In justice to both men, it must be held as probable that they were charged with several crimes they did not have anything to do with, simply because of their bad reputation.

As nearly as can be ascertained, none of the cases against the two gangs ever came to trial. It is claimed that they were dismissed because the acts had been authorized. The court records show, however, that these cases were never dismissed; they were docketed for trial at each successive term of court for a number of years, but the defendants apparently could not be apprehended. All of them left the county, and it is presumed the sheriff was without power to bring them back even when they could be located. McCollum was later shot by

---

*History of Georgia, Avery, p. 257.

a drunken policeman at Hampton, Ga., where he was practicing law; the fate of the others is not known.

It is a curious fact, and one not generally understood, that the membership of the two gangs which operated so extensively in Pickens was not drawn from this county. Neither McCollum nor Jordan was a citizen of Pickens County, nor did more than a handful of their men live here. Of the approximately forty names appearing in criminal actions together with that of either McCollum or Jordan on the minutes of the Pickens Superior Court, only six are shown in the Census of 1860 for Pickens County, and it is doubtful whether several of these did not signify altogether different persons.

Some Phases of the Aftermath

I need hardly emphasize that the spirit of gangsterism and organized outlawry was altogether repugnant to the people of this county; nor did such a spirit typify any element of the citizenry. It is true, though, that with the close of the Civil War, Pickens County found itself a part of that no-man's-land of the South in which the people were torn among themselves by conflicting sympathies and sentiments. Where the actual presence of war had made it necessary for all factions to unite in a common cause, the absence of such a need now acted to renew and intensify old differences. The resultant displays of feeling were simply a part of the general emotional release which swept over the South during that trying period we now know as the Aftermath.

In Pickens County these displays were confined, on the whole, to the channel of politics. In the days when the "carpet-bagger" was in the land, a political candidate was *ipse facto* "for" the Union or "for" the Confederacy. Obscuring all other issues was the burning question of whether he favored the North or the South. Intense popular interest accompanied every race for office, whether local or national, and personal violence was not so rare in political arguments as to be entirely unheard of. In fact, the discussion over candidates would sometimes lead to the urgent necessity for a doctor to patch up the wounded.

Eventually, of course, the dissension and bitterness wore itself down. Differences began to be forgotten, neighbors started speaking to each other again, and something like a national viewpoint began to take the place of strictly Northern or Southern attitudes—as was happening everywhere else. About the time this first period of expression was passing, though, another began to take form; and this time true lawlessness was to rear its head.

The second period, although it did not come until some years after the carpet-bagger era, may also be considered as a phase of the Aftermath since it represented the conflict between a Northern viewpoint and that of a certain class of Southerners. The United States government had placed a tax on whiskey for revenue, and had employed officers to collect the tax and to put an end to illicit distilling. This very vitally affected certain inhabitants of North Georgia.

Now I can not say whether "moonshining" was more or less prevalent in Pickens County than it was in the rest of this section at that time. There was certainly some of it going on here. In fact, the grand jurors often took note of the circumstance; and in 1864, when public corn was being given to needy families of the county, the jurors advised care in the distribution of this corn because, they complained, some of the citizens were making whiskey out of it.

Be that as it may, the effort of the federal government to collect a tax on all liquor manufacturers was regarded by the mountaineer distiller as an invasion of his personal rights and liberties. To add to his grievances, a spy system, rewarding any person who reported to officers the location of an illegal still, was instituted. The popular attitude then became more bitter toward a "reporter" than toward the revenue officers.

Out of this situation grew the feeling that men were compelled to band together for mutual protection, and there was organized in Pickens County a society by the name of "Honest Man's Friend and Protector." The activities of the society were directed against both the officers and the "reporters." An officer was killed and a number of homes belonging to "reporters" and others in sympathy with the new revenue law were burned to the ground. Masks and other regalia worn by the members of the "Honest Man's Friend and Protector" served both to disguise the wearers and, probably, to frighten and impress their unfortunate victims. Something like a reign of terror ensued as the bold crimes of the gang mounted up. It was short-lived. One day the officers captured one of the younger members, and he turned state's evidence. The officers were led to the gang's meeting-place. One of the members escaped, but the rest, numbering about a dozen, were taken into custody.

Put on trial for their lives, the entire band were found guilty, with a recommendation of mercy, and were given long prison sentences. Thus ended one of the most trying periods in the history of our country, and the only instance of organized crime on the part of any group of its citizens.

In an effort to escape from the penitentiary, one of the men was killed; several others died in prison; and one of the younger members was later released, is now living in our county, and has made a worthy citizen.

During the closing chapter of this organization's history, popular excitement ran high and a strong fight was made to wipe out the band. A Baptist minister, the Rev. Elias Allred, was a leader in this fight, while to intrepid Judge George F. Gober and Solicitor-General George R. Brown, who was assisted by Col. Carter Tate, later Congressman from the Ninth District, the county also owes a debt of lasting gratitude for their part in the restoration of law and order in this section.

From this time on, our county has made great progress in all lines, and in recent years it is the exception when our Superior Court, which sits twice a year, holds for more than three days. An old citizen, upon being asked to what he attributed this great change and improvement, said:

"To the schools and to an educated ministry."

Confederate Soldiers From Pickens County

COMPANY E, 23d REGIMENT
GEORGIA VOLUNTEER INFANTRY

Officers:

Samuel Tate, Captain
Paschal F. Ferguson, 1st Lieut.
Leander A. Simmons, 2d Lieut.
Stephen A. Cox; Jr. 2nd Lieut.
Robert V. Kelly, 1st Sgt.
Thomas P. Forrester, 2d Sgt.
Z. J. Williams, 3d Sgt.

William Pool, 4th Sgt.
James P. Mullins, 1st Corp.
G. K. Mullins, 2d Corp.
John W. Hanie (or J. R.), 3d Corp.
H. H. Loveless, 4th Corp.

Privates:

John F. Agan
W. H. Atkins
James Bailey
Jesse P. Berry
W. J. Berry
James H. Blanton
William G. Blanton
J. B. Bottoms
Jesse F. Boyd
R. C. Brock
Caleb Brown

Jacob Brown
Samuel Brown
William T. Brown
Russell Bryant
Charles Carroll
Lorenzo O. Carver
William J. Clark
Benjamin Corbin
Joseph Corbin
J. N. Corbin
S. S. Covington

George W. Cox
James M. Cox
Jesse C. Cox
Jackson J. Craig
H. K. Crow
Joseph Crow
Elnathan Davis
B. F. Dorsey
A. S. Dowdy
Benj. J. Dunagan
Martin Eberhart

Thomas N. Eberhart
Nathan Evett
William Ferguson
J. D. Fouts (or
  Foutes)
Joshua Gilbert
Wilson Gilbert
F. M. Godfrey
Siloam Goode
Jasper Gravett
Robert M. Griffin
John Hambrick
John E. Hamby
Stephen L. Hammon-
  tree
S. T. Hammontree
William H. Hanie
B. M. Hazlewood
Isaac Hazlewood
J. J. Holcombe
W. W. Holcombe
Patterson Hood
John M. Hutson
Joseph P. Jackson
Jordan Jackson
L. N. Jackson
Thomas M. Jenkins
Joel Johnson

Alfred W. Kaylor
David Kaylor
A. M. D. Kelley
D. A. Lansdown
John T. Legan
M. Jackson Lovelady
A. W. Loveless
Evan Loveless
James Loveless
Samuel Loveless
J. M. Mann
A. W. Mullins
S. J. Mullins
J. M. Murphy
John McBee
William Neal
Leroy K. Padgett
H. J. Pettit
Jordan Pressley
E. P. Price
Burton Quinton
Sanford V. Ray
Robert R. Reed
J. H. Roper
William Seay
Michael R. Shadwick
Henry R. Simmons
P. R. Simmons

William A. Simmons
D. M. Sosebee
D. N. Sosebee
H. J. Sosebee
A. J. Stancell
William Swafford
J. S. Tabereaux
E. S. Tapp
A. B. Taylor
James M. Taylor
Joseph H. Taylor
J. A. Taylor
Edward Townsend
George H. Turner
W. P. Uldrix
A. J. Waters
M. H. West
John W. Wetherby
C. B. Wilbanks
W. H. Wilbanks
Zachariah T. Wood
Russell G. Woodall
Alfred W. Worley
Ambrose Worley
J. L. Worley
J. W. Worley
P. E. Worley

COMPANY L, 36th REGIMENT
GEORGIA VOLUNTEER INFANTRY
(With Army of Tennessee)

Officers:

Thomas Williams, Captain
D. S. McCrary, 1st Lieut.

J. W. Brown, 2d Lieut.
James H. Williams; Jr. 2d Lieut.

Privates:

Ransom Bennett
Rankin Brown
James E. Burch

J. R. Chasteen
Jacob Childers
Reuben C. Childers

J. A. Collins
Thomas Craig
Pearson E. Fields

Jasper Fowler
William S. Franklin
Ansel Godfrey
James C. Godfrey
Lewellen Godfrey
N. Godfrey
James A. Griffith
J. Guyton
Sylvanus Hambrick
Ira A. Harris
William K. Hopkins
Ryan E. Jackson
Larkin Jones
W. R. Jones
Henry D. Keater
James A. Killian
W. A. King
John M. Long

William A. Long
Alex P. Martin
Elijah Morrison
Sylvanus Moss
Benson J. Mullinax
James Mullinax
Robert Mullinax
W. H. McClure
John McEntire
Augustus B. Morrell
David Oaks
John Pack
J. L. Roach
C. B. Roe
John W. Roe
William R. Roe
Elisha Roper

Solomon D. Roper
J. N. Smith
A. J. Stephens
James A. Stephens
John W. Stephens
D. L. Stewart
William A. Stewart
R. B. Stripling
Elisha P. Thomas
Samuel Thomas
W. J. Thomas
David Wallis
M. V. Watts
R. B. Wilkins
Richard S. Williams
Levi Yancey
Spencer B. Yancey

COMPANY C, 43d REGIMENT
GEORGIA VOLUNTEER INFANTRY
"Pickens Volunteers"

Officers:

Benjamin F. Hanie, Captain
Philip R. Simmons, 1st Lieut.
Newton C. McClain, 2d Lieut.
Robert L. Simmons, 2d Lieut.
John M. (or J. R.) Hanie; Jr.
    2d Lieut.
William Arthurs; Jr. 2d Lieut.
Thomas G. Stearns; Jr. 2d Lieut.
Jabez B. Morris, 1st Sgt.

John D. Dorsey, 2d Sgt.
Chessley D. Corbin, 3d Sgt.
Mordecai F. West, 4th Sgt.
Francis P. Long, 5th Sgt.
Leonidas V. McArthur, 1st Corp.
William B. Nations, 1st Corp.
W. B. Allred, 2d Corp.
Harrison Whitfield, 3d Corp.
Nathaniel Ward, 4th Corp.

Privates:

John C. Allred
R. E. Allen
William J. Allen
Mark Arnold
James D. Ausburn

Robert F. Ausburn
William K. Austin
Wm. M. Blackburn
David Boling
Alvin D. Brady

Benjamin F. Brady
Lewis Brady
Thomas Bray
E. R. Brock
Joe Brock

J. R. Brock
Benjamin P. Brown
Hugh M. Brown
James M. Browning
Robert J. Brown
William P. Brown
James C. Brown
James M. Brown
Jabe Burch
Alfred J. Cash
Clark M. Cash
Dillard H. Cash
Preston C. Cash
Rayford A. Cash
Thomas D. Caswell
William H. Carl
Stephen D. Caudell
B. F. Caudell
James H. Caudell
William M. Caudell
Peter P. Chapman
James M. Chitwood
Richard Chitwood
William Chitwood
James M. Cochran
John S. H. Coker
B. Coker
Marion R. Coker
John M. Coker
J. C. Cotton
R. C. Crump
J. T. Darian
A. J. Davidson
G. M. Davis
William M. Davis
Robert A. Dill
Wilmot Fagans
Thomas T. Gaswell
Pressley Gault

Jesse J. Gunn
Berry Hambrick
Floyd Hambrick
R. C. Hardy
John H. Higgins
Thomas F. Hill
Thomas T. Hipps
L. B. Hardy
William D. Hooper
Z. L. House
Almond Hulsey
Charles H. Lane
John Lane
William Lane
J. A. Lawrence
Jackson Lewellen
John Lewellen
James G. Loftis
M. A. Loftus
Edward Lowry
F. A. Mabry
Greene S. Martin
Truman W. Martin
W. L. Martin
John L. Meeks
Burton Meeler
Matthew Meeler
B. F. Miller
James M. Miller
Robert F. Miller
Thomas A. Mize
Hampton B. Morris
James H. Morris
McKinney A. Morris
John C. Moss
Thomas J. Motes
Alexander Murray
James D. Murray
James F. Murray

James L. Murray
William F. Murray
W. B. Nations
William J. Nunnally
James W. Parker
Augustus A. Porter
Lewis A. Pritchett
Empson Pruett
Charles T. Ragsdale
O. S. Ragsdale
George W. Ramsey
John T. Richards
Martin Sanders
Moses H. Sanders
S. Savage
Kimsey Segars
Seth S. Segars
Thomas Segars
Taylor Savage
W. A. Segars
Francis M. Sewell
Caleb C. Smith
Henry J. Smith
John Smith
William Smith
W. J. Sloan
Robert Stow
Robert P. Varner
Henry S. M. Wade
Daniel C. Ward
James Ward
Levi Ward
Joshua White
Berry Whitfield
Harrison Whitfield
William Whitfield
John H. Willis
Jasper Wills

COMPANY L, 43d REGIMENT
GEORGIA VOLUNTEER INFANTRY
(With Army of Tennessee)

Officers:

Merrick H. West, Captain	Eber Wofford, 4th Sgt.
Leander A. Simmons, 1st Lieut.	William N. Swafford, 5th Sgt.
Hezekiah M. Parris, 2d Lieut.	Thomas M. Cook, 1st Corp.
Richard L. Simmons; Jr. 2d Lt.	John Reece, 2d Corp.
Jacob Wofford, 1st Sgt.	Sam Tatum, 3d Corp.
Henry R. Wofford, 2d Sgt.	Joseph Hazelwood, 4th Corp.
Augustus C. Taylor, 3d Sgt.	

Privates:

Silas Akens	James P. Hammett	John M. Poole
John N. J. Anderson	J. R. Hazelwood	William S. Poole
John C. Bradley	M. V. Hollingshead	Martin Priest
Lucius C. Bradley	Ben F. Holtzclaw	Warren M. Reese
Rufus C. Bradley	James F. Johnson	William M. Reese
William Calhoun	Charles Jones	John Rice
Thomas M. Cline	William Jordan	William Reece
Jasper Corbin	William Kennedy	Zaddock G. Rogers
James Crane	Lewis Calvin King	Allen Sawyer
William Crane	James W. Ledford	Franklin S. Simmons
John B. Dearing	Dred Ledford	Andrew J. Sosebee
William Davis	Leonard L. McArthur	James L. Sosebee
John Denny Dorsey	Leonidas V. McArthur	Jeremiah Sosebee
James H. Evans	James C. Manley	John W. Sosebee, Jr.
Marcus Evans	Franklin J. Morrison	John W. Sosebee, Sr.
Van Buren Gibbs	Francis M. Mears	Joseph W. Sosebee
John P. Hales	Griffin Mullins	Allen Stanfield
Reeves Hales	Martin Parris	Henry Suttles
Warren Hales	Joseph Paul	Miles Swafford
William Hales	Jasper Pool	

COMPANY I, CHEROKEE LEGION
GEORGIA VOLUNTEER INFANTRY
"Pickens Raid Repellers"

Officers:

James Bruce, Captain	C. M. McClure, 1st Lieut.

Joseph Williams, 2d Lieut.
William Forrester, 2d Lieut.
E. P. Watson, 1st Sgt.
Eli C. Coffey, 2d Sgt.
William K. West, 3d Sgt.
L. H. Bohannon, 4th Sgt.

Martin Collins, 5th Sgt.
J. W. Freeman, 1st Corp.
Thomas Dean, 2d Corp.
Hiram Reid, 3d Corp.
Joseph Simmons, 4th Corp.

Privates:

M. V. Bruce
J. N. Barron
J. K. Brown
J. C. Bailey
Virgil Bailey
T. J. Byron
A. Brooks
T. L. Bryan
James Childers
Leander Childers
Wiley Carver
Ransom Collins
James Clarke
S. A. Cox
James Craig
W. R. Carbin
J. M. Ducket
James Eaton
George Evans
G. D. S. Green
Benjamin Goss
J. M. Goode
Harrison Gipson
A. J. Glenn
W. M. Griffith
T. J. Honea

Henry Honea
John B. Hopson
Theo. Holcombe
Thomas B. Hudlaw
Alpheus Hice
John L. Hanie
Thomas Hanie
George Joins
James Kell
Abel Kaylor
John L. Keeter
Henry Kelly
David Kaylor
L. C. Levelty
L. W. Larmon
Gabriel Moss, Sr.
Gabriel Moss, Jr.
Berry H. Martin
John F. McElroy
Alfred McCollum
Richard McFarland
J. H. McFarland
Abel Medlin
Leroy McCrary
J. E. T. Mullineane
Thomas Nicholson

B. P. Padgett
John H. Paxton
John Pendley
T. T. Pendley
A. J. Pierce
Robert Roland
James Roe
M. B. Rutledge
James Sharyer
James R. Smith
E. C. Smith
J. M. Stewart
Andrew Steele
Joseph Simmons
Lewis Thompson
John W. Tatem
Joseph Thomas
D. S. Wilson
Hezekiah Williams
James West
H. Wilkins
Obediah Yancey
Samuel Yancey
Samuel Young

COMPANY I, 8th REGIMENT
3d BRIGADE, 1st DIVISION OF GEORGIA STATE TROOPS
"Captain Day's Company"

Officers:

William T. Day, Captain

Bayles Bruce, Captain

Wm. D. Cunningham, 1st Lieut.
Lemuel J. Allred, 2d Lieut.
Eli C. Coffey, 3d Lieut.
John W. Heath, 1st Sgt.
Seaborn Hill, 2d Sgt.
Michel Moreland, 3d Sgt.

Leander H. Price, 4th Sgt.
Patterson H. Lyon, 5th Sgt.
S. A. Darnal, 1st Corp.
George W. Byers, 2d Corp.
Robert F. Wigington, 3d Corp.
Merret B. Mealer, 4th Corp.

Privates:

John C. Bradley
Virgil Bradley
Martin Coffy
Toliver M. Carr
John L. Chapman
George W. Clark
Silas Cantrell
John G. Coffey
William Davis
Jason Evans
William L. Fields
Thomas J. Fields
Jonathan Fann
Ansel Godfrey
William L. Gravett
Reuben Gravett
Henry S. Goss

Joseph J. Goode
Abram Goode
Mitchell Goode
Robert Honea
John M. Hall
William A. Joice
Elijah A. Joice
Andrew C. Kuykendall
George W. Lindsey
Philip M. Lenning
Henry A. Lankford
Jackson A. Lansdown
James McMahan
Wm. H. Nicholson
Isaac B. Nicholson
John Oakes
James O. Phillips

John Pendley
Hezekiah M. Parris
George W. Ponder
Robert Rowland
John Rice
Ephriam T. Riddle
Starling Ray
Allen D. Smith
Charles H. Sawyers
Miles Swafford
Hugh L. Thompson
Martin V. Teems
William Varner
Warren Wiginton
Joseph D. Walker
Allen Wright
Joshua Watkins

On the official muster roll of this company is shown its pay roll from December 5, 1861, to January 1, 1862, at Camp Jackson, as follows:

Pay _____$ 932.62
Clothing _____ 480.00

Amount _____$1,412.62

It is also explained here that the regiment including "Captain Day's Company" was "commanded by Lieutenant-Colonel J. S. Fain, called into the service of the state of Georgia, under the provisions of an act of the legislature passed December 18, 1860, by Joseph E. Brown, governor of Georgia, from the 5th day of December, 1861, date of this muster, for the term of six months, unless sooner discharged."

MUSTER ROLL OF PICKENS COUNTY MILITIA
As of March 4, 1862

T. A. Cantrel, Capt.
R. L. Henderson
C. H. Taylor
John King
James George
M. Forester
Daniel Turner
James McCutchen
Jasper Carr
S. C. Stoner
Isaac Shelton
Thomas Taylor
James Turner
John Turner
John Parker
J. V. S. Stoner
Jeremiah Holcomb
Benjamin Holbert
R. G. Griffith
C. J. Cornelison
Augustus Taylor
Thomas K. Cook
Thomas H. Cook
R. V. Cook
T. P. Grover
Henry Ingram
John M. Johnson
D. R. Reese
James B. Mosely
J. P. Arwood
John West
W. B. Chambers
W. B. McHan
Floid Yeancy
S. Silvey
B. F. Lewis
S. B. Yeancy

Mansel Friendley
J. J. Dean
Jasper Fowler
Z. G. Roggers
James Heath
Mariab Spears
P. E. Jackson
Noah Clark
William Temples
Henry Tabley
William Anderson
R. B. Fulton
Nathan Cobb
Levi Yeancy
Ransom Bennett
James Killian
D. S. McCrary
T. L. Johnson
John P. Murphy
William Collins
J. J. Bradley
K. Burgan
John Pack
P. Fields
James Adair
John Roe
F. M. Forester
Isaac Yong
Sam Yong
Humphrey Chadwick
William Parker
J. L. Newman
Harrison Pendley
Joseph Wilkins
William Gravits
J. J. Cowart
Andrew Cowart

Reuben Fields
Nathan Sherley
William Arthur
Robert Eubanks
Harvy Pendley
Louis Holtsclaw
Leander Neal
Martin Wilkens
S. H. Abbett, Captain
A. L. Padgett
A. P. Padgett
J. M. Haney
F. M. Blackwell
R. J. Boling
B. Q. Disharoon
G. J. Jackson
C. C. Newman
R. T. Davis
J. Herndon
W. R. Barnett
J. F. McElroy
W. P. Dobson
Robert Ivins
B. Padgett
Green Moss
N. Bradley
James H. Williams
James Eaton
George Vaughn
Rubin Childers
Jacob Childers
Daniel Steward
Daniel Johnson
Calvin Jones
Henry Kelly
J. E. Burck
Martica West

D. S. Wilson
Elija Roper
Thomas Deen
Thomas Bryan
Ahaz Gibson
William C. Atherton
A. J. Carrol
John Parper
Green Dover
Henry Roach
Wilson McMullin
David Oaks
Marion Stokes
John Tatum
Marvin Silvers
G. Willis
Samuel Willson
Monroe Dover
Jack Hensley
G. Silver
L. A. Cantrel
William B. Jones
Lewis Bohannon
R. S. Williams
James Childers
Martin Collins
Baylis Thompson
T. J. Rutledge
R. Cansbery
James Mullinax
J. A. Harris
C. L. Carlin
Samuel Thomas
Elsha Benett
Thomas Balin
Matison Bruce
S. P. Bohannon
Vedo Bohannon
James A. Craig

Leander Childers
A. J. Corbin
C. D. Corbin
James Cobb
Joseph Chastain
Thomas Craig
Asa Dinkins
John Evans
Edward Clark
John Eddelman
William Forester
E. W. Forester
Nathan Fendley
Booker Gravly
D. W. Dobbs
T. J. Eubanks
W. H. Gordon
R. H. Gordon
Z. C. Glascow
L. H. Hide
William Hale
Waran Hale
Thomas Hudlow
John Haad
Miles Jackson
Silas Nichalson
J. A. McCutchen
E. O. Mann
R. B. McCutchen
C. P. Pence
William Partan
W. J. Padgett
William Berry
Pinkney Lambert
Johnathan Rowland
J. H. Reaves
Jeremiah Sosebee
J. W. Sosebee
R. L. Simmons

G. R. Smith
W. C. Thompson
Joseph Varner
Joseph Wofford
Samuel Waldrop
John P. Wofford
J. McMann
William Swafferd
Thomas Cowart
S. V. Gibbs
Thomas T. Gordon
Hiram Harris
J. A. Graham
Thomas Champion
R. D. McGoah
Elish Briant
G. W. McGoah
B. R. McGoah
J. L. Pendley
F. M. Godfrey
W. B. Pendley
Francis Welchel
Thomas Howell
George Wiginton
Thomas Pinion
Hiram Cain
William Heays
Thomas Heays
T. F. T. Wadkins
Joseph Eubanks
James Pendley
John Taylor
Butler Jones
John Sea
L. V. McArthur
Ben Evans
John G. Coffe
Michael Goode
W. C. Ammons

R. Anderson
Ealey Adams
B. F. Akins
L. C. Bradley
R. C. Bradley
James Bailey
William Carlwell
John Howard
Enice Collett
Van Tatum
William M. Swofford
G. G. Sims
Joel Blackwell
William Blackwell
G. W. Blackwell
V. H. Monroe
G. N. Padgett
G. W. Elrod
G. B. Rackley
John Ridens
D. Cantrell
J. Thompson
Joseph G. King
William T. King
W. T. Fitzsimmons
J. B. Morris, Captain
G. T. Green
William Crow
Reuben Hopkins
Joel Keeter
Pinkney Morris
Cuthbert Wilbanks
Rufus F. McKinny
Thomas Pinion
Ezekiel Patterson
Ed. Crow
John D. Nelson
John Bishop
John Brooks

Daniel Taylor
Ed. Patterson
Joseph Morris
Thomas Blackwell
Samuel Brown
John Stokes, Jr.
Henry Ledford
Wiley Carver
Wilky McHan
Robert H. Robarts
John N. Ferguson
Alfred Moor
Joseph Griffin
J. M. Evans
E. A. Herendon
L. Ferguson
N. S. Boseman
Allen Sawyer
J. C. Manley
William Jordan
Franklin More
William Bearden
Terry Fitzsimmons
William McHan
Franklin Johnson
G. W. Brown
Gus Cantrell
William Woods
Absolem Presley
John Tally
Absolem Loveless
William Davis
John Darnel, Capt.
H. T. Fitts, 1st Lt.
S. B. Cowart, 2d Lt.
Asa Holcombe
M. V. Kuykendal
J. N. Whitemore
Andrew Goode

B. B. Brooks
Henry Quinton
Stephen Kelley
Wash Kelly
Daniel Beachum
James McDanel
C. W. Hames
George Stephens
Solomon Smith
Edward Smith
James Chastain
David Chastain
Dudley Mulky
William Mulky
Abrieham Mulky
Jesse Wilkey
Lawson Baker
Rubin Jackson
P. G. Moss
John Moss
Isaac Guyton
Abriham Guyton
Henry Blaylock
Edward Wilkey
Thomas Haley
Joel Haley
David Anderson
Solomon Anderson
Larkin Jones
M. L. Forester
James Pack
Moses Pharr
Silvanas Moss
Wade H. Moss
Levi Speerman
John Stegal
Russell Howel
Simon Huff
John Boseman

F. Arthur
Newton Darby
Reubin Darby
D. W. Padgett
G. W. Collet
Thomas Wilson
Jackson Buchannon
David Worley
H. J. Partain
James Worley
J. T. Green
R. Biddey
E. C. Disharoon
Francis Heath
P. Herendon
W. Padgett
W. J. Mills
J. M. Goode
James Darby
N. Biddy
W. F. Byers
S. Richards
J. Hodge
James Grogan
Terrel Hall
E. W. Biddy
V. V. Barnett
Thomas Haney
William Price
Carvil Hutchens
Joseph Williams
Robert Childers
William Stone
James W. Darnel
James A. Griffeth
W. R. Griffeth
Wash Balew
Silas Balew
J. W. Balew

A. J. Dooly
J. N. Chastain
E. F. Ivie
George Ivans
Sam Silver
P. I. Gaddis
W. G. Brown
John Pool
James Ferguson
B. H. Holt
L. A. Simmons
John Brock
E. W. Allred
Clark McClain
Graftain Adair
Richard Howell
E. R. Sosebee
Crawford Coward
F. S. Simmons
Thomas R. Bradley
M. D. Beery
Griffin Cason
B. J. Compton
H. C. Hobson
Silvanous Hambrake
Davis Hightower
Henry Haney
F. M. Hightower
J. S. Johnson
Lewis Larmon
Simmons Martain
William Johnson
Stewart McCollum
Alvin McCollum
John McIntire
Gabrel Moss, Jr.
William McNearrin
Clark Godfrey
James Mullinax

Robert Mullinax
W. J. Murphy
William McClews
Solomon Roper
Sidney Stover
Jacob Stover
H. W. Snider
A. F. Smith
Elija Thompson
Lewis Thompson
Jefferson Thomas
Joseph Thomas
Elisha Thomas
H. P. Williams
Hezakiah Wilkins
R. B. Wilkins
Nathan Yeancy
Levalden Godfrey
Silas Akin
James Carr
Mat Carr
Francis Nicholison
Jacob Padgett
Barney McHan
John Reese
John Dykes
R. P. Kelley
William Champeon
Butler Williams
Ephraim Mabry
William Westbrooks
Whit Westbrooks
Deney Dorsey
S. B. Barker
L. S. Cunningham
H. Bailey
Allen Stanfield
Joe Simmons
B. F. Steel

Joseph Shyers
Eli Summer
T. G. Stox
Harvey E. Stearns
Samuel T. Tatum
Samuel Tally
Elias Turner
David Wallis
W. H. Wood
M. V. Hollenshed
Reeves Steele
Samuel Crider
Abner Dunagin
J. D. Dorsey
John B. Dearing
Thomas Godfrey
J. J. Garrett
J. H. Hazlewood
Henry Hazlewood
R. W. Ingram
William W. James
Joseph C. Jones
James Kell
Calvin King
W. A. Long
J. M. Long
F. P. Long
Dred Ledford
Andrew J. Lewis
E. Morrison

G. R. Mullins
S. Mullins
D. L. McArthur
E. M. McArthur
L. L. McArthur
L. H. McArthur
L. J. McArthur
Leroy McCrary
Wesley Mullinax
A. P. Mullinax
William Nicholson
Joseph Paul
William M. Reese
J. W. Reese
N. M. Rea
W. C. Rippy
William Riggins
J. A. Stephens
J. M. Stanfield
William Hopkins
Simeon Hopkins
Henry B. Bozeman
Stephen Crow
William Hazlewood
Reuben Corbin
William Tate
James J. Keeter
William Rea
Eli Richards
Washington Ledford

J. D. Emery
Albert Mosely
W. H. Mann
Robert Mann
Ez. Fownsend
Hosey Hopkins
Jes. Brown
William Tankesly
Jas. Swanson, Capt.
J. A. McGoah
Elbert Coffy
Rolin Kimmons
Thomas Ray
J. W. Bramlett
Marrion Stanfield
Hiram Coward
J. M. Cowart
Joshua Darnel
F. Wadkins
J. E. Burlison
W. B. McGoah
Peter Cantrell
Meredy Neal
Savere Fereby
J. B. Tabreaux
Mad. Strickland
B. M. Cowart
Nelson Ledford
Pet. W. Fitzsimmons
R. C. Allen

The foregoing list represents the membership of the Pickens County militia as it stood on March 4, 1862. This list, or "muster roll," was sent by A. K. Blackwell, colonel of the 107th Regiment of Georgia Militia, to Gen. W. C. Wayne at Milledgeville, on March 5, 1862; and together with his letter to General Wayne is preserved in the records of the state.

The letter is as follows:

"Jasper, Pickens County
"5th of March, 1862

"General W. C. Wayne,

"Milledgeville, Ga.

"Dear Sir:

"Enclosed I send you the list of the Volunteers on the 4th inst., called for and also the names and number of the Militia now under my command.

"I hope I have persued strictly the orders sent me. I am glad our company responded promptly to the call made on her for one hundred men. They are ordered to Camp McDonald. I have also filed the lists required with the Clerk of the Superior Court all right.

"Very respectfully,

"Your obedient servant,

"A. K. Blackwell,

"Col. of the 107 Reg., G. M."

A tabulation at the end of this list gives the total number of militiamen as 572 and the number of volunteers therefrom as 104. There is also the following certificate:

"I, A. K. Blackwell, Colonel of the 107 Regiment, G. M., Pickens County, Georgia, do certify that in obedience to the proclamation of His Excellency Governor Brown of the 11 of February last and the several orders from the Adjutant and Inspector General's Office that I have caused the Militia to assemble as requested and that one hundred and four volunteers responded to the call and that the above list was taken on the day to wit: the 4 day of March, 1862, and I think it is correct. I have also as requested have filed a copy with the Clerk of the Superior Court of Pickens County both of the Militia and Volunteers and have ordered them under the Captain B. F. Hanie to meet on the 10 of March the present month at Jasper and take up the line of march for Camp McDonald. Given under my hand and official signature this 5 of March, 1862.

"A. K. Blackwell, Colonel,

"of the 107 Regiment, G. M.,

"Pickens County, Georgia."

World War Soldiers from Pickens County

ARMY

Officers:

Craig C. Day, 1st Lieut.

John Ralph Henley, Major
  (U. S. regular Army)

William McKinley Hopkins, 2d
  Lieut.

Maynard Mashburn, Field Clerk

Kate McClain, Field Clerk

William Robert Snyder, 1st Lt.

Howard Tate, Captain

Luke Tate, Food Administrator

Charles Edwin Thomas; Jr. 2d
  Lieut.

John Pierce Turk, 1st Lieut.

Privates:

John W. Anderson

Henry C. Asby

Lucius H. Atherton

Dock Atkins

Henry J. Atwood

Mack L. Ballard

John T. Baker

James H. Bates

Charles M. Barrett
  (deceased)

John W. Barrett
  (deceased)

Augustus Bell

John H. Boatfield

Glenn Brady

Carl Bryan

Dallas W. Byess

William O. Cagle

William V. Cagle

Carter Callahan

James L. Cantrell

James W. Cantrell

Robert L. Cantrell

Hobart M. Cape

Waldo E. Cape

Homer Carver (de-
  ceased)

Bunyon Castleberry

John M. Champion

William E. Champion
  (killed in action)

Walter S. Champion

Jacob M. Childers

William A. Childers

John C. Chumley

Carter C. Cloninger

John W. Cloninger

Homer Otis Cochran

Luther D. Cochran

Lewis R. Coffey

Fell Conn

Clyde M. Cornett

Walter C. Corbin

Jesse J. Cordell

William Cowart

Farris Carter Cox

Henry V. Cross

William Crow

Collie E. Daly

John C. Darnell

Walton Davis

Cicero Charles Dearby

Tom B. Dickey

Willie L. Dickson

Charley Disharoon
  (deceased)

Henry Duncan

John F. Eaton

Willie A. Eaton

Robert M. Edge

Robert T. Edwards

Frank Elrod (killed
  in action)

Leon H. Feagin

Dallas H. Fields

Olie Fields

Ardia E. Fitts

Ernest W. Fitts

Henry G. Fitts

James C. Fitts

Seth M. Fitts

Warren I. Fitts

Granville W. Forest

C. W. Foster

Edgar B. Fowler

Dallass C. C. Free

Homer W. Fricks

William H. Gibson

Lester Godfrey

Tom Godfrey

John Milton Gorham

Marion Goss
Benjamin H. Grant
Benjamin H. Grant
(two of same
name)
Glover Green
Thad Green
John Grizzle
William H. Hales
Charley Hammontree
D. C. Hamrick
Horace G. Hamrick
William G. Harper
Elbert L. Hawkins
John I. M. Hefner
Charles O. Hitt
Ed Holder
William McKinley
Hopkins
Thomas V. Hughes
Major T. Humphrey
Albert W. Hutton
William E. Ingram
William H. Inman
Harry Jackson
Lee Jackson
Paul Jackson
Roscoe W. Jackson
William E. Jackson
Buman Hill Jarrard
Charles O. Johnson
Robert L. Jones
Adolphus P. Jordan
Paul Kennemur
James Kent
Fred King
James Carson King
Ralph B. King
Benj. Kuykendall
Fred H. Lamine

James E. Lenning
Charles R. Long
John W. Long
Henry T. McArthur
Joseph T. McArthur
William V. McBee
(deceased)
Veach M. McPherson
Baker S. McCall
Lawrence McCan
George A. McGaha
Carter McHan
Joseph McHan
John C. McIntire
Arie McPherson
Willie R. Martin
David Henry Merrick
Homer Lee Minter
(deceased)
Loy Montgomery
Arnold M. Morris
Arthur H. Morris
Thomas G. Morris
Claude Moss (killed
in action)
Victor Moss
James A. Mowell
John W. Mullinax
Willie T. Mullinax
Elford A. Mullins
Grover C. Nelson
David E. Nix
W. P. Nix
Andrew H. Padgett
Ernest B. Padgett
Noel T. Padgett
Ollie Homer Padgett
Homer Parker
James Parker
Pearl B. Parker

Carter Patrick
Jeff Patrick
Sam P. L. Pendley
Charles Pendley
(deceased)
Sherman R. Priest
Paul Prather
James F. Pruitt
Silvey L. Ray
James A. Richards
William E. Richards
James E. Roach
James Lester Roberts
Arthur Roland
(killed in action)
Willie H. Scudder
William Wesley Seay
Daniel Simmons
Howell C. Simmons
George B. Sorrels
Silas Charles Stegall
Hillya G. Stokes
Willie Strickland
Hobert M. Tabereaux
Yeargan T. Tarpley
Charles C. Tatum
Joe Tatum (de-
ceased)
William L. Tatum
Enzlo L. Teem
William L. Teem
Joseph Teague (de-
ceased)
Joe C. Teems
Everett Thomas
William D. Tuck
Chesley Vincent
Carter T. Ward
Howard Washington
Lewis Washington

Julian W. Watkins   Walton C. Whitfield   Samuel Wooten
Alison P. West   John W. Wiginton   Baxter Worley
Arthur C. Wheeler   Henry J. Wilson   Charles M. Young
James G. Whitfield   Merritt R. Wofford

NAVY

Loron Clifford Bearden

John Hollman Bell

Clyde Hurman Brown

John Erman Cagle

Ollie Sherman Clinton Cagle

Sherman Clark Cagle

Thomas Hobson Cantrelle

Walter Jacob Childers

Forrest Carter Tate Conner

William Jennings Bryan Conner

Benjamin Cowart

Columbus Paul Dilbeck

Paul Crawford Fitts

Theodore Gailey

Allen Walker Grant

James David Hammontree

Bryon Clay Hamrick

Martin Quillian Hamrick

Mercer Jesse Harbin

Lolan Heath

Joseph Lamual Holbert

Robert Thurston Hopkins

Patrick Claiborne Keeter

Sanford Clay McClain

Leon McWhorter

Sherman Lee Morris

Cleveland Montgomery Morrison

Gordon Mosley

Emmett Howard Moss

James Fonsy Parker

William Wesley Seay

Jasper Leander Shirley

George Hubert Stancil

Homer Stanfield

William Stanfield

James Brady Turner

Chapter V ★ ★ ★ ★
FIFTY YEARS AGO
IN PICKENS

•

(Author's Note: The sketches which appear in this chapter present the "human side" of an interesting period in the history of Pickens County—that of the late 'eighties and 'nineties. They have been written for this book by Judge William Alonzo Covington, now of Meigs, Ga., but a native of Cherokee County, and, for several years of his early life, a resident of Pickens. Judge Covington tells here, in distinctive and interesting style, of some of his experiences and impressions in Pickens County fifty years ago.)

----

by W. A. COVINGTON

I SPENT six months in Jasper, in the fall of 1884 and the first part of 1885, setting type and printer's-deviling on *The Mountain Boys*, the first newspaper published in Pickens County; and in the years 1889, 1890, and 1891 I was bookkeeper for the Atherton brothers at their cotton factory three miles south of Jasper.

During the time I was in Pickens I had many contacts with the people of the county, especially with the farmers who did business with the Factory; and of them I carry none but pleasant memories. The people were eminently moral and well-behaved; the men were honest, and there was never a word of "talk" about any of the women of my acquaintance. Three-fourths of the adult population were church members. I do not believe there was a community that excelled them in the world; anyhow, I liked them, and so it is a pleasure to record their merits.

It is pleasant, also, to know that such of my acquaintances there as yet survive still bear a kindly feeling toward me. When I was a stranger they took me into full confidence in their homes; and having no family, I came in handy in going for the doctor and in "setting up" with the sick. They were a loving and a lovable people.

Hospitality was one of the traits of those people that stands out in my mind. There was practically no hard poverty among the farmers, or in fact anywhere in the county. But even in the poorest homes, a chance guest was always welcome—"if you can put up with our fare." In some cases it might require a good bit of polite "mannering" to get all hands to bed, and out, with nobody seen *deshabille*; but it had been done thousands of times, and was done numbers of times when I was present. Sherstone, whose classic runs:

> Whoe'er hath traveled life's weary rounds,
>   Where'er his travels may have been,
> May sigh to think he still has found
>   His warmest welcome at an inn,

had—poor man—never stayed all night with a Pickens County farmer. No inn I ever saw furnished the genuine hospitality or the sure-enough feather ticks of an old-time Pickens farm-home.

Health conditions seemed good in Pickens. The men and women were strong-looking and there were plenty of children playing in the average yard. Pretty girls were so plentiful that it was confusing to the boys in their sparking. It was too hard to pick a steady sweetheart. I have in mind, yet, more than one perfect specimen of female beauty raised on the farms—partly due to the climate, I think.

Many a time I have been reminded of some good friend of the old days in Pickens; and it would not be hard for me to set down a list of them so long that you might not read it. A few will have to do. There were Robert Hopkins, a dear young fellow, and his bachelor brother, Bill; Richard Cox and his good wife and children; Steve King, at whose house I once attended a country dance where I beat the straws for the fiddler and where a Mr. Trammel, son of Georgia's first railroad commissioner, "patted" to the music; W. B. Mc-Creary and his brilliant boy Andrew; Frank Collins and his hospitable family, with whom I once spent the night; A. W. Johnson and his brother; John Allred and his two young sons and their pretty wives, daughters of Mr. Bearden at Mineral Springs; Miss Kate Davis, a maiden lady, and her pretty niece; George Owens and his fine family; old Dick Cook, a picturesque character; William Thompson and his brother Lewis, big cotton-producers of near Jerusalem; William Timmons, a substantial farmer near Bethany; John, James and Robin Henderson, sons of a widowed mother who was spry and active at seventy; Gabe Martin, a "wit to the manor born"; Robert Lee Allred; the Cagles over at Cagle's Mill and old man Buck Dowda; Jim Atherton, one-time clerk of the superior court and later in the legislature; Mrs. Maggie Barrett, my school-teacher in 1883; and Mr. and Mrs. John Henderson and their daughter Janie, a family that set a high-water mark in entertaining the stranger—or the friend—within their gates.

One of the prominent families of Pickens was the Allreds. There were three brothers, Elias, John, and Lemuel J., who removed to Pickens some time in the 'forties from Habersham County. In 1889-91 Elias was a man of independent means and a Baptist minister. John Allred was a Baptist layman, a substantial farmer, and a United States commissioner, living at Mineral Springs. I had no personal acquaintance with either of these two, but I formed a close friendship with Lemuel J. Allred, and although he was seventy-five and I was about twenty, we visited each other frequently.

Lemuel J. Allred represented Cherokee County in the legislature from 1851 to 1854, while that county still contained part of Pickens. His opponent in the first election was James Harbin, of Waleska, a great-uncle of mine. Uncle Jim had told me before I met Mr. Allred that it was a close race, Allred's majority being only four votes which finally developed in the "Dug Road" District (now in Pickens), where Allred had served gingerbread and apple-cider at the polls.

Mr. Allred was defeated for his third term, but on the day that his successful opponent left Canton for his legislative duties at Milledgeville, Mr. Allred appeared to go down with him. Gov. Joseph E. Brown had appointed him to the position of executive secretary, a position he held to the end of Brown's administration at the close of the Civil War.

From 1872 to his death, Mr. Allred was doorkeeper of the Georgia senate. He was probably the best-posted man in Georgia as to the public men in the state from 1853 to 1893, about which latter date he died. I heard a great many fascinating tales from his lips; it is a great pity that he did not keep a diary.

The Allreds were descended from French Huguenots and the name, I understand, was originally "De Alred." I knew Brantley Allred, a cousin of Lemuel J. He was the father of three mighty pretty girls—Palestine, Adora, and Adina, the first of whom still survives and is the wife of one of the county's fine citizens, a Mr. Cagle.

A history of Pickens County would be incomplete without

some attention to the Rev. William Cagle. Although uncultured, he was one of Nature's noblemen.

One Sunday my employer, William C. Atherton, and his family attended services at Salem Baptist Church, southwest of Jasper; and they brought home to dinner the preacher of the day, Rev. William Cagle. Mr. Cagle had preached near my home in Cherokee when I was a child, and, as I could understand it, was almost as much against the Methodists as against the devil. This day I saw him for the first time; and I watched and listened to him narrowly. He was a strapping, handsome man, and full of vitality. Of course, since he was the guest of Methodists, all controversial subjects were avoided; but I recall one of the incidents he told about. His mother, he said, had become seriously ill on one occasion, and "I was sent for to go to see her." She talked to him a while about family matters; then she said, "Son, you are a preacher now, and before you go, I want you to make me one promise." "I asked her what it was," Mr. Cagle told us, "and she said, 'Never by word or deed bring reproach on the cause of Christ.' I took her by the hand and I said, 'Mom'—we always called her that—'Mom, I'll never do it; I'll die first.' "

Well, it was very simple and impressive to hear, and when next year the Rev. William was a candidate for the legislature, I eased in a vote for him. It was voting for a man who was both a Republican and a Baptist—an "awful mixtry," as the old woman said of her liquor, but I downed it.

Mr. Cagle was elected and made a creditable representative. He later moved to Oklahoma, but his family continued to be well represented in Pickens. Indeed, this is a good place to make mention of the fact that the clan Cagle has been for nearly a hundred years prominent in Pickens and the upper part of Cherokee. And I, at least, never heard a word against one of them. They were and are a God-fearing folk and they kept His commandment to "multiply the face of the earth."

Churches that I remember from the old days in Pickens were Salem Baptist, two miles to the right of the Mineral Springs road and four miles southwest of Jasper; Refuge, three miles south of Jasper on the old road to Canton; Bethany, eight miles south of Jasper on the Waleska road; and Jerusalem, over south of Ludville, toward Salacoa. All these were Missionary Baptist churches. I recall two Methodist churches at Ludville—one Northern and one Southern. And, of course, there were a Baptist church and a Methodist church at Jasper.

In the 'eighties, most of the revival preaching in the country districts was done by Rev. William Cagle and Rev. Thad Pickett. Both knew how to get results, and both were natural orators. I bear in mind a "protracted meeting" at Refuge Church once, that was not going very well. "Bill" Cagle passed along, one night, going to Jasper. He climbed off his mule, went inside, and preached. Soon the "mourners" were going up to the front in droves, and shouting as they went. His mission accomplished, Cagle got back up on his mule and rode on.

One Sunday afternoon—and it was a hot one—I sat at an outdoor meeting on a bench with no back to it, listening to the Rev. Thad Pickett preach a sermon lasting over two hours. He "hilt" me right through it.

A lot of the settlers of Pickens were descended from the Scotch Highlanders who left the land of their birth after the suppression of their klans by the English monarchy, following the unsuccessful uprising of 1745 led by the "Young Pretender" Stewart. Occasionally one of the Pickens yeomanry of 1889-91 would drop out an expression from Walter Scott's novels. I recall one day relating to an aged, toothless man some local incident of a somewhat tragic nature, whereupon he exclaimed, through his nose and with all the naturalness in the world, "Good lack-a-day!" It was the only time I ever heard that expression so used.

The predominantly Anglo-Saxon origin of the people who settled Pickens has always been evident in the independent spirit of those settlers' descendants. Illustrating this spirit was the popular sentiment of the 'eighties against the revenue tax on distilling, and the popular contempt for "informers" which gave rise to the "Honest Man's Friend and Protector" —a phenomenon mentioned, I believe, elsewhere in this book.

Now, at the time I knew the county, while drinking was by no means uncommon, it was on the decrease, the common sense of the country people recognizing that liquor was habit-forming stuff; that it made men wild, and shortened their lives. The women and girls did not drink at all; and I do not think they ever did. But during the time that Jasper was a sort of headquarters, back in the 'eighties, for the suppression of illicit distilling, with some ten or twelve "deputy marshals" and "deputy collectors" in the town drawing good pay and faring sumptuously, I know that the people generally had little sympathy with the officers and the statute they represented; they felt it difficult to respect a law that licensed a thing to be done for a cash consideration and then put you in jail if you did that thing without paying.

The independent spirit that came down from the pioneers of Pickens was not confined to the men of the county. I remember once hearing a story whose heroine was the wife of Clark McClain. Mr. McClain was the oldest man in Jasper when I lived there; a "forty-niner" who had made his stake, and a Confederate veteran. He was a remarkable character, but his wife was no less remarkable. The story went that when Ben McCollum of Cherokee was raiding Pickens with his bushwhackers, he came to the house of Mrs. McClain while her husband was in Lee's army. She had a little pony hid in the smokehouse, and when it whickered a welcome to the horses of the band, McCollum promptly put a bridle on it. At that point, out came Mrs. McClain, axe in hand, offering to split McCollum's head if he did not put the pony back. He put the pony back. One loves the woman yet.

Pickens has always been a "politically-minded" county; from the earliest days its citizens seem to have been uncommonly interested in candidates, platforms, and elections. And since, as I understand it, this Southern county has never gone Democratic in any presidential election except the last one, it is reasonable to infer that the citizens of Pickens have not at all times lived together in complete political love and harmony. But some of the elections that took place during my stay in the county must have been high points in the way of excitement, and among these elections I think the local Cleveland-Blaine contest in 1884 impressed me most.

It was in October of 1884 that I ran away from home—I lived near Waleska—and went to Jasper to become a printer's devil on Pickens County's first newspaper, *The Mountain Boys*. T. B. Heard, the first editor of that paper, had been visiting his people in Waleska and I went back with him, riding double with him on a saddle-horse.

The whole country was in the throes of the Cleveland-Blaine presidential race, and Pickens, never averse to a row and especially a political row, was talking of nothing else. Walter Simmons had written a three-column editorial for *The Mountain Boys* in the last issue before I got there. It was the hottest thing the people had ever read dealing with Blaine's public record, and when one commenced to read it there was no stopping till the end—except to cuss, if you were a Republican. Mr. Simmons was, incidentally, a young grandson of James Simmons, one of the six protesting members of the Secession Convention.

The Simmons article raised a great howl from the Republicans, and especially from the dozen or so federal revenue agents in Jasper, some of whom cursed freely about it. However, there was no personal violence—possibly because Simmons was gone and the editor was a cripple.

Blaine carried the county by forty majority. The next morning I got with Isaac Grant, the depot agent, and we went up to the depot for news on the national returns. When Grant found out who had won, he jumped as high as he could (he was from South Carolina), and yelled, "Boys, Cleveland has carried the solid South, New York, New Jersey, Connecticut, and Indiana!" And more than once on his race back to town, Grant would stop and dance a jig in the snow.

There had been a lot of money staked by the "revenue crowd" on Blaine, at nice odds, and most of it had been taken by Jack Lovelady, a young business man of Jasper. He made a killing.

The final result of the election, however, was in suspense for some days, depending on the official count of New York state. Finally it was settled, Cleveland carrying New York by a plurality of less than 1,100. That night, the Jasper Democrats pulled off a celebration. Two anvils were secured, and a lot of gunpowder. The hole in one of the anvils was filled with powder and a trail of powder-grains was arranged leading to one side; then the other anvil was laid on top of the loaded one. When everything was ready, Clark McClain, a veteran of Lee's army, applied the spark from the burning end of a long pole. The result was a detonation calculated to wake the dead; the sound of it reechoed from the string of mountains on the east.

This was done time after time that night. During his work, "Old Clark" paused once to say, "Boys, they are having this joyful noise away over at Sharp Top Mountain, where there's neither God nor law."

The celebrants also amused themselves by tearing up the hat of every Republican in sight; but Republicans, for that one night, were scarce in Jasper.

Chapter VI ★ ★ ★ ★ ★
TOWNS AND INDUSTRY

●

Pickens County's economic picture includes the industrial and commercial activities carried on in her three incorporated towns—Jasper, Talking Rock, and Nelson—and two towns that are unincorporated—Tate and Marble Hill. In the three last-named places are centered the activities of The Georgia Marble Company, one of the state's leading industrial concerns; and all five towns, while comparatively small, are favorably located to serve prosperous farming sections.

A short description of each of these places follows.

Towns of the County

Jasper, the county seat of Pickens, is one of the most beautifully located towns anywhere to be found and is a fitting namesake for the gallant soldier whose name it bears. It looks out upon the mountains and is supported by the valleys of Pickens.

As already related, Jasper came into being as a town after a spirited election held during the early days of the county on the question of where to locate the county seat. The present site winning over one farther to the west, Jasper was laid out as a town and it soon acquired a sizable population. It was incorporated in 1857.

Jasper is now the principal trading center of Pickens County, besides serving as its center for legal and official matters. It supports thriving Chevrolet and Ford agencies;

and is the distributing point for Standard Oil and Texas Company products for this section of the state. It also has drug stores and general stores which furnish splendid accommodation and service. The Georgia Power Company maintains an office and salesroom here, through which its service and general business in the county are carried on. There are two industrial enterprises: a lumber mill which sells its finished product, and a marble plant which finishes the stone and deals in monuments. There is also a harness and shoe shop started many years ago by the Groovers, which still does a very good business and is now owned and operated by Mr. Lee Prather, who served his apprenticeship under the former owners.

Jasper has one of the most up-to-date public schoolhouses in the section and maintains an excellent high school, the official high school of Pickens County. The building is of brick construction and is well-equipped throughout.

Nelson. As the marble industry developed in the county, the need for another finishing plant caused The Georgia Marble Company to purchase the property of John Nelson, located on the railroad near the Cherokee County line, for this purpose; and the town that sprang up there logically took the former owner's name. Mr. Nelson was a farmer and also a gunsmith of considerable note, and today there are many Nelson rifles throughout this section which are highly prized by their owners.

Since the beginning of the marble industry at Nelson, the stone for many important buildings throughout the country, and many beautiful works of art in marble, have been finished here. Among the skilled workmen at Nelson have been a considerable number from Italy and Scotland, where they were also workers in stone, and some have remained to become citizens.

The town has a Baptist and a Methodist church, and not

far from the limits is a second and very old Baptist church which antedates the town by many years. Nelson also has one of the best and most beautifully laid out high-school plants in this part of Georgia, and a corps of efficient teachers.

Nelson was incorporated by the legislature in 1891. The extreme southern part of the town lies in Cherokee County, and the 1930 census showed ninety of the 798 inhabitants of Nelson as living in Cherokee.

Talking Rock. Several legendary accounts are given with regard to the naming of Talking Rock; one is the story of an unusual echo that was supposed to come from a nearby rock cliff; while another story, already mentioned (page 28), tells about a rock with which some of the Indians played a trick on one another.

Talking Rock is situated on the creek of the same name, in the upper part of the county. Being on the Old Federal Road, it was one of the earliest settlements in this region, and some of the earliest churches and schools in Pickens were at or near the present site of the town. Talking Rock is also close to the site of the old Indian village Sanderstown. One of the earliest cotton mills in Georgia was started at Talking Rock by William C. Atherton, and flourished until the Civil War, when it was destroyed by Sherman's raiders.

The Talking Rock neighborhood was settled by a number of Presbyterian families, including the Coleman, Morrison, Kelley, Glenn, Freeman, and Allen families, most of whom came to Pickens County about the time of the Indian removal. The town, however, was not incorporated until 1883.

Talking Rock is a good business center, and for many years was the only railroad outlet for a sizable area. It is located on the L. & N. Railroad and the Atlanta-Knoxville highway, and is in the midst of a fine farming section.

Tate. Widely known as the home of Georgia marble is the little town of Tate, an unincorporated and scattering village of about 1600 people. The main quarries of The Georgia Marble Company are located here, as well as one of its large marble works, although most of the product of the quarries is shipped to other plants to be made into monuments or prepared for its place in buildings.

Tate is situated in the southern part of the county, on the Atlanta-Knoxville highway and the L. & N. Railroad. It is estimated that the area served by the railway station and post office here has a population of over two thousand.

This is one of the oldest settlements in Pickens County, and in fact was the site of the very first election and court held in the newly organized Cherokee territory, in 1832 (page 44). The settlement was then called Harnageville, after Ambrose Harnage, in whose house the early court was held. The post office at this place was officially known as Marble Works for a period of years; then it was re-named Harnageville; and when the railroad came through in the early 'eighties the town and postoffice received their present name of Tate.

There are two churches at Tate, Methodist and Baptist, and also one of the finest high-school buildings in the United States. The latter is built of Georgia marble and equipped with every modern convenience. Like the model church, it was not built for show but to house the teaching of lessons and truths more durable than the stone of which it is built. It was made possible by the interest and liberality of Col. Sam Tate. The school is handled by a most efficient staff of teachers, who are making it one of the best high schools in the state.

Marble Hill, another unincorporated village, is located four miles from Tate at the northeastern end of the marble-quarry area, and has a population of approximately three hundred. As in the case of Tate and Nelson, the mercantile enterprises are supported largely by the workers in marble, but there is also considerable business done with the neighboring farmers. There are a Methodist and a Baptist church here and a splendid schoolhouse with capable teachers.

The town lies between several mountains, at the head of Long Swamp Valley—a region of great natural beauty.

At one time the only Catholic church ever built in our county was located here, when a number of marble-cutters of that faith came into the Valley to do some work for the old Piedmont Marble Company. They erected and dedicated this church and worshipped in it for a time, but when their jobs were done and they returned to their former homes the church went into decay and now it would be hard to pick out the exact spot on which it was located.

In addition to the towns mentioned, Pickens has several smaller communities where trade is active, including Ludville, Hinton, Blaine, and Jerusalem.

Ludville, west of Jasper, was the first community in Pickens County to establish a high school or academy (page 278), and it now has one of the many first-class schools of the county. Ludville is located in a splendid farming section and has long been a trade center for the western part of Pickens.

Hinton. At Hinton the road forms a parting of the ways, one branch going to Talking Rock and the other to Jasper. As a result Hinton has long been a trading point of some importance for the western part of Pickens County.

Old Talking Rock, now called *Blaine,* is a small community near Talking Rock, and marks the former site of that town. It is not on the line of the railroad, and the town of Talking Rock sprang up in its present location after the railroad came through. Blaine is also near the site of the old Talking Rock Cotton Factory, and the site of the old Indian village of Sanderstown.

Jerusalem is not so much a settlement as the name of a

thriving Baptist church and a community settled over fifty years ago.

ECONOMIC PROGRESS OF PICKENS COUNTY

Economically, Pickens County is noted chiefly for one of the state's outstanding industrial concerns, The Georgia Marble Company, which is the outgrowth and culmination of the efforts of several individuals and organizations, over a long period of time, to develop the county's most precious and remarkable mineral resource.

A little farther on in this account is given the early history of Pickens County's marble industry, together with some of the pioneer names in connection therewith. One of these names is that of Henry Fitzsimmons, a stone-mason and contractor who came to Pickens about 1836 and shortly afterwards started the first marble-mill in the county. Col. Samuel Tate, who purchased marble lands here in 1834, was another early figure in the realization of the county's present industrial program.

Until the coming of the railroad in 1882, Pickens County of course saw no large activity in the marble business, or in any other branch of industry. There did exist, however, the small, scattering "industrial" enterprises usual in settler regions, such as milling, brickmaking, metal-working, and so on—as well as a few of a slightly more unusual nature, as for instance the making of wooden shoes and the manufacture of plug tobacco. Such enterprises as these, together with the slowly developing marble industry and a small though successful project in the textile-manufacturing field, comprised the industrial activity of the county in the days before the railroad came to Pickens.

Rather numerous were the old water-mills where corn was ground into meal and, sometimes, wheat into crude flour;

and many an older resident of the county will recall his early responsibility as a boy of "going to the mill" on horseback with bags of shelled corn slung from his saddle. Another highly essential industry was conducted at the neighborhood smithies where plows and other agricultural tools were made and horses shod with home-made shoes and nails.

The wooden-shoe "industry" was carried on by the Taberaux family—S. Taberaux and his sons, J. B. and Jelang—who had come from Belgium, lived several years in Floyd County, Ga., and moved to Pickens shortly before the Civil War. When the war forced the price of leather shoes out of ordinary reach, neighbors of the family found a substitute in the wooden shoes always worn—and made—by the Taberaux, who thereupon found quite profitable, for a while, the trade they had learned in the old country.

Tobacco-raising was an important phase of agriculture in the western end of the county for a number of years before the Civil War, and several small factories were put up for the manufacture of the weed in its various forms. The tobacco-growing section of Pickens was very similar in its natural features to the Salacoa Valley, a few miles to the south in northwestern Cherokee County, where the "Little Virginia" colony of settlers also raised and manufactured tobacco for many years; and like their neighbors to the south, many of the settlers of western Pickens were from Virginia and came to this county during the 'fifties. Some of the families who early settled around Hinton, where most of the tobacco-raising was done, were the Gravleys, McHans, Pattens, Fullers, Jeffersons, Dunns, Eatons, and others. Ephram Jefferson was one of the "manufacturers"; his plant was located near Sharp Top and he specialized in the making of plug tobacco.

The experiment of the settlers around Hinton was more or less successful for some years, but following the Civil War a high tariff was put on tobacco and raising the crop became so unprofitable that the planters were forced to turn to cotton-farming.

One of the most important industries of other days in Pickens, especially from a historical standpoint, was that represented by the early cotton-mills of the Atherton brothers, who may be said to have founded the textile industry of North Georgia. These brothers, William, Thomas, and James, had immigrated to this country from Manchester, England, in their boyhood. The family settled in Paterson, N. J., but the three brothers later came south and engaged in textile work in various localities. William Atherton went to Roswell, Ga., about 1840 and started the old Roswell Cotton Mills. Seven years later he moved to Pickens County and bought a mill-site on Talking Rock Creek, where he put in a grist-mill, a wool-carder, a sawmill, and a cotton-gin. These were destroyed by raiders during the war. Immediately following the Civil War, the three brothers came together and pooled their resources, and erected at this same place the old Talking Rock Cotton Factory, the first textile mill in Northwest Georgia.

The principal product of the Talking Rock factory was "bunch yarn," which was used for home weaving. For several years the Athertons conducted their business successfully; then the factory was destroyed by fire. William Atherton moved to Waleska, in Cherokee County, and put up a cotton-mill on Shoal Creek. A few years later, however, he returned to Pickens and with his brother Thomas opened up the Harmony Cotton Mills, three miles south of Jasper, at Alice. Later this property was sold to P. M. Tate, who operated it till it was destroyed by fire about 1897.

The Harmony Mills came to have a considerable output under the skillful management of the Athertons, producing various kinds of yarn for both local and Northern consumption. Some of the yarn was used as warp for the home-woven cloth widely used in the mountain section of Georgia at that time, while a special kind of twist was shipped to carpet-manufacturers in Philadelphia. In addition to the yarn factory, a wool-carder was operated at the same place, and here raw wool was made into "rolls" to be spun into yarn by the mountain housewives. The woolen yarn was then used as "filling" for jeans woven on the primitive looms which were to be found in nearly every country home. Such jeans were colored with walnut-hull dye or other vegetable dyes and then cut out and sewed into clothing.

Besides being highly competent in their profession, it is said of the Atherton brothers that they were especially sensitive about commercial honor, and that if they owed a farmer for cotton and he did not come for his money on the due date, it was carried to him the next day. There is no question that their early enterprises in Pickens County had much influence on the growth and development of the textile industry in Georgia.

There was another industry in Pickens County which, despite its less-than-reputable nature and the fact that it was here confined to a limited number of citizens, had a certain influence on the social and political thought of the last century and should receive a place in this account. This industry was the manufacture of intoxicating liquors—an occupation which had the full sanction of the federal government when the legalizing fees were duly passed but which constituted an imprisonable crime in the opposite event.

It is said there were some eight or ten legal or "government" stills in the county during the 'eighties, and at each of these places the federal government employed a "gauger" to watch and measure the output. An internal revenue tax of from ninety cents to $1.10 a gallon was imposed on the distiller, who generally sold his product to the Atlanta saloons—retailing in the county was forbidden by local laws

—and who got very little more than the tax on it. Under these circumstances, business was naturally good for "moonshiners," who evaded the tax, and these unauthorized or extra-legal distillers gave the federal authorities trouble for many years—especially since popular sentiment was on the side of the moonshiners because of the "infamous" revenue tax. One of the outgrowths of this situation was the "Honest Man's Friend and Protector" society mentioned in a preceding chapter, and another was the widely popular feeling that convictions and imprisonments under the revenue law were in no sense a disgrace to the moonshiner, who after serving a short term on the chain-gang usually returned home more or less a hero. It was not the law and its enforcers that finally prevailed against this state of affairs; the gradually-increasing influence of churches and schools was the factor that ultimately turned popular sentiment against the business of liquor-making—whether legally conducted or otherwise—and thereby brought about its decline.

In 1883 occurred an event of major importance to the development of industry in Pickens County—the coming of the railroad. This was also one of the contributing elements to the advance of the county in many other ways, for the reason that it gave to the people a contact with the outside world that the old wagon-train had been inadequate to furnish.

The railroad was known for a period of years as the "Atlanta, Knoxville & Northern," and it is now a part of the Louisville & Nashville system; but it began its existence as the "Marietta & North Georgia Railroad" because it started at Marietta and was intended to help exploit the great natural resources of the more northerly counties of the state.

The Marietta & North Georgia Railroad was almost entirely a local enterprise; that is, it was organized, financed, and managed in its early period chiefly by citizens of North

Georgia. Gen. William Phillips, of Marietta, was one of the leading spirits in the building of the railroad and headed the incorporating company for some years. A number of prominent business men and citizens in the various counties to be traversed were also active in promoting and building the railroad. There was great popular excitement when it began to appear that a railroad through Cherokee and Pickens was an assured fact. Stock was subscribed by a large number of people living in these counties; some paid in labor, some in cash, and some were not to pay at all, but to all those who subscribed the credit is due that they helped along a worthy cause by their enthusiasm if in no other way.

The people of Pickens County took an important part in the building of the railroad. Not only did many of them purchase stock in the enterprise, but they secured permission from the legislature to endorse bonds of the railroad company to the extent of $150,000. In addition to this, the construction of the right-of-way through a part of Cherokee and Pickens was carried out by the firm of McAfee, Tate & Company, composed of J. M. McAfee and E. Fields, of Canton, and Stephen C. Tate, of Tate, the latter being one of the early sponsors and supporters of the railroad and later influential in bringing it into Pickens County.

Construction of the railroad began in 1878, and in November of 1879 the first train arrived in Canton, then the northern terminus. In May, 1882, the railroad reached Ball Ground, a few miles south of the Pickens County line, and by September, 1883, it was finished to Jasper. Gradual progress extended the line through North Georgia, and finally, to Knoxville, Tenn.; but 1883 may be marked as the year in which the transition to industrialism was made in Pickens County. Almost immediately plans were made to develop on a large scale the marble deposits of the county, and in

1884 the present Georgia Marble Company was organized, of which more will be said a few pages farther on.

NEWSPAPERS OF THE COUNTY

Contributing to the economic advance of Pickens County, and to its moral and social progress as well, have been the various newspapers published here during the last fifty years.

Prior to 1884 Pickens County had no newspaper. Before that time various outside publications served to carry the official advertising of the county, the *Ellijay Courier* and the *Marietta Journal* being among those most often used for this purpose.

The first newspaper published in Pickens County was *The Mountain Boys,* which made its initial appearance on January 1, 1884. T. B. Heard, a young man from Waleska, was the editor and publisher. The paper consisted of eight small pages, and was printed on a little hand-press in the courthouse at Jasper.

The Mountain Boys did not survive for quite two years. It changed hands several times between Mr. Heard and two other Waleska boys, J. Hardy Rhyne and his brother Lester A., with John W. Henley and M. C. McClain of Jasper also associated with it at times; and it even had its name changed, becoming *The Jasper News* early in 1885; but despite the efforts of everyone concerned, the paper was forced to suspend during its second year.

The county remained without a newspaper from the demise of *The Jasper News* until October 14, 1887, when the *Pickens County Herald* came on the scene, with W. B. Mincey as editor and publisher.

The *Herald* was a Democratic newspaper, and it soon had competition. On March 29, 1890, the *Piedmont Republican* appeared in Jasper, edited by J. S. Peterson. The *Re-*

publican was established by a stock company, of which John
M. Allred was president and John W. Payne, John M.
Allred, W. F. McHan, F. C. Richards, and Eli L. Darnell
composed the "finance committee." In 1892 C. C. Haley,
W. S. Clayton, and W. Franklin became the editors; in
1894 Mr. Clayton and F. W. Padgett took charge. Tom
Davis became the leading spirit in the stock company, and
Sion A. Darnell, a noted lawyer of the county and a staunch
Republican, was a regular contributor to the paper. The
Republican was suspended and then revived several times,
but in 1900 it disappeared for good.

Mr. Mincey continued the publication of the *Pickens
County Herald* until 1892, when he was succeeded as editor
and publisher by Albert L. Turner. A few years later the
paper was bought by Col. Farish Carter Tate, but Messrs.
Mincey and Turner were named as editors. Colonel Tate was
then a member of Congress and Mr. Turner became one of his
secretaries. Mr. Turner severed his connection with the *Herald*
in 1898 and Mr. Mincey continued the paper alone for a
few months longer; then it suspended. It was revived, however, in September of 1899 under its present name of the
Pickens County Progress.

Ben F. Perry, who had formerly edited the *Cherokee
Advance* at Canton, was the first editor of the *Progress,* and
John W. Nations was publisher. After a few weeks Mr.
Perry resigned and Mr. Nations took complete charge. In
1900 Rev. G. A. Bartlett leased the plant and edited the
paper for a little over three years, during most of which
time W. T. Day Jr. was in charge of the mechanical work.
Tolleson Kirby then published the paper for something over
a year, after which it was got out for a few months by the
Jasper Publishing Company, headed by Capt. Howard Tate.
In 1904 the paper was leased by E. K. Akin, who conducted
it for one year; then it was taken over by Cooper Edge,
whose term of editorship lasted nine or ten months.

In 1906, Claude F. Edge, a practical printer whose health had broken down in Atlanta, leased the plant and became editor of the *Progress,* with his sons, Claude Jr. and Robert, handling the mechanical work. For several months prior to his death in September, 1916, Mr. Edge edited the paper from his home. Following their father's death, Claude and Robert Edge bought the plant, which had been operated under lease, and have continued the publication of the *Progress* up to the present time. They are both capable newspapermen and under their efficient management the *Progress* has been of great benefit to the county in the advancement of all its interests, material and otherwise.

HISTORY OF THE GEORGIA MARBLE INDUSTRY

The question has been asked when Georgia marble was first quarried and finished. This can not be answered definitely, for at the Tate homestead there are steps which were in use when the white men first came into this part of the country. These steps furnished the approach to an Indian cabin situated on this same spot, and some of them are now in use at the approach to a garden. They have been exposed to the weather and to the tramp of human feet for more than one hundred years, and although they were hewn from weathered outcroppings they show little sign of wear and no sign of disintegration.

Further showing that the marble was first used by the Indians, there is also at this place a connahaynee bowl cut from marble which remains in a good state of preservation, with the exception that the bottom of the bowl is broken.

Reference has already been made to the acquiring of marble lands by Samuel Tate in 1834. Land Lot No. 147, of the 4th district and second section, was the nucleus around which the Tate marble properties grew. This lot has an in-

teresting history, having been the location of the noted old
house of Ambrose Harnage where the first court and election of Cherokee County were held. Near the Harnage
home there was also one of the first postoffices in the Cherokee district, established, according to federal records, early
in 1832. Older citizens inform me that this postoffice was
located in a store near the crossroads.

Lot No. 147 was held by Harnage until the lottery dis-
placed him in 1833, when the lot was drawn by a man named
Fawns, of Chatham County. In July, 1834, William Green
bought the lot from Dr. Jesse Green, attorney-in-fact for
Mr. Fawns. The following month Dr. Green himself purchased the lot, and in October of the same year he sold
it to Samuel Tate. The foregoing transfers are shown in
the early records of Cherokee County.

Concerning the beginnings of the marble industry in
Pickens County, *Stone Magazine* for May, 1895, gives the
following account:

In 1840, Henry Fitzsimmons began quarrying marble on a small
scale in Long Swamp Valley, near Tate. This seems to have been
the first systematic work done in developing the marbles. The stone
worked is said to have been obtained from outcroppings and weathered boulders, and was often of a poor quality. All of the work
being done by hand, the more or less laminated varieties were
selected on account of the ease with which they could be worked.
All the marble then taken out was worked up into tombstones, which
were so costly that only the wealthy could buy, and consequently
the trade was small. In 1844, Fitzsimmons erected the first mill in
the county. It was on the east branch of Long Swamp Creek near
what is now Marble Hill postoffice, and contained one gang of saws.
It was a rude and primitive affair, but the method was the same as
now used in the best mills.

Summy & Hurlick built a mill on the west branch of Long Swamp,
near Jasper, which was in operation at various times for a period of
four or five years.

In the year 1850 the firm of Tate, Atkinson & Company opened a quarry in the vicinity of The Georgia Marble Company's present location. The tool marks of the old hand drills show sharp and clear, and to the present day show very little if any signs of disintegration. Two mills, each of two gangs of saws, were erected by this company, one above and one below the quarry, and owing to this increased capacity many tombstones were turned out. An agent was employed to travel North Carolina and solicit orders. Delivery was made by a six-mule team.

In 1852 the firm of Rankin, Summy & Hurlick succeeded this company and were the last to do any work in that vicinity until the present Georgia Marble Company was organized in 1884. In 1854 Summy & Hurlick, who had opened a quarry east of Jasper, resumed work at that point. They erected a mill with four gangs of saws and did a successful business for about six years, or until the breaking out of the War. Closely following the close of the War, the quarry was operated by Robinson, Richardson & Besinger for nearly two years, and then that property passed into the hands of the Perseverance Marble Company, who built a steam mill and operated the quarries for three years.

What may be called the marble belt of Georgia, and Pickens County in particular, was remarkably free from the ravages of the late war. Some detachments of both armies occasionally marched through the territory, but the only noticeable relic of their presence is pointed out near Colonel Stephen Tate's residence. It is told that several companies of Federal cavalry were encamped there for a week. They had brought with them hay for their horses and the seed therefrom were scattered on the ground. The following spring a luxuriant growth of grass sprang up and has continued to grow and spread. It is blue grass, though it is still referred to as "Yankee grass."

The coming of the railroad, in 1883, brought a renewed interest in the marble deposits of Pickens County. Again quoting from the same issue of *Stone Magazine*:

In the year 1883, Mr. J. A. Dewar, of Kansas City, Missouri, while traveling in the south, had his attention directed to the marble deposits of North Georgia, as a business investment. After a thorough personal investigation, he became convinced of the wonderful richness of these deposits and interested Mr. Frank Siddall, of Philadelphia, in the marble beds of Pickens County, as the most desirable and richest in the state. Through Mr. Siddall's solicitation, Messrs. H. C. Clement and O. F. Bane, of Chicago, were induced to visit the section. They, like Mr. Dewar, were surprised and pleased with the outlook, and at once entered upon the work of securing by purchase and lease, the control of all that part of the marble lands which appeared to them the most desirable properties.

This work occupied most of Mr. Clement's time during the months of March and April, 1884, and on the first day of May that year the present Georgia Marble Company was organized. The company was capitalized at $1,000,000, with the privilege of $3,000,000, and later the capital was increased to $1,500,000.

The first officers of the company, elected at the time of organization, were: H. C. Clement, president; F. H. Siddall, vice-president; L. B. Bane, secretary and treasurer; and J. A. Dewar, general manager. In 1885 O. F. Bane was elected secretary and treasurer, George W. Hoffman vice-president, George H. Keeler general manager, and the office of assistant secretary was filled by Mr. S. H. Wright.

When active operations were begun, The Georgia Marble Company had leased all the marble lands owned by the Tate Estate, comprising about 5,000 acres, and had acquired by purchase an additional 2,000 acres, on which latter tract was the property on which the now valuable Kennesaw quarry is located.

The first carload of stone shipped by The Georgia Marble Company went to Atlanta and was used in the Kimball House.

It is interesting to note that when the marble for Georgia's state capitol was offered for the cost of production, transportation and work of finishing, the committee in charge questioned whether there was a sufficient quantity to build the capitol. The controlling factor, however, was an estimated cost against a price made by the Indiana limestone interests.

A potent factor in the development and growth of the Georgia Marble industry has been its especial adaptability to fine interior finish in public and private buildings, and to this branch of its manufacture the works of George B. Sickels & Company, of Tate, Georgia, are exclusively devoted.

The Sickels company, organized in 1886, was sold to Sam Tate, Luke Tate, J. M. Eaton et al. in 1907, and was

continued under the same name until the consolidation of
the various plants already mentioned, which occurred in
1915.

The Blue Ridge Marble Company, organized by the
Dewars at Nelson, Georgia, and now a part of the Georgia
Marble Company, has through the efforts of Mr. Harry
Dewar and Mr. Alex Anderson been responsible for a great
part of the use of Georgia marble for exteriors.

The Georgia Marble Finishing Works, at Canton, Georgia,

COL. SAM TATE

organized and developed to a point of great efficiency by
Captain Thomas M. Brady, has maintained its independence
and is still operating as an independent manufacturer under
the management of E. A. McCanless. Mr. McCanless is an
experienced marble man and had his training under Captain
Brady, who, incidentally, designed and carved the "Lion of
Atlanta" as a memorial to the Confederate dead. He is
said to have derived the inspiration for this work from the
noted "Lion of Lucerne."

Inseparably connected with the marble industry in Georgia
is the name of Tate. It was Samuel Tate who first purchased

the marble lands, nearly a hundred years ago, and who was instrumental in the early development of the industry. It was Stephen Tate, his son, who was largely instrumental in the building of a railroad through Pickens County and in the organization of The Georgia Marble Company, of which he was for years a director and officer, besides serving in similar capacities the Blue Ridge Marble Company, at Nelson, and the Kennesaw Marble Company, at Marietta. And it has been under the presidency of the present Colonel Sam Tate that the Georgia marble industry has been consolidated and brought under one management, and that the industry has enjoyed its era of greatest prosperity. The company which he heads has taken its place among Georgia's foremost industrial concerns, and Georgia marble, the world-famous product of Pickens County, has earned a most enviable reputation throughout the United States and wherever it is known.

It has been Colonel Sam Tate's life work to make The Georgia Marble Company one of the largest marble companies in the world and Georgia marble the material of the world's leading sculptors, architects and builders. Out of this marble was fashioned the Lincoln figure in the Lincoln Memorial, at Washington, D. C.; Lorado Taft's "Columbus Memorial" fountain at Washington; the "Maine" monument at Havana, Cuba; the Piave World War memorial at Rome, Italy; the McKinley Memorial at Niles, Ohio; the Harding Memorial at Marion, Ohio; the Buckingham Memorial Fountain, in Chicago (largest fountain in the world); numerous public buildings, including the New York Stock Exchange, the Royal Bank of Canada at Montreal, the Corcoran Art Gallery at Washington, the House Office building and part of the Supreme Court building at Washington, the state capitols of Rhode Island and Minnesota, the capitol of Porto Rico, Shedd Aquarium and Field Museum in Chicago, the

Bok Tower in Florida, and many others too numerous to mention here.

While enough Georgia marble has been removed to make this material—and the county from which it comes—famous the world over, geologists assure us that the immense deposit of Long Swamp Valley has hardly been scratched. The deposit is a solid mass, from five to seven miles long, one-half mile wide, and in some places estimated by geologists to be 2,000 feet deep. It has been quarried to a depth of 225 feet. To a person standing on any bluff overlooking Long Swamp Valley, the twenty enormous quarries appear only as rabbit holes in the field; yet each of these quarries would hold a large office building. One government expert has estimated that if marble were removed from the Long Swamp quarries at the rate of 200,000 cubic feet a year, it would take more than one million years to exhaust the store.

Equally as remarkable as the size of the deposit is the formation of, and wide range of colors found in, this famous marble. It is of crystalline formation, which characterized the ancient Parian marble. The Taj Mahal, in India, generally conceded to be the world's most beautiful structure, is built of marble which so closely resembles Georgia marble that experts can not tell them apart. Authorities say that no stone (other than the Pentelic and Parian marbles) possesses both the beauty and enduring qualities of crystalline Georgia marble.

In variety of coloring and patterns, Georgia marble is probably unique. The great range of shades and markings are divided for convenience into half a dozen general classifications, known by the trade names of Etowah, Cherokee, Creole, Silver Gray, White Georgia, and Mezzotint. Etowah marble is colored in widely ranging shades of delicate pink; Cherokee is light to dark gray, with wavy or cloudy effects; Creole is rich dark blue against a white background. White

Georgia is colorless, or practically so, and of striking translucence; Silver Gray is of evenly toned grays; and Mezzotint is a combination of dark designs on a gray background.

Thousands of visitors annually come to the quarries at Tate to watch the interesting processes of quarrying and fabrication employed there. The work of wresting a huge block of Georgia marble from the "mother lode" is, of course, a Herculean task. There can be no blasting or splitting loose, for the marble in its natural bed is a solid, compact mass. Skilled workmen and highly efficient equipment are necessary for the task. One of the most interesting machines used by the quarrymen is the "double channeling cutter," which operates two long arm-like devices at one end of which is a holder which contains drills. These are driven up and down cutting a channel on each side of a track upon which the machine moves slowly, giving thereby an even depth to the channels. The drills chip away at the surface until they dig a crack or crevice in the floor of the quarry; then the "undercutting" takes place. This is done by drilling a series of horizontal holes in a straight line beneath the block and so close together that when the wedges are driven into these holes the block can be sufficiently raised to permit a heavy chain to be fastened around it. One after another, blocks are cut on the same level, working toward the walls of the quarry. The blocks as cut from the quarries are raised to the surface by a huge steam derrick, and loaded on flat cars to be shipped or hauled to the storage yards. Large locomotives and enormous traveling cranes handle the marble in the mill yards. Acres of marble surround the mills. Here are huge blocks weighing many tons—just as they were taken from the quarries. Here also are sawed blocks and slabs of every size, ready to be selected for the finished product.

In the mills—four of which are operated: one at Tate, one at Nelson, one at Marietta, and one at Marble Hill—the marble blocks are sawed, planed and finished. The sawing is done by saws which contain no teeth, being simply long strips of steel that are set in gangs of a dozen or more to each frame. As the frame swings back and forth, the abrasive material—sand—is fed into the slowly deepening grooves as needed, and is washed underneath the moving blades. This is called the slabbing or block process—sawing to approximate dimensions. Then on huge cast-iron disks revolving horizontally, the blocks are rubbed down to definite sizes for finishing. Great lathes turn out circular pieces, the largest machines being capable of shaping a column six feet in diameter and thirty feet long.

The work of further finishing the marble is of such a character as to require skilled workmen of high degrees of specialization. The intricate carving and sculptured work turned out by the company's craftsmen, some of whom have spent their lives perfecting their craft, has received the praise of nationally known artists.

The Georgia Marble Company employs over one thousand men, mostly natives of the section, who work in ideal surroundings for something more than a living wage. Their families are housed in modern and comfortable homes with gardens; churches thrive, jails are unknown and crime rarely occurs. Every child under eighteen years of age goes to school, and the company not only supplies the schools but employs the teachers. Each school has its playground and its auditorium. In addition, each of the communities has its social center, its community building and gymnasium. These conditions are the result of a regime that began in 1905, when Colonel Sam Tate took over The Georgia Marble Company from the northern capitalists who had leased the marble lands from his father. In the conduct of these industrial communities is seen a striking example of the exemplary methods Colonel Tate has followed in unfolding the industrial dream of his pioneer grandfather, the first Sam Tate, and of his father, the late Stephen Tate.

The growth and development of Pickens County from
its first days of organization has, of course, been in no small
measure the reflection of the growth and success of The
Georgia Marble Company. For that reason I have thought
it proper to give here a somewhat full account of this company and to mention, at least, those persons who were responsible for its founding and development. I have also felt that
the rather unusual character of this industry, together with
its social significance in the communities where it operates,
would tend to make such an account of considerable interest
even aside from its historical importance. In connection
with this idea, and as conclusion to the story of the Georgia
marble industry, the following verses by J. G. Daneker will
give a picture that should prove interesting:

> "At the foothills of the Blue Ridge
>   In the Long Swamp Valley fair,
> Lies the town of Tate, in Georgia,
>   With its treasure rich and rare.
> Here the centuries in their passing
>   Worked their wonders 'neath the sod;
> Time alone made Georgia marble—
>   Here the handiwork of God.
>
> "In this valley Indian tribesmen
>   Featured early history pages,
> Knowing naught of future grandeur
>   In these miles of 'Stone of Ages,'
> Needing only touch of craftsmen
>   And the brains of future time,
> To create commercial structures,
>   Rare memorials—shrines sublime.
>
> "Here a kindly-hearted hill-folk
>   Live at peace devoid of care,
> Work in real Arcadian freedom;
>   All contribute—each his share.
> Here sincerity is treasure,
>   Here the brotherhood of man
> Is the touch that makes all kinsmen
>   Through a true Utopian plan."

Chapter VII ★ ★ ★ ★ ★ ★
SCHOOLS AND CHURCHES

●

If one were to ask what influences have made the greatest contribution to the life and progress of our county, he might get a variety of answers but certainly the pulpit and the schoolhouse would head the list, and properly so.

The religious and educational advantages possessed by the people of the county today reflect not only their own enlightened desires but also the desires, plans, and struggles of earlier generations who founded and helped to develop these things for their posterity. Surely it is in connection with such activities that present citizens of the county stand most indebted to those of earlier days.

Not always, of course, have churches and schools been so numerous and easy of access as almost to be taken for granted; and this has been particularly true, in our county as well as in our country, of schools. The public-school movement is itself of more recent origin than many people realize, not having got well under way until the middle of the last century. Georgia's public school system dates back only as far as the year 1868. These matters are mentioned here because it will be shown that, in the light of comparison, earlier residents of Pickens County were more alert and progressive in educational matters than might at first be supposed. Still—they and their children had no easy time of it to obtain an education; many people had to forego such privileges entirely, and many others were able to obtain

only the bare rudiments of the "three R's." From their day
to ours is a long cry educationally; and it is with the county's
progress in this respect that we now concern ourselves here.

ANTE-BELLUM SCHOOLS OF GEORGIA

It will help us, in tracing this progress, if we first take a
brief glance at the condition of education in the state as a
whole during the first years of the county's life—that is, just
before the Civil War. Incidentally, the discussion of this
rather general topic in the present volume is further justified
by a very interesting historical sidelight on the subject from
the records of our own county—but more of that later.

The fact has often been commented upon that Georgia,
now ranking high among her sister states in the quality of
her educational institutions, both public and private, was in
earlier days so backward in educational matters that not until
the Civil War was over did her children first enjoy the advantages of a public school system.

It is also pointed out that when this finally did occur, it
was mainly as a result of the efforts of the "carpet-baggers"
—those unsavory statesmen in whose irresponsible hands
rested the government of Georgia immediately following the
War; for it is commonly accepted by historical authorities
that the first system of public schools in the state was provided by the Constitution of 1868, framed by the notorious
"Carpet-Bagger Convention."

These two circumstances—that Georgia was tardy in es-
tablishing public schools for her boys and girls, and that even
then they had to receive such benefits from the hands of
legislative usurpers and swashbucklers—form a rather puz-
zling episode in the history of the state. It is hard to reconcile
these points with the undoubted humanity and intelligence
of many of Georgia's early statesmen, or with her ante-
bellum ideals of culture and citizenship. They remain, in

fact, as the basis of some rather adverse criticism of our state.

Of course, any praise of the carpet-baggers in this connection can hardly be serious; they did not establish public schools out of humanitarian motives but simply to reap the votes which their colored clientele (and white too) might gain by the ability to read and write. But before convicting Georgia's earlier lawmakers and citizens of the crime of neglecting the welfare and enlightenment of their children, it is well that we pause for further facts.

PICKENS COUNTY HIGH SCHOOL (AND JASPER GRAMMAR
SCHOOL), JASPER, GA.

Long before the Civil War there were in every settled part of Georgia institutions known as "tuition-schools" and "academies," where good educational opportunities were provided at reasonable cost; and there were also "poor-schools," supported by a state fund, where children of indigent parents could obtain an education of sorts without payment. The poor-school fund was entirely inadequate and its fruits were sorry; but Georgia was not alone in keeping this institution alive after the nation had outgrown it. It is to the discredit of the wealthy planter class of the whole ante-bellum South that they regarded poor-schools as good enough for "other people's children." The hardy, inde-

pendent settlers of the hill sections, such as those of Pickens
County, had little use for the undemocratic poor-school. And
yet there is no doubt that it served a good purpose, on the
whole.

We see, then, that even with a makeshift and rather unsatisfactory system, education was by no means neglected in
Georgia before the Civil War; but there is another fact
to consider, and that is that provision for free public schools
was really made by the state several years prior to the war.

The First Public Schools

This is a fact which does not seem to have its due prom-
inence in the history of education in Georgia, but it can
be brought out here with some emphasis, being supported
by certain documentary evidence in the form of an early
Pickens County grand jury presentment. This presentment,
or recommendation, which was written in March of the year
1859, shows conclusively that a true public school system
was in the process of being established in Georgia several
years *before* the Civil War, and that if the attitude of
Pickens County was a fair example, the counties of Georgia
were only stopped from putting the plan into full operation
by the crushing blow of the War of '61.

A word of explanation is necessary here. It is a matter
of public record that in 1858 the Georgia legislature passed
an act* providing that education should be made free to
all white children between the ages of eight and eighteen.
To the meager poor-school fund already existing, the legislature added a yearly appropriation of $100,000, together
with "whatever surplus funds" the treasury might contain
from time to time. The act then provided that all these
moneys should be pro-rated among the counties according to

*Acts, Georgia, 1858, p. 49.

the number of children of school age, to be spent along with county school-tax money in whatever way the county officials deemed best for educational purposes.

The provisions of the act of 1858 were not essentially different from those embodied in the Constitution of 1868— or, for that matter, from the school laws we have now; and yet the latter date is generally given for the establishment of Georgia's public school system. The weakness of the 1858 legislation seems to have been that it was not made a part of the constitution, as it thus had to put the matter up to the counties on an optional basis. Its operation was necessarily imperfect, the more so by reason of the state's inexperience in public education. Governor Brown made this point in his message to the 1859 legislature, adding that "so great a work must be progressive; a succession of wise enactments, guided by the light of experience, can alone perfect it."

And yet—public schools had been started. Special research lately conducted on this point by the State Historian shows that the act of 1858 was immediately put into operation in nearly every county in Georgia, and that the schools affected were thenceforth considered to be *public* schools, as evidenced by the designation of the state money, after 1858, as the "educational fund" instead of the "poor-school fund." (The educational fund of a state would naturally be limited to use for *public* education.) These points indicate that, if the use of the word "system" is not disallowed by reason of the optional character of the act of 1858, Georgia really started her public school system ten years earlier than the date she is now credited with. It might be noted here that this would put her a good many years ahead of most other Southern states and even the great and progressive state of New York, which collected tuition in its "public" schools until 1867.

In the final analysis, the test of the matter would seem to rest as much in the intention of the lawmakers as in the results of their law; and it is on this point that the Pickens County jury presentment appears to have a valuable historical bearing, through its interpretation of this act of 1858 by a representative group of contemporary Georgians. If the jurors knew the spirit of the legislature, and we have every reason to believe they did, there can be little question that the act was intended to inaugurate what was in every sense of the term a system of public schools for Georgia. The presentment, with its cordial reception of the legislature's plan and its well-considered outline of procedure, is, I think, of unusual interest among the county records of Georgia, and shows the extent to which early Pickens Countians were interested in educational matters.

You will find this presentment quite worth the reading, and I am reproducing it here in full (italics are mine where they occur):

The grand jury chosen and sworn for the March term 1859 of the county of Pickens having taken into consideration the provisions of the Act passed by the last legislature for the education of the children of the State between certain ages, and in accordance with the provisions of said Act, do recommend and present as follows:

First, that the time allowed to bodies organized as we are is too short to enable us fully to consider and properly to digest an educational system. We therefore recommend to the next legislature to vest the power given to the grand juries under the above stated act to some more permanent body. But as that Act cast the whole fund into the poor-school system unless we take some step in the matter, *and as we are satisfied of the inefficiency and radical defects of that system,* we make the following recommendations for the present year and until altered by law:

Second, we recommend that the ordinary of this county after consultation with the county treasurer, tax collector, and clerk of the superior court shall divide this county into school districts to be determined when the number of children and their location shall be returned as shall hereinafter be provided for. The school districts to be laid off by the most distinct and convenient boundaries which the nature of the case will permit. That [the ordinary shall?] cause a map of the county to be drawn with the boundaries of said districts marked thereon and keep the same on file in his office. That the ordinary appoint three trustees for each school district.

Third, said trustees shall hold their office until successors shall be appointed and qualified, subject to removal by the ordinary. A vacancy in their number may be filled by the ordinary.

Fourth, in laying off said school districts the ordinary shall see that no district shall contain less than twenty children between the ages of eight and eighteen years and none shall contain more than one hundred, unless when the returns are made a greater or less number may be thought advisable by the ordinary to suit the convenience of certain localities.

Fifth, the trustees thus appointed shall take an oath before the ordinary to discharge the duties of their office without bias, partiality or prejudice, and for the best interests of the cause of education in the county.

Sixth, the trustees in each district shall have power to select a site for a school house, keeping in view conveniences to all the children and a central position to all portions of the district. The trustees however may exercise a wise discretion to disregard a central location where other circumstances require it.

Seventh, the trustees shall have power to arrange for the erection of a suitable school house and the site thus selected; may receive contributions; and shall procure the title to the land and school house which shall be conveyed in trust to the ordinary and his successors in office for said district and be forever dedicated to the purposes of a public school.

Eighth, the trustees shall have power to select a teacher (he or she having complied with the eighth section of said Act) and to make such contract with such teacher as they see fit by and with the advice and consent of the ordinary, but *in every case said school shall be perfectly free to every child between said ages in said district for at least three months in every year.*

Ninth, the instructions of children in said school shall be confined to the elementary branches of education.

Tenth, the ordinary shall distribute the educational fund received from the state and school tax for this county among the several school districts pro rata according to the number of children between said ages in said districts and shall pay over the same to the teachers on certificate of the trustees; that the number of children shall be determined by the returns of the tax receiver as provided in section 3 of said Act.

Eleventh, the trustees of each district shall before the 20th day of October in every year return to the ordinary a statement of the condition of their school, the number of children taught, the salary paid the teacher, and any other information of interest. And no teacher shall draw any part of the school funds until the trustees make such return. But the same shall be held by the ordinary while the return is made. These returns shall be copied by the ordinary, the originals filed in his office, and the copies given to the senator from this county to be laid before the Senatus Academus.

Twelfth, no teacher in this county shall receive any part of the school fund except the teachers of district schools, as herein provided.

Thirteenth, the boundaries of school districts when once established shall not be changed except on recommendation of the grand jury.

Fourteenth, if trustees appointed refuse to be qualified and to serve, the ordinary may appoint [others?] in their places.

Fifteenth, the daily reading of the Bible shall be part of the exercises of every public school.

Sixteenth, and for the immediate inauguration of this system the justices of the peace and constables of each militia district be and they are hereby respectfully and earnestly requested to procure the names, ages, sex and locality of all the children between the ages of eight and eighteen in their respective districts, and that on the first Tuesday in May said justices meet in the ordinary's office and report to the ordinary, that the districts may be so laid off as to meet the wants and conveniences of all the citizens.

Seventeenth, that when the trustees have selected and secured a suitable site for a schoolhouse in their respective districts, the citizens of the district by contribution or otherwise build good, comfortable, and suitable school houses, and that no part of the school fund be paid to said district until such school house shall be received by the trustees.

Eighteenth, that in the event the officers appointed by the 16th section refuse or neglect to perform the duties therein specified and to report by the first Tuesday in May to the ordinary, then the ordinary appoint three suitable persons in each district to perform said duties and report to the ordinary on the first Tuesday in June next, as provided for in the 16th section.

Nineteenth, that the districts shall be distinguished by numbers.

Twentieth, that the trustees of each district be requested and are earnestly desired to use their best efforts to secure the services of some good, competent, philanthropic person or persons in the district to teach regularly a Sabbath school in said district school house, which school shall not be denominational or sectarian. Of course no such teachers would expect any part of the educational fund though the result of their labors if faithfully performed can only be calculated by Him who is all-wise which is the good man's reward.

We have thought it best not to levy a tax for school purposes for the present year. We have determined to build our school houses by public contribution and our own labor, and that the buildings should be comfortable and convenient. This will require an indirect tax more than fourfold of county and state tax. We will also secure the site for the school houses by private contributions and vest the title in the ordinary to be dedicated forever and ever for school purposes.

We have also determined not to use one dollar of the state fund for any other purpose than to pay the teachers, but at the same time we expect the people and the citizens behalf [?] that for the future such a tax will be recommended and levied as should with the aid of the state fund *educate every child in the county in* the elementary branches.

We hail with pleasure this first step of the Empire State in the right direction in the way of educating the masses. The poor-school system utterly failed. The present system can but succeed if the people of Georgia are true to themselves and their best interests, and we know Pickens will do her duty.

The reader will want to know whether these recommendations of the jury were carried out, and if so to what extent.

It is known that Pickens *was* one of the counties to follow the plan outlined by the legislature, but unfortunately there is little information available as to the extent of the plan's development here. The county records that would illuminate this point are missing, probably having been destroyed during the Civil War as many other records were. The court minutes show a presentment of the next grand jury—that of September, 1859—recommending that the legislature increase the educational fund and take steps to "perfect the common school system," but no details are given here or in any of the other existing records of the county as to the actual progress of the system locally.

It is chiefly from the records of the state that evidence of this county's participation may be gathered, certain state treasury receipts showing that payment of sums from the educational fund was made to Pickens County officials in 1861, 1862, and 1863. Confirmation is also found, however, in several jury presentments of this county, written during the Civil War period, which indicate that "common schools" had then been in existence for some years although they were just then in very bad shape. At least we can say that the original public-school system was adopted by Pickens County, and that it went into effect here not later than 1861.

EDUCATIONAL PROGRESS OF PICKENS COUNTY

In reviewing the history of education in our county, it is hardly necessary to go into the period before the county was formed, other than to say that the schools were like those already described for Georgia in general; and the same situation existed after the creation of the county, up to the time of the public schools provided by the act of 1858. Mention of that early institution, the poor-school, is made by the grand jury in 1856 in recommending that a county tax amounting to 20 per cent of the state tax be levied for the poor-school fund; and in 1857, raising this levy to 25 per cent.

It might be noted here that the tuition-schools of this section were not separate from the poor-schools; the teacher merely received his tuition, for certain pupils, from the state and county instead of from the parents, and all the

HIGH AND GRAMMAR SCHOOL BUILDING AT TATE, GA.

pupils went to school together. I had not come across any description making this point clear, although I do not suppose there is any general misconception on it.

In 1860, which was evidently the last year for the poor-school-tuition-school setup in this county, the census shows that 919 children attended school in Pickens, out of the 1219 children of school age who lived here. It will be seen that the county's educational showing in 1860 was very good for that day, with three out of every four children being given some schooling. This proportion, moreover, must have been true for some years previously, as the system was the same.

The stimulation of the act of 1858, when it went into effect in Pickens, shows up in the early figures for the county's share of the state educational fund. From $1,169 in 1861, the figure rose to $1,311 in 1862, and then to $1,737 in 1863, indicating a corresponding increase in school attendance.

Of course, it must be remembered that in that day the annual school term was seldom more than three months long, and it was many years before this term was increased for the average school. On the whole, however, education in Pickens County appears to have been in a rather flourishing condition even at this early period of the county's life.

Then the Civil War came along to cast its terrible blight on the people and institutions of the South, and to deal the cause of education a tremendous and overwhelming set-back. The disastrous effect on schools was almost immediate, and continued well into Reconstruction days. In Pickens, as in many other counties, practically every school was forced to close before the war was over.

The county records tell the story very graphically. In March of 1864 the grand jurors, stating "we are sorry to learn that there were but few schools taught in our county last year," urged the school trustees to use every means in their power to revive the schools in their districts. In the following March, the jurors observed with regret that "the cause of education is languishing in our county." In September of 1865: "Feeling the all-importance of educating our children, we hope that some measure will be taken at an early day to *recommence* this great work. Though we have been greatly depressed by the trying times through which we have passed, yet we feel that with good schools and free churches, God in his providence will yet bless us as a people." In April, 1867: "In the impoverished condition of our country, education is neglected and our poor children are growing up in ignorance. *This we deplore more than the loss of property.* We urge upon our citizens the necessity to do all in their power to remedy this evil." (Italics are mine.)

In 1868, Georgia made her first constitutional provision for public schools, and the cause of education took on new life all over the state. From that time on, there has been no lapse in the functioning of a state system of public education; and the steady growth of this system through the years is now crowned by the efficient schools that are possessed by every county in Georgia.

THE OLD LUDVILLE ACADEMY BUILDING. MOVED FROM LUD-
VILLE TO TALKING ROCK IN THE EIGHTIES, THIS BUILDING
HAS RECENTLY BEEN REPLACED AT TALKING ROCK BY A
MODERN SCHOOL STRUCTURE.

In Pickens, there have been certain mileposts along the educational road that deserve special mention here even though justice can not be done the subject in the way of a lengthy discussion. One of these mileposts was the establishment of the old Ludville High School, in 1877. This was the first high school in our county and one of the first in "Cherokee Georgia." It was promoted and built by Hiram Mills, Granison Moss, Sylvanus Hamrick, Jim Killian, Sant Tolbert, Hurd Tolbert, James Eaton, John Johnson, Dave Hightower, John Guerin, Booker Gravley, and Dave Anderson. Located at Ludville, in the western end of the county, this school was patronized by people from all parts of the county and even by some who lived outside of Pickens. On account of financial difficulties the school was sold to Chesley Vincent, an early educator whose work at this place and elsewhere was of much benefit to the section. Professor Vincent operated the school at Ludville for a time and when the railroad came to Pickens in 1882 the building was moved to Talking Rock.

The "educational honor roll" of Pickens County would surely include the names of the men who founded the Ludville High School, but to complete the roll would require many other names. Col. Sam Tate built a schoolhouse at Tate in 1866, and this institution was also important in the life and progress of the community it served. The school was later rebuilt on a larger scale by his son, Stephen Tate; and there now stands in the village, due principally to the interest of the present Sam Tate, an imposing marble structure that is one of the finest and best equipped school buildings in the United States.

The "honor roll" would also include those early teachers of the county whose work in training the youth of their day was of such great benefit to this section. Mention should be made of one especial group, whose efforts had wide influence. At the close of the Civil War, Emory College at Oxford, Ga., made an offer of free tuition to disabled Confederate veterans, and four men from Pickens County took advantage of the offer: George King, Ed Prather, Eber Wofford, and Jess Berry. All of these men came back to Pickens and taught school here, making a valuable contribution to the enlightenment of their county and section.

One of the important names in Pickens County's educational history is that of John W. Henley, an early teacher, lawyer, and county school commissioner. Mr. Henley was a native of Lumpkin County and attended college at Dahlonega. Upon his graduation in 1879, he came to Jasper and established an academy, which he taught for three years. He then became county school commissioner, and

PRESENT SCHOOL AT LUDVILLE

during the fifteen years that he held this post his wise and able administration of school affairs spread the gospel of education to every corner of the county.

Only a few have been named of the many men and women who have contributed a part to the upbuilding of education in this county, but the work of all stands as a monument to their efforts. Today, Pickens has an enviable place in the ranks of education, and her schools are of a quality that insures the proper equipment of her future citizens and reflects credit on her people.

The present system of the county includes, in addition to adequate rural and grammar schools, good high schools at Tate, Nelson, Marble Hill, Ludville, and Jasper, and a new high school has recently been built at Talking Rock to replace the old academy building which was moved there from Ludville during the 'eighties.

Let me say also that the door of opportunity has not been closed to the negro. There are schools for colored children at Jasper, Tate, and Nelson, the one at Tate carrying some of the high school grades. The colored children have a great thirst for knowledge and these schools are doing a very useful and efficient work.

CHURCHES

The forces of education and religion always go hand in hand; and in our county, educational progress has been not only accompanied but greatly aided by the development of religious interests, the leadership in both matters having even been the same in many cases.

We come now to a subject which has meant more perhaps than anything else to the welfare and general progress of the county's people, and that is the part which churches and religion have played in our history. "With good schools and free churches," the old grand jury declared, "God will yet bless us as a people." This realization on the part of our county's earlier citizens, and their efforts to preserve and develop these institutions, have meant much to us of today and should not be forgotten.

The history of churches in Pickens County includes the contributions made by several denominations. Although the Methodists and Baptists have always predominated here and today have the only regular churches in the county, there have been several other denominations here in the past, including the Presbyterians, the Campbellites, the Catholics, and the Universalists—all but the latter having had churches in the county at one time or another.

Methodist Churches. The earliest Methodist church in Pickens County was one established at Hinton, in the western end of the county, some years before the Civil War and probably before the formation of the county itself. A log house was built for the purpose by Benjamin Murphy and a Mr. Hinton, and here the members met for many years. I am told there were seven charter members; one was Mrs. Jim Eaton but I have not been able to get the names of the others. A Rev. Mr. Harris was one of the early pastors, if not the first pastor, of this church.

The first camp-ground and probably the first Sunday-school in Pickens County were also at this place. Scared Corn Camp-Ground, the former was called; and to explain this unusual name the story is told that corn on a nearby creek-bottom grew so fast the neighbors said it was "scared." Scared Corn Camp-Ground was established about the same time as the Hinton Methodist Church. The Sunday-school at Hinton was started shortly before or during the war, with Moses Pharr as its first superintendent. A Methodist Sunday-school was also started at Jasper about this same time by Col. William Simmons. (There were no Baptist Sunday-schools here then, the Baptist Association not being favorable to them.)

After the War Between the States and its resulting dissensions, the members of the church at Hinton split up into two factions, Northern and Southern; and a Northern Methodist church was built only a short distance away from the original building. The first pastor of the new church was named Haley, while Rev. Jim Sullivan was the first pastor of the Southern church after the division.

Not long after the church at Hinton was started, another

Methodist church was organized in Pickens County at Jasper, under the leadership of Charles M. McClure, James Lovelace, and James Simmons; and a building was begun here in 1860. Rev. J. B. M. Morris was the first pastor. He served until the outbreak of the war, when he enlisted as a private in the Southern army. A Rev. Mr. Murphy then preached here for a time, and after the war the first pastor was Rev. Will Sullivan, who later joined the Northern Methodist Church. The early pastors at Jasper preached also, more or less regularly, at other points, including Duncan's Chapel, Fairview, Waleska, and Ball Ground—the latter three in Cherokee County.

Local preachers served the Jasper Methodist Church for a number of years after its organization, but in 1868 the charge was placed under the North Georgia Conference, in the Dahlonega District. Only the one church seems to have comprised the conference charge at this time. It had a membership of 330 white and four colored persons. At the meeting of the conference held in 1868 at Griffin, Ga., one local colored preacher, William Payne, was elected and ordained a deacon.

The development of Methodism in Pickens County includes the establishment of churches at Tate, Marble Hill, and Nelson, besides the one at Jasper; and there are also a considerable number of Methodist churches in the rural communities. At different times in the past these churches have been re-grouped or re-separated as conference charges, and the Jasper charge has usually included one or more other churches.

I am giving here a list of the pastors who have served the Jasper charge since it became part of the conference. The Methodist church at Tate has been a part of this charge during a great deal of this time and of course had the same pastors during those years. The list is taken from conference records and also shows the presiding elders, up to 1893, whose districts included this charge.

1868. A. C. Cason, supply pastor; W. A. Simmons, presiding elder.

1869. A. C. Cason, pastor; William T. Caldwell, P. E.

1870. Charge placed in Dalton District; supply pastor named. William J. Scott, P. E.

1871. John N. Sullivan, supply pastor; William J. Scott, P. E.

1872. Joseph M. Hardin, pastor; R. W. Bingham, P. E.

1874. Charge placed in Gainesville District. J. J. Harris, pastor; J. R. Parker, P. E.

1876. Charge placed in Dahlonega District. J. H. Mashburn, pastor; J. W. Stipe, P. E.

1877. Jasper and Pickens Mission. J. H. Bentley and N. E. McBreyer, pastors; J. W. Stipe, P. E.

1878. R. B. O. England, pastor; D. L. Anderson, P. E.

1879. Jasper Circuit, membership 164. W. T. Bell, pastor; D. L. Anderson, P. E.

1880. Membership now 490, with four local preachers. W. O. Butter, pastor; W. A. Candler, P. E.

1881. J. Rembert Smith, pastor; W. R. Branham, Jr., P. E.

1882. G. W. Thomas, pastor; W. R. Branham, Jr., P. E. J. N. Austin, supply pastor.

1883. T. J. Simmons, pastor; W. R. Branham, Jr., P. E.

1884. F. O. Favor, pastor; A. C. Thomas, P. E.

1885. A. W. Smith, pastor; A. C. Thomas, P. E.

1886. T. J. Warlick, pastor; A. C. Thomas, P. E.

1887. M. S. Williams, pastor; A. C. Thomas, P. E.

1888. W. B. Dillard, pastor; J. T. Gibson, P. E.

1889. Charge placed back in Dahlonega District. W. D. Shea, pastor; M. J. Cofer, P. E.

1891. Ford McRee, pastor; M. J. Cofer, P. E.

1892. Ford McRee, pastor; M. L. Underwood, P. E.

1894. G. W. Farr, pastor.

1895-96. Loy Warwick.

1898-99. W. E. Tarpley.

1903. G. D. Stone.

1904. E. K. Akin.

1905-08. Felton Williams. Junior pastor, 1908-09, G. W. Hamilton.

1909-10. W. H. Clark.

1910-11. T. L. Rutland, Jasper. (During these two years Jasper and Tate were separate appointments.)

1910-11. G. W. Barrett, Tate.

1912-14. Nath Thompson.

1915. Neal A. White.

1916. G. L. King.

1917. Firley Baum.

1918. H. C. Emory.

1919-22. W. T. Watkins.

1923. W. E. Brown.

1924-25. C. L. Middlebrooks.

1926. J. R. Allen.

1927-28. A. L. Hale.

1929-32. J. S. Thrailkill.

1932-date. D. P. Johnston.

One of the most interesting features of rural Methodism in earlier days was the old "camp-meeting." There are still a number of camp-grounds in this section where meetings are held every year, but the day of their greatest usefulness and popularity passed long ago with the coming of automobiles and highways and the increased opportunities for social communication.

There were two well-known camp-grounds in Pickens County, the one already mentioned at "Scared Corn" and one at Four Mile, east of Tate, which is a Baptist institution and was attended by some very able ministers. Large numbers of people attended the services at these old camp-grounds in years gone by. "Meeting-time" was in the fall, just after the crops were laid by. A family would have its house or tent on the grounds and here they would go *en masse* to stay for the duration of the meeting, usually a week. Many social contacts—and matrimonial contracts as well—were made at the old camp-meetings, which were always eagerly looked forward to and which filled a very real need in the lives of the people.

The "Georgia Camp-Meeting" has long been famous in song and story but I think some of the songs and stories are unworthy of the sentiment of the pioneers who began this institution and of those who sought its spiritual and social enlightenment.

The camp-meeting seems to have been principally a Methodist institution, although people of other denominations were by no means barred from attending and often came to enjoy its religious inspiration and social contacts.

Baptist Churches. The first Baptist church and probably the first church of any denomination in what is now Pickens County was the one at Talking Rock. Land for this church was deeded by James Morrison soon after the Indians were removed in 1838. Mr. Morrison was a Presbyterian but was interested in the religious life of the whole community. A log church house was built and the Baptists began to hold their services here in about 1839.

The first records of the Talking Rock Baptist Church, which have recently come to light, give the names of some of the earliest members. On October 5, 1839, the following persons joined this church: Dicy James, Eddy Gibson, Jane Phillips, Jane Robertson, Hannah Blalock, Malinda Jones, and Milly Dickson. On October 31, 1839, the following were taken in: David R. Blalock, Isaac Mullinax, and Charles James, deacons; William Evans, Aaron Robertson, Jacob Gibson, Richard Howard, Grief Williams, John James, and Moses James. The early records show that a number of negro slaves were members of this church along with their owners.

The first pastor of the church at Talking Rock was Rev. Robert Jordan. Other early pastors were Rev. Basil Harris,

Rev. Jimmy West, Rev. B. M. Stephens, Rev. E. Akins, Rev. Willis West, Rev. W. F. Fleming, a Rev. Mr. Chastain, Rev. Thad Pickett, Rev. J. R. Allen, Rev. William Cagle, Rev. Jim McHan, and Rev. E. W. Allred.

In 1859 this church gave some land for a schoolhouse, and a school building was erected in the churchyard which served the Talking Rock community for many years. During

JASPER BAPTIST CHURCH

the four years of the War Between the States, the church held its services as usual and often helped families in destitute circumstances caused by the war.

In 1884, a heavy snow falling on the last night in February broke in the roof of this church. When the Baptist people came together to discuss rebuilding, some of them wanted to build the new church about half a mile away in the little village of Talking Rock, which had sprung up in the meantime. On account of sentiment, this proposal was voted down and the church was rebuilt on the original site. This is the present building, which still serves a rather large country membership. There is a cemetery in the churchyard here, and some of the graves are a hundred years old or more.

One of the early organizers of the Baptists in this part of the country was "Uncle" Albert Webb, a planter of Dawson County and a very forceful preacher of the Baptist doctrine. He organized a number of Baptist churches in Pickens County and his efforts along this line were greatly augmented by Rev. Jesse Padgett, a resident of the eastern part of the county.

Besides the church at Talking Rock, there are a number of other Baptist churches in Pickens County with long and honorable histories. At the present time the Baptists have thriving churches in the five principal towns of the county and also in many of the rural communities.

Lebanon Presbyterian Church. Although the Presbyterians have no active church in Pickens County now, they were once represented by one of the county's most flourishing religious organizations—the Lebanon Presbyterian Church at Talking Rock. This was one of the earliest churches in the county, and the only Presbyterian church ever established here.

The records of this church have apparently been lost, but I understand that it was organized in 1839 or 1840, soon after the Morrison family came to the Talking Rock community from North Carolina. This family, consisting of three brothers—James, Andrew, and Joseph—and three sisters—Elizabeth, Mrs. Johnson Long, and Mrs. Patton Watson—together with their own families and Mrs. Nannie Coleman and a Mrs. Duckett, constituted the first members of Lebanon Church. Among the early pastors were a Rev. Mr. Brown, a Rev. Mr. Millican, Rev. Paul Morton, Rev. Will Morton, Rev. Will Milner, Rev. Richard Milner, and the same Rev. Mr. Harris who preached at the Hinton Methodist Church.

It is said that an excellent library was maintained by the Lebanon church, containing many of the best books of the day, and these books were used in the Sunday-school instead of the literature used today. Some of them are still in existence.

The Civil War took a heavy toll of the young men members of Lebanon Church, and many of the older members also died during that period. "Uncle Jimmie" Morrison, the leader in the religious life of that section, was an invalid for several years before his death in 1874 and could not take an active part in religious affairs. After his death, Lebanon Church began to decline. On the last night of February, 1884—long afterwards known as the "night of the big snow"—the roof of the church building was broken by the weight of the snow that had fallen on it. (Curiously enough, the same thing happened that night to the Baptist church at Talking Rock.) After this, the Lebanon church was never repaired, although it stood for twenty years or more. Services were abandoned, and the remaining members moved away or joined the nearby Baptist or Methodist congregations.

Lebanon cemetery, which was in the churchyard, was noted for its large and beautiful cedar trees. After the church building was finally torn down, a number of these cedars were cut down as they had grown too large to be left. They had been planted too near the graves. Passing along the Atlanta-Blue Ridge highway a little north of Talking Rock, the observer today will notice a number of tombstones clustered together. This is all that remains at Old Lebanon Church. Some of the graves marked by these tombstones are a little apart from the others. Here lie several negro slaves—near, in death, to their "white folks" whom they served in life.

Other Denominations. As stated before, there are no

290 HISTORY OF PICKENS COUNTY

churches in Pickens County now except those of the Methodists and Baptists, but several other denominations have had churches here in years past which made their contributions to the religious life and development of the county.

I do not have details concerning the Christian or Campbellite denomination in Pickens County, but there have been a number of Campbellite churches here in the past. Their congregations became scattered and the denomination lost ground in this section, and today its churches are practically abandoned here.

The Universalists built no churches in Pickens but many adherents to that faith have lived in the county.

One Northern Methodist church still remains—the one at Hinton. After all, it is on "foreign soil," and it has not prospered much.

In the 'nineties, the Catholics came to see us. Like the Jews, Catholics are not often found in virgin territory, but many of them were at work in the marble industry at Tate and Marble Hill and a church dedicated to the Catholic faith was built near Marble Hill. Mr. John McGrath, father of the present Father McGrath, was one of the members and principal supporters of this church. For lack of support it has been discontinued, and the field has been left to the Methodists and Baptists.

Chapter VIII ★ ★ ★
FAMILY ACCOUNTS

●

(The personal accounts appearing in this chapter include only those families from which the necessary data was received, and therefore do not include as complete a list of the pioneer families of the county as could be desired. For information concerning other early families, however, the reader is referred to Chapter III, which gives the name, age, and native State of every person residing in Pickens County when the Census of 1860 was taken; and which includes nearly all the pioneer residents of the county.—L. E. T.)

ANDERSON

Alex Anderson Jr. was born in Banffshire, Scotland, on May 6, 1873, and came with his parents to New York in 1882. He was educated in the schools of that city, and served his draftsman's apprenticeship in the office of Stanford White, the noted architect. He came to Georgia in 1896 to go with the Blue Ridge Marble Company. Mr. Anderson is an expert in all lines of the marble industry and has been an important factor in the development of The Georgia Marble Company, of which he is now first vice-president. He is also an enthusiastic lover of sports, being well known as a hunter and fisherman.

In 1904 Mr. Anderson married Miss Vinita Tate, daughter of Col. Stephen C. Tate, and they have two daughters.

ATHERTON

William C. Atherton, one of the founders of the textile industry in North Georgia, was a native of Manchester, England. At an early age he came to America with his brothers, James and Thomas, and the family settled at Paterson, N. J. William Atherton moved to Georgia and in about 1840 settled at Roswell, where he started the Roswell Cotton Mills. Seven years later he moved to Pickens County, and in the late 'sixties he and his two brothers erected the old Talking Rock Cotton Factory, the first textile mill in the entire section (see page 250).

William Atherton went to Cherokee County for a time and operated a yarn factory on Shoal Creek in partnership with J. V. Keith, but after a few years he returned to Pickens and with his brother, Thomas, opened the Harmony Cotton Mills south of Jasper.

J. T. Atherton, son of William C. and Catherine Dutcher Atherton, was born in 1859 at the old Talking Rock factory and lived there until he was a young man. He then moved to Waleska, where he married Miss Florence M. Barrett. Going thence to Alice, Ga., he superintended the Harmony Cotton Mills for a number of years, moving to Jasper in 1897. He was elected clerk and treasurer of Pickens County in 1900 and served four years in office, and also represented the county in the legislature during 1909-10. He was in the mercantile business for eighteen years at Tate, and now conducts a similar business at Jasper.

BRADLEY

The Bradleys were one of the first families to settle in what is now Pickens County. Nauphlet Bradley, father of B. B. Bradley of Talking Rock, was one of the men who helped to gather the Indians of this section into the fort at Sanderstown in 1838. The family came from North Carolina.

B. B. Bradley was born in 1861 and is one of the oldest and most respected citizens of Talking Rock. He recalls many interesting events in the history of the county, including the founding of the old Ludville High School, one of the first institutions of higher learning in the entire section, and the establishment by the Atherton brothers of the Talking Rock Cotton Factory. A. B. Bradley, a brother, was a member of the General Assembly in 1915 and 1916.

DARNELL

Hon. Sion A. Darnell was born in Pickens County on December 28, 1845. He attended the first school in Pickens County in 1855, and afterwards such schools as this section afforded. At an early age he developed a thirst for knowledge and began to read extensively. At the age of seventeen he taught a large and flourishing school near his home.

He was familiar with the patriotic speeches of Clay and Webster and when the vicissitudes of war broke up his school, he with his father and a younger brother escaped from the Confederacy. They, like many others in Pickens County, were opposed to Secession. They were captured by Confederate scouts and condemned to be shot. Taken to the place of execution they were rescued and released by Union soldiers. Sion Darnell became a private in the Union army and was honorably discharged at the termination of hostilities.

In January, 1866, Mr. Darnell was elected tax collector of Pickens County, and at the next election he was chosen to represent Pickens County in the General Assembly as a republican. In September, 1872, he was admitted to the bar, and in March, 1873, he was appointed special commissioner of claims for Georgia. He held this appointment until January, 1879, when he resigned to accept an appointment as U. S. attorney for the district of Georgia, which he held until March, 1882, in the meantime representing the federal government in cases from Georgia before the French-American claims commission, then in session at Washington. In July, 1882, he was appointed U. S. attorney for the southern district of Georgia and served four years in this capacity. In 1889 he was appointed U. S. attorney for the northern district of Georgia by President Harrison, and served here another four years.

Mr. Darnell was active in politics and an ardent supporter of the Grand Army of the Republic, becoming post commander of two G. A. R. posts in Georgia and a delegate to the Milwaukee convention in 1889. He was always a strong supporter of the schools and churches.

He married Miss Susie Hotchkiss, of Marietta, Ga. Surviving are a son, Sion A. Darnell, Jr., and a daughter, Mrs. Will Jones, both of Atlanta.

DAY

Hon. William Thomas Day, a widely-known lawyer and jurist of Pickens County, was born September 30, 1828, in Walton County, Ga., and died June 10, 1916, at his home in Jasper, Ga. Colonel Day was highly esteemed for his valuable services to his county and state and for his many good qualities as a citizen.

His grandfather, William Day, was born in Virginia and served under Washington during the Revolutionary War. William Day moved to South Carolina and married a Miss Munday. To this union was born Lewis Day, who came to Georgia and married Miss Alpha Dixon. They settled in Walton County, but in 1842 they moved to what is now Pickens County, with their son, William Thomas Day.

Colonel Day had in his youth such educational advantages as the section afforded, and he applied himself diligently to his studies. At the age of twenty-six he began to study law with Daniel H. Byrd, of Canton, and on October 4, 1854, he was admitted to the practice of law by Judge David Irwin, of the Blue Ridge Circuit. His ability at the bar soon won him many clients.

He was a delegate from Pickens County to the Secession Convention of 1861, and there opposed Secession; but at the outbreak of the Civil War he immediately enrolled in Company I, Eighth Regiment of Georgia Volunteers. He served honorably for three years and emerged from the war with the rank of captain.

On May 14, 1866, he was appointed solicitor of the Pickens County Court. In 1877 he served as a delegate to the convention called to revise the state constitution. In 1880-81 he represented Pickens County in the general assembly, and in 1884-85 and 1909-1910 he represented his senatorial district in the same body.

Colonel Day built up a large law practice and was known as one of the state's ablest criminal lawyers. He was also interested in matters of public welfare and served several years on the county board of education. He belonged to the Methodist Church and to the Masonic fraternity.

He married Miss Theresa Craig, of Harris County, on September 18, 1866, and six children were born to the union. Mrs. Day died February 11, 1894. The following children survived Colonel Day at the time of his death: Mrs. W. A. Hamrick, Ludville, Ga.; Mrs. William J. Russell, Athens, Ga.; C. P. Day, Atlanta, Ga.; W. T. Day, Jr., Jasper, Ga.; and Craig Day, Birmingham, Ala.

EATON

The family of Jim Eaton was one of the first to settle in the western part of Pickens County, coming here from Forsyth County near Cumming. Mrs. Jim Eaton, formerly Mary Jackson, had come from South Carolina. She was one of the six charter members of the early Methodist church at Hinton. The children of Jim and Mary Eaton were: Zim, Jule, Joe, Will, Milt, Sarah (Mrs. Dunn), Emma (Mrs. Bradley), and Ophelia (Mrs. Cross).

Joe M. Eaton, son of Jim and Mary Jackson Eaton, is a successful business man of the county, with mercantile, banking, and marble interests. He lives at Marble Hill.

FITZSIMMONS

Henry Fitzsimmons, a pioneer in the marble industry of Pickens County, immigrated from Ireland to this country in the early 'twenties at the age of about twenty-four, and married Almyra Thebert, of Greenville, S. C. They moved to Lawrenceville, Ga., where Mr. Fitzsimmons pursued the occupations of contractor and stone-mason, erecting several of the early public buildings of that section. About 1836 he moved to the Long Swamp Valley in Cherokee (now Pickens) County, and purchased land in the vicinity of the present Marble Hill, where he developed three marble quarries and built a small marble mill for monumental purposes. The product of this mill was transported by six -or eight-mule teams to Middle and East Georgia and South Carolina. A monument which he made in 1845 now stands in Dahlonega, Ga., as a memorial to seven men massacred by order of the Mexican commander at Goliad, Tex.; and bears his name and the address "Long Swamp Marble, Cherokee Post Office, Cherokee County, Ga." He also furnished the 138 marble mileposts for the state-owned Western & Atlantic Railroad from Atlanta to Chattanooga, which are still in use. Mr. Fitzsimmons died on December 24, 1845, and was buried in the family lot at Marble Hill.

William T. Fitzsimmons, the oldest of four sons of Henry and Almyra Fitzsimmons, was an early stone-cutter in Pickens County and served in the War with Mexico. (See page 65). Elizabeth and Ovaline Fitzsimmons, two of his sisters, married, respectively, John Stegall and Bethel Q. Disharoon, both early figures in the marble industry of the county.

HAMRICK

Sylvanus Hamrick, a prominent business man and planter of the last generation, was born in North Carolina and with his parents moved to Pickens County while a young man. He lived here until his death on March 13, 1913.

Mr. Hamrick was esteemed for his high moral character and was a faithful member of the Methodist Church for over fifty years. He was a staunch democrat and a Mason. He took prominent part in the public affairs of his section, holding for forty years the office of justice of the peace and being one of the committee who located the county site of Pickens County. He also helped to establish the first high school in the county, at Ludville.

When the Civil War broke out, Mr. Hamrick enlisted in Company L, 36th Regiment, Georgia Infantry. He was captured at the Battle of Vicksburg, July 4, 1863, and was paroled July 9, 1863. He fought in the war until its close.

Mr. Hamrick was married September 1, 1853, to Miss Harriett Killian, daughter of Lawson Alexander Killian and Martha Bedford Killian, of Dahlonega, Ga. Eleven children were born to this union: John A., James L., Robert T., George W. (all of whom were prominent in church and political affairs in the county and state), Martha E., Rachel A., Lola Belle, William A., Jesse M., Henry M., and Horner A. The last four survive. Mrs. Hamrick died October 8, 1881, and Mr. Hamrick married Miss Mary Jane Smith, of Gordon County, on November 6, 1883. Two daughters survive this second union, and one son, William A. Hamrick, was married December 6, 1893, to Miss Fannie Day, daughter of Col. William T. Day and Theresa Craig Day, of Jasper, Ga., and with his family reside in Pickens County where he

has large farming and mercantile interests. Sons of Robert
T. Hamrick are engaged in the mercantile business at
Ludville.

HENLEY

John W. Henley, prominent among both the lawyers and
educators of Pickens County, was born in Murray County,
Georgia, on March 28, 1852. Though left fatherless when
a very young boy, he availed himself of every opportunity
to obtain an education. In 1874 he attended Fort Mountain
Institute for a short period and then taught school in Gordon
and Murray Counties. In 1874 he entered North Georgia
Agricultural College at Dahlonega, from which he graduated
in 1879. He then established an institute in Jasper and
taught there for several years. This institute later became
a public school.

Mr. Henley studied law under the direction of the Hon.
George R. Brown, of Canton, and became assistant solicitor-
general of the Blue Ridge Circuit and later an assistant
U. S. district attorney. In this capacity his qualifications
were such that he was retained through the changes of administration to the time of his death.

Mr. Henley served for a time as Pickens County school
commissioner. He was accurate, painstaking and untiring
in all his work and in all respects was an exemplary and
useful citizen and greatly respected.

HOBSON

The Hobson family is of Irish-English extraction and
came to Georgia from South Carolina, where they had moved
from their original home in Virginia. John Hobson, who was
born in 1813, came to Pickens County before the Civil War
and made his home in the Holt Settlement. He became a
captain of militia, and at the outbreak of the Civil War

he and his company joined the Confederate ranks. Captain Hobson served throughout the war, fighting with General Johnston against Sherman during the latter's march through Georgia. At the close of the war he moved to Bartow County where he died about 1890.

Henry Hobson, a son, born in 1843, married Mary Jane Thompson, daughter of Lewis Thompson. The Thompsons were another pioneer family of the same community. Henry Hobson also served in the Confederate Army throughout the war. He was with General Forrest's cavalry a part of the time and saw almost continuous service around Chattanooga and through Georgia, being with Forrest at Cartersville and Rome. He died in 1866 of disease resulting from his war service.

A son of Henry and Mary Jane Hobson, John Henry Hobson, is now living.

Long

Mortimer S. Long was born at Morganton, Fannin County, Georgia, on June 2, 1867, a son of John Michael Long and Martha Emily (Crawford) Long, who were both born in Fannin County. All the grandparents, George I. Long and Polly (Falls) Long and Samuel Horton Crawford and Celia (Jones) Crawford, came to Fannin County from western North Carolina.

Mrs. John M. Long died in 1924 and her husband in 1927. Of their eight children, six are living: M. S. Long, of Jasper, Georgia; Molly McCleer, of Atlanta; Horace, of Tate; Nellie Simpson, of Middletown, Ohio; O. W. Long, of Russellville, Alabama; and Frank H. Long, of Atlanta, Ga. Two are deceased: Mrs. Bertie Copps, of Charlottesville, Virginia, and Mrs. Edith Pool, of Jasper, Georgia.

M. S. Long was married April 23, 1893, to Lillie Day Wofford, daughter of Benjamin J. and Malissa Furgerson

Wofford, of Pickens County, Georgia. Six children were born to these parents: John, Clarence S., Charles Reid, Lillie Vera, Emily Faye, and Helen May, who died in infancy.

Mr. Long received his education in the common schools of Fannin County and at North Georgia Agricultural College, Dahlonega. He was employed in the mechanical department of The Georgia Marble Company for twenty-five years, during fourteen of which he was master mechanic. He was elected ordinary of Pickens County in 1916, appointed by Governor Hugh M. Dorsey as commissioner of roads and revenues of Pickens County in 1920, and reelected in 1924, 1928, and 1932. Mr. Long's incumbency has marked Pickens as one of the most progressive counties in this section in the development of roads and highways.

A man of kindly and genial nature, loyal to his friends, and possessed of an ambition to serve his community, Mr. Long has been one of the county's most respected and able officials; and the positions which have been bestowed upon him are a fair measure of how well he has succeeded in his civic ideals.

Horace Long, also a son of John and Martha Long, was born in 1874 and received his education in the public schools of Tate and at Reinhardt College, Waleska, Ga. He has spent the greater part of his business career with The Georgia Marble Co. He is now in charge of the finishing work in the monumental department of that company's plant at Tate.

McClain

R. L. McClain, Jasper banker, is the son of Newton Clark McClain and Mary Arthur McClain, who were among the pioneer settlers of Pickens County. His grandparents moved from South Carolina in 1824 and later came to what is now Pickens County.

Mr. McClain was born December 6, 1872, in Pickens County, and was educated in the public schools of Jasper. He began his business career as clerk in a general store at Tate, was later bookkeeper for the Blue Ridge Marble Company at Nelson, shipping clerk for The Georgia Marble Company at Tate, and then traveling salesman for the same company. He was elected treasurer of The Georgia Marble Company in 1910, but resigned in 1920 to enter the banking business.

Mr. McClain is president of the Bank of Jasper, the only bank in Pickens County. He has always taken an interest in matters of public moment in his town, county, and state; and was a member of the Georgia legislature in 1929.

PICKETT

Hon. Roscoe Pickett, one of the leading lawyers of Pickens County, was born July 10, 1883, and was educated in the public schools of Pickens and the University of Georgia, from which he received the B. L. Degree in 1909. He is the son of Rev. Thaddeus Pickett, who was prominent in the religious and political affairs of his day, and Sarah E. Worley Pickett.

Mr. Pickett is an active member of the Baptist Church and, politically, is prominent in the affairs of the Republican party, having been a delegate to the Republican national convention in 1908. He has also served as chairman of the Republican state central committee, and is now a member-at-large of that body. He was a member of the lower house of the Georgia assembly in 1911-12, and represented his senatorial district in the legislature during 1915-16.

SIMMONS

James Simmons was born in Spartanburg County, S. C., in 1803. When he was less than a year old his family moved to North Carolina, where they lived until 1831. He married Miss Elizabeth Ramseur and after living in Hall County, Ga., about a year he moved to what was then Gilmer but is now in Pickens County, on the Old Federal Road about two miles north of where Jasper is now located. For several years his nearest white neighbor to the south was Sam Tate on Long Swamp, who had purchased in 1834 the Fawns tract of land from Dr. Green. He lived for several years among the Indians and was their esteemed and trusted friend.

In 1861 Mr. Simmons was elected delegate to the Secession Convention. He was elected as a Union man and did not vote for secession, giving as his reason: "I thought secession would involve us in war and was too hasty; that the proper remedy would be to petition Congress for our constitutional rights and then if we did not get them it would be time to secede." Mr. Simmons was also elected to the state senate in 1861 and again in 1863.

The children of James and Elizabeth Ramseur Simmons were: Adolphus and Rufus, both of whom lost their lives in the Civil War; Philip, Augustus, Richard, Frank, and Julia.

SIMMONS

Col. William Hill Simmons was born in Monroe County, Ga., on April 1, 1824, the son of William H. and Elizabeth Simmons. His great-grandfather, John Simmons, and grandfather, James Simmons, had come from Virginia to North Carolina in an early day, and thence to Georgia in 1784, settling in Hancock County near Sparta. There they worshiped at Post Oak Methodist Church, of which no trace now remains.

The elder William H. Simmons was born in a fort erected by the settlers of Hancock County for protection against the Indians. He was married to Elizabeth Maddux, daughter of Joseph Maddux, in 1815, the subject of this sketch being the fourth of their nine children. The family moved to what is now Pike County, and the children grew up on the old homestead near the present town of Williamson.

At the age of nineteen, William Hill Simmons left home for the Lumpkin County gold mines, but he stayed there only a short time and then went to Forsyth County where he organized and taught a tuition-school. On December 26, 1844, he met and married Adliza Elizabeth Allen, daughter of Beverly W. Allen. He began the reading of law with Hiram Parks Bell, at Cumming, and was admitted to the bar in Dahlonega, before Judge Joseph E. Brown, in 1855. The following year he began the practice of law in Jasper, where he continued to live until his death.

From 1862 to 1877 Colonel Simmons held the office of ordinary of Pickens County, and in 1878 he was elected state senator from Pickens. While in the senate he introduced a bill, which passed, reducing the enormous fees then charged by tax receivers and collectors, saving the taxpayers of the state many thousands of dollars. Later he further served his county as school commissioner.

Colonel Simmons was widely known and respected for his legal ability, and he was also loved by all who knew him for his kindness and helpful spirit. Always deeply interested in the spiritual welfare of those about him, by precept and example he served to guide both old and young. He was a steward in the Jasper Methodist Church for more than thirty years, superintendent of the Sunday school for thirty-two years, and Worshipful Master of Pickens Star Lodge, F. & A. M., for thirty-five years. His death, on January 31, 1891, was mourned by a great number of friends in his county and state.

STEGALL

John Stegall, an early planter and landowner of Pickens

County, was born June 13, 1820, and in 1843 came with his father, Blackwell Stegall, to Lumpkin County, Ga., from South Carolina. His grandfather, Richard Stegall, born in Virginia on July 4, 1754, of a family which was later represented by several Revolutionary soldiers, had immigrated in 1793 to Pickens County, S. C., where he had become a prosperous farmer.

John Stegall married Elizabeth Fitzsimmons, daughter of Henry Fitzsimmons of Long Swamp, Cherokee (now Pickens) County, Ga., in 1846. He mined gold in Lumpkin County until 1851, when he and his brother, Hensley Stegall, went to California and mined gold until 1854. Returning to Pickens County, he with his brother-in-law, Bethel Q. Disharoon, purchased the major part of the Henry Fitzsimmons estate and marble properties. John and Elizabeth Stegall had eleven children. Mr. Stegall died November 1, 1878.

TATE

Samuel Tate, the first of his family to settle in what is now Pickens County, was born in Morganton, N. C., on May 25, 1797. He was the son of John Tate, who served in the Revolutionary War, and Anne Oliphant Tate. The family had come from Pennsylvania to Virginia, from there to Burke County, North Carolina, and later to Franklin County, Georgia. In about 1834 John Tate moved to what is now Gilmer County, and he is buried in the cemetery at Ellijay.

In 1834 Samuel Tate purchased lands in the Long Swamp Valley, then in Cherokee but now in Pickens County; and members of the family have resided at the homestead here since that time. Samuel Tate was a farmer, a government land agent, and an early developer of the marble business in this section. He was Pickens County's state senator in 1857-8. At the outbreak of the Civil War he went out as captain of a company of volunteers from Pickens. On account of illness he was honorably discharged at Yorktown, and he returned to his home in Pickens where he died September 20, 1866. Samuel Tate married Mary Griffeth, of Habersham County. They had seven children: Caleb R., Julia Anne (Mrs. Martin Davis), William, Stephen C., Jane Sophronia (Mrs. John Davis), Martha Hester (Mrs. John Maddox), and Farish Carter Tate.

Caleb R. Tate, son of Samuel and Mary Tate, was born December 9, 1824. He married Winnie Pendley on October 1, 1890.

William Tate, son of Samuel and Mary Tate, was born July 15, 1827, in Lumpkin County. During the Civil War he enlisted from Cass (now Bartow) County in Captain Cook's company of the First Georgia State Troops, was made a major in 1864, and engaged in the seige of Atlanta and the Battle of Jonesboro. He was the first clerk of the Pickens County superior court, serving from 1854 to 1862. He married Mary Bird, of Gordon County, and was survived by three daughters and three sons: Mrs. E. M. Cole, Mrs. R. N. Holland, Mrs. Preston Rambo, Farish Carter Tate, Dr. William B. Tate, and P. M. Tate, who was a banker, merchant, manufacturer, and farmer of the county.

Farish Carter Tate, son of Samuel and Mary Tate, was born October 26, 1834. He served in the Confederate Army as a lieutenant in the Lewis Volunteers, 18th Georgia Regiment, and died of measles in a military hospital at Richmond, Va.

Col. Stephen C. Tate, son of Samuel and Mary Tate, was born in Lumpkin County, Georgia, June 9, 1832, shortly before his parents moved to Pickens. At the age of twenty he went to California to mine gold, but he returned in 1855 and established a successful mercantile and milling business at Cartersville, in Cass (now Bartow) County. During the

Civil War he enlisted from Cass County in the military service of the state and was assigned to duty on the state road, where he served throughout the war. Returning then to the homestead in Pickens, he engaged in farming and also turned his attention toward the development of the marble industry here, being instrumental in bringing the railroad to Pickens in 1882 and in the organization of The Georgia Marble Company in 1884. At the time of his death, which occurred in April, 1901, he was vice-president of The Georgia Marble Company at Tate, the Blue Ridge Marble Company at Nelson, and the Kennesaw Marble Company at Marietta; and had served as postmaster at Tate for nearly forty years. Colonel Tate was married, in 1857, to Eliza D. Buffington, of Griffin, Ga., and they were survived by six daughters and three sons. The daughters were: Mrs. Levi Darnell, of Jasper; Mrs. M. S. Williams, of Atlanta; Mrs. A. S. Hinton, of Summerville; Mrs. Alex Anderson, of Nelson; Mrs. I. P. Morton, of St. Louis, Mo.; and Miss Florence Tate, of Tate; of whom the last three are still living.

Farish Carter Tate, son of William and Mary Bird Tate, was born November 20, 1856. He had a notable legal career and was in public life for over thirty years, serving terms as legislator, congressman, and U. S. District attorney. His wife was the former Julia Bell, of Forsyth County. He died February 7, 1922.

Howard Tate, son of Farish Carter Tate and Julia Bell Tate, was born October 6, 1884. For several years he served as assistant U. S. attorney, and during the World War he was a captain in the U. S. Army and also connected with the military court. He died on December 2, 1928.

Col. Sam Tate, son of Stephen C. and Eliza Buffington Tate, was born June 13, 1860, and received his education in the common schools and at North Georgia Agricultural College, Dahlonega. He first engaged in the mercantile

business with J. M. McAfee at Canton; then from 1883 to
1905 he conducted a similar business at Tate. In 1905 he
became connected with, and since 1907 has been president of,
The Georgia Marble Company. Colonel Tate is a director in
the First National Bank of Atlanta and vice-president of the
Bank of Canton. From May, 1929, to March 1, 1930,
he served as chairman of the highway board of the state.
He is an active Methodist and a trustee of Wesleyan College,
Emory University, and Young Harris College, and has made
liberal contributions toward the causes of the church, education, and public welfare generally. Colonel Tate holds the
honorary degree of Doctor of Laws, conferred by the University of Georgia in 1931.

Stephen L. Tate, son of Stephen C. and Eliza Tate, was
born February 6, 1866. He was educated in the local schools
and at Gordon Institute, Barnesville. Until the time of his
death, August 10, 1897, he was associated with The Georgia
Marble Company, and also engaged in the mercantile and
banking business.

Walter E. Tate, son of Stephen C. and Eliza Tate, was born
December 1, 1877. After receiving his education in the common schools and at Webb School, Bell Buckle, Tenn., he
became associated with The Georgia Marble Company, of
which he is now general manager and a vice-president. He
married Miss Bessie Atwood, of Franklin, Tenn., and they
have three children.

Luke E. Tate, son of Stephen C. and Eliza Tate, was born
March 27, 1879; attended the common schools and Emory
University at Oxford, Webb School at Bell Buckle, Tenn.,
Virginia Military Institute, Columbian University at Wash-
ington, D. C., and the University of Georgia (A. B. and
B. L. degrees); volunteered for service in the Spanish-
American War; served as Pickens County food administrator
during the World War and also in Red Cross work; has

engaged in the practice of law, the banking and mercantile businesses, and the marble, cotton-mill, and oil industries; and since 1930 has represented Pickens County in the legislature.

WHITFIELD

William Gray Whitfield and his wife, Annie Murray Whitfield, came from North Carolina to Banks County, Georgia, and from there they moved to Pickens County about 1845. Mr. Whitfield was a farmer and also an early worker in the marble industry of the county.

The children of William G. and Annie Murray Whitfield were: John C., Caleb, Tom, Steve, Aramissa (Mrs. Tom Hopkins), Martha (Mrs. Pink Morris), Mary (Mrs. Fayette Stancil), Narcissa, Syceria (Mrs. Jim Dowda), and Julianne (Mrs. Mort Little).

• INDEX